VIETNAM RECONSIDERED

VIETNAM
RECONSIDERED
LESSONS FROM A WAR

EDITED WITH AN INTRODUCTION BY

HARRISON E. SALISBURY

HARPER TORCHBOOKS

Harper & Row, Publishers, New York
Grand Rapids, Philadelphia, St. Louis, San Francisco
London, Singapore, Sydney, Tokyo, Toronto

"VIETNAM RECONSIDERED": THE VIDEO TAPE SERIES

A 32-hour series on the four-day symposium "Vietnam Reconsidered: Lessons from a War" is now available. The video tapes, in color, may be ordered either by individual panel (including question-and-answer session), or in their entirety. For further information please contact:

Vietnam Conference Series
USC School of Journalism
University Park, GHS 315
Los Angeles, CA 90089-1695
Attn: Shultz/Domanick
(213) 743-2391

Copyright acknowledgments appear on page 336.

First HARPER TORCHBOOKS edition published 1985.

Designer: Amelia Lau Carling

Library of Congress Cataloging in Publication Data

Main entry under title:
Vietnam reconsidered.

"Harper Torchbooks."
Papers presented at a symposium held Feb. 1983 at the University of Southern California, Los Angeles.
Includes bibliographical references and index.
1. Vietnamese conflict, 1961–1975—United States—Congresses. 2. United States—History—1945–   —Congresses. I. Salisbury, Harrison Evans, 1908–

DS558.V54	1985	959.704'33'73	83-48382

ISBN 0-06-015266-4   84   85   86   87   88   10   9   8   7   6   5   4   3   2   1
ISBN 0-06-132052-8 (pbk.)   90   10   9   8

The basic materials of this book are drawn from a four-day conference conducted February 6–9, 1983, at the University of Southern California, Los Angeles, under the sponsorship of the School of Journalism, Center for Humanities and School of International Relations in cooperation with the Immaculate Heart College Center.

The USC Advisory Panel which arranged the conference comprised: Ronald Gottesman, A. J. Langguth, Charles Powell, Mark Kann, Luther Luedtke, and Michael Fry. The energy and imagination of Jack Langguth, himself a former Vietnam correspondent, was vital in the organization of the conference.

Special thanks go to Larry Ceplair for his outstanding and painstaking work in shaping, collating, and editing the conference materials for this book.

CONTENTS

ABBREVIATIONS

AID—Agency for International Development
ARVN—Army of the Republic of Vietnam (South Vietnam)
ASEAN—Association of South East Asian Nations
CIA—Central Intelligence Agency (American)
COINTELPRO—Counter-Intelligence Program (Federal Bureau of Investigation)
COMECON—Council of Mutual Economic Assistance (USSR)
CORDS—Civil Operations and Revolutionary Development Support (American)
COSVN—Central Office for South Vietnam (Communist headquarters of the guerrilla war, based in Cambodia)
DMZ—Demilitarized Zone (Border area separating North and South Vietnam)
DOD—Department of Defense (American)
Five O'Clock Follies—Daily press briefings for Saigon journalists by MACV
MACV—Military Assistance Command, Vietnam (American)
NLF—National Liberation Front (South Vietnam-based opponents of the Republic of Vietnam)

NVA—North Vietnamese Army

OSS—Office of Strategic Services (American, forerunner of CIA)

USIA—United States Information Agency

VC—Viet Cong (Derogatory term given by the Republic of South Vietnam to the NLF)

Vietminh—Vietnam Doc Lap Dong Minh (Vietnamese Independence League), formed in 1941 by the Vietnamese Communist Party

INTRODUCTION

Harrison E. Salisbury

Vietnam—the war that seems to have no ending, the war that lies heavy on our hearts and still awakens us in nightmare—how did it come about; what machines set it in motion; what passions fueled its escalation and left as residue in American lives such debts— human, political, moral, social, philosophical?

For four days in Los Angeles in February 1983, some eighty or more Americans (newsmen, historians, diplomats, military and intellegence men) and a handful of Vietnamese probed the embers, seeking answers, seeking solutions, seeking to isolate those factors from which can be constructed some lessons of that traumatic involvement which brought America face-to-face with regions, peoples, nations hardly known to Americans before World War II and not much better known by the government's planners and policymakers and diplomats in the years to follow.

What were the roots of involvement and in what soil did they take so fearful root?

The task of inquiry is made more complex by the fact that within two years of the Paris accords of 1973, Vietnam simply fell apart. The military and political strength of Saigon washed away like a castle of sand. On American minds was left the fateful imprint of the Hueys (helicopters) removing the last personnel from the U.S. Embassy and the clutching hands and fearful faces of the

Vietnamese who were left behind.

It is not accidental that the most expensive Hollywood film made about Vietnam depicted hallucinations of the apocalypse illuminated with characters drawn from Conrad, Dostoyevsky, and Melville.

The tragedy, the malaise, the cost in lives, shattered families, hospital wounded, psychoses, economic stress, fragmentation of political and social structures, president after president blown away by perceived and unperceived Vietnam legacies, the impacted frustration of the U.S. military—this represents a disaster such as the United States has not known previously, or at least not since the Civil War. We cannot simply "put Vietnam behind us." Those who seek the roots of the new catastrophes of the Reagan era, economic, social, and political, would do well to reexamine Lyndon Johnson's utopian, heroic concept, doomed from inception, to have *both* guns and butter; to have a war that was not a war, an undeclared war resting precariously on that principle which the late Arthur Sylvester, deputy secretary of defense for public affairs under President Johnson, so honestly asserted: the inherent right of the government to lie to the people. Sylvester was not the first to follow this practice; he was only more honest about it. His predecessors and successors simply call it "public relations" or "opinion management."

To William Appleman Williams, the origins of the American actions in Southeast Asia are to be found in the vision of the New England fathers of what they called "The City on a Hill," a society raised high above others by its moral probity and God-given values, a society in which the doctrine of an evangelical, crusading America was encapsulated: America as the force of light striving against a world of evil.

Such a philosophy—active or subliminal—Williams believes, underlies the containment theory of George Frost Kennan and the first critical steps taken under that rubric by President Truman and Secretary of State Acheson toward involvement in Vietnam.

If this be so, the city on a hill has been badly shaken.

Hardly anyone seems prepared to ask the questions: What went wrong in Vietnam? What happened? How can it be prevented from happening again? Our political leaders have perceived Vietnam as a still-glowing coal. To seize the question might sear their careers. The public has turned away from the issue in confused despair. The American military hardly mentions Vietnam. Not a single major assessment has been made of what went wrong and what went right. Instead, the military have comfortably wrapped themselves in star-spangled blankets and whispered, "No more Vietnams, no matter what president suggests a small assistance mission in some distant land."

The military have blamed the politicians and the press; and we journalists have not done much better. The bookshelves overflow with follow-ups by such astute observers as Gloria Emerson, Frances FitzGerald, David Halberstam, William Shawcross, and many more. But not much has been done lately. Bright new headlines have beckoned. Long before Vietnam had been tucked away in its bloody wrapping sheets we were whooping and hollering off on fresh tracks—very fresh and very important, those of Watergate, of the CIA, and COINTELPRO.

There have been a few exceptions: Neil Sheehan laboring year after year like some medieval monk on the book about John Vann, which we all hope will bring the American experience into focus; Seymour Hersh with his classic exposé of Henry Kissinger, Richard Nixon, and the whole Dr. Caligari's cabinet of deceits and illusions; and John Del Vecchi's realism masquerading as novel, *The Thirteenth Valley.*

To James Thomson, a man of missionary background, there appear in the American intervention in Vietnam subtle symptoms of a transference of American emotion and philosophy from the "lost" China to an adjacent alternative objective in Southeast Asia. We lost China, but would regain our missionary goals by "saving" Vietnam—not noticing that we were plunging into a domestic civil war. Through most of the analyses contained in this volume and the discussions over four days at the University of Southern California which produced them, there runs like a red thread the question of ignorance—the ignorance of the policymakers; the ignorance of the military; the ignorance of the public; the ignorance of the press as to what Vietnam was, what it was about, and even where it was geographically. Sometimes the ignorance was deliberate and contrived—actually a deception; but often enough it was genuine, a sheer lack of knowledge or understanding. No one bothered to ask the experts, and there were precious few to ask.

There was, alas, much self-deceit.

With the end of the war, not much has changed. Post-Vietnam has been for the most part a gray wasteland in which few wish to occupy their minds with difficult and painful questions. On this horizon so bereft of landmarks, we can begin to see the emergence of gruesome absurdities, poisonous tales of paranoia reminiscent of those which emerged in post-Wilhelmian Germany and eventually destroyed the Weimar Republic: tales of the stab in the back, the war lost by press and TV, the noble military handcuffed by puerile politicians—the makings of the kind of legend that in Germany spawned Hitler and the terrible disaster of the Third Reich.

It is time to call a halt to such escapism—escapism is the only word for it—and turn to the serious task of establishing the facts of Vietnam and drawing from them some conclusions for the future. I do not agree with Hegel, who once asserted that neither the people nor governments have ever learned anything from history or acted on principles deduced from history. I believe that only by analysis of history can we understand our present and gain some notion of the future. If we do not understand our mistakes, we are doomed to repeat them.

Ronald Steel suggests that the power vacuum left at the end of World War II by the exhaustion of the world's imperial powers impelled the United States into roles unthinkable in the past. With Japan prostrate, China engulfed by civil war, and Europe's empires in ruins, the United States was drawn almost magnetically into Southeast Asia. Many Americans believed that the United States was better qualified than any other state to assume the role of mentor and protector of the benighted nations of the world and to guide them toward democracy and enlightenment. Steel feels it a mistake to suppose that Kennan intended the containment doctrine to apply to Asia. It had as its goal halting the threat of Soviet aggression in Europe. But John Foster Dulles, following in Dean Acheson's footsteps, applied it to Asia and stretched its dimensions to the ultimate.

By the time the United States began backing the French more and more heavily in Indochina, not many Americans remembered the warning of Franklin D. Roosevelt against assisting France to restore its rule in Indochina. Nor had the initial signs of eagerness by Ho Chi Minh to collaborate with the United States (reported here by Archimedes L. A. Patti and Robert Shaplen) left much trace. Instead, Vietnam had begun to be perceived as a building block of Communism and a good place to hit back at Moscow. That otherwise prescient American diplomat, David Bruce, warned from Paris that if Indochina fell, Burma, Thailand, and Malaysia would fall as well, "like ripe apples." (Of course, to this day they have not fallen.)

So the forces built up. There were American military men who were eager for a showdown in Indochina. They wanted to finish what they felt they had been denied by the truce in Korea—a resounding victory in Asia over the Communists. Some perhaps dreamed of an escalation from Indochina into China itself. U.S. funds began rolling into Saigon. They hit two billion dollars in 1955–56. By this time the French had left, and President Eisenhower had sent in four hundred U.S. "advisors." President Kennedy would up that total to sixteen thousand, and Lyndon Johnson would "cross the big river" and make it an American war.

It got bigger and bigger. Even so, Lt. Gen. W. R. Peers still feels it did not get big enough and was too slow in growing. The fatal mistake, he believes (and he is not alone among the military), was in not biting the bullet at the start—declaring war, nationalizing the National Guard, putting the nation on a war footing, and pouring in huge troop increments at the beginning to force a quick decision. Instead he thinks we nibbled Vietnam to our own death.

But the papers herein contained make abundantly clear that President Johnson never had a mandate from Congress or the nation for that kind of war. Even his own kind of now-you-see-it, now-you-don't escalation finally proved self-defeating. The political trouble at home grew and grew. The war just didn't work. As John Mueller notes in these discussions, the Vietnamese were consistently underrated and underestimated. They suffered casualties at twice the rate of Japan in World War II and came on for more.

No one in the U.S. command, no one in U.S. intelligence, no one in the U.S. political structure understood the Vietnamese dedication to their country and its defense against the U.S.A. Sometimes the American intelligence was good, sometimes it was not. There was always the peril of skewing the intelligence to fit perceived political precepts—especially those of the White House.

Again and again in these discussions emerge the issues of

ignorance, deceit, misperception, and the inability to understand the enemy or the war it waged.

At times it became quite clear that the U.S. military was fighting the wrong war at the wrong time in the wrong place. General Peers notes that the crack American divisions sent to Southeast Asia were trained to fight in Europe, not the jungle. Their weapons, their equipment, their tactics were geared for war against the Soviets in Europe, not a guerrilla struggle in the tropics.

And it was fought on a short-term basis—the men went in for a year; the officers just to punch a ticket, to get combat citations on their career profiles.

The problems of Vietnam tumble out of the assessments like logs into a spillway.

What, then, are the lessons of Vietnam? That remarkable man, Robert McNamara, whose fertile innovation and too-logical mind was responsible for some of the most revolutionary experiments contemporary military men have attempted, seems today unique in his capacity for early recognition that the prime need after Vietnam was a clear, sharp, brutal postmortem. I have been a newspaperman for fifty years, and the number of politicians I have met who have been willing to submit their policies to such an inquiry is limited to one—Robert McNamara.

That is why the fate of the Pentagon Papers, the great, free-wheeling, McNamara-initiated and sponsored inquest on Vietnam, must be accounted so great a tragedy. I will defy any group of well-informed Americans to recall its findings. The conclusions reached by this study over which Leslie Gelb, Daniel Ellsberg, and so many others labored; the long-suppressed files they uncovered; the duplicitous interpretations, tricks, deceptions, conflicts, and discrepancies—all of the evidence has slithered down the memory hole. No one has wanted to remember; no one has wanted to learn the truth.

The gravamen of McNamara's magnificent bequest to this country was lost in the blaze of legal and political controversy which attended its emergence in June 1971. National interest was diverted from what the Pentagon Papers revealed to the question of whether press and public had a right to print and read them. The fuss and fury buried the words of the papers like an avalanche. The papers have never been read, and even today are largely ignored by contemporary scholars who, busily putting an academic varnish on "revisionist theories" that exculpate those responsible, hope thereby to win fame and fortune.

The wonder, perhaps, is not that McNamara's work was swept into the rubbish heap of the unread, but that it ever saw the light. Few nations are truly eager to learn what they have done wrong. Had it not been for a few individuals and a handful of courageous newspapers, the papers would still be gathering dust on the top shelves of a Pentagon strong-room. The truth and the crusty ingredients of history are not apt to be thrust freely into the hands of citizens, reporters, or historians. We must take as an axiom that the possessor of authority wants the world to know only those facts which will add gloss to his reputation, his policies, his decisions. Since few reporters and historians are willing or able to dig out the other facts, most often what is suppressed is *the* story.

This is a lesson which anyone who worked on Vietnam learned so well that it would not seem to need repetition. But I repeat it because the lesson is not unique to Vietnam; it is the basic instruction which should be engraved on the mind of every citizen in every country in every time. Not long ago I picked up Guy Chapman's study of the Dreyfus affair.[1] It was the first time I had read about that classic example of government and social blackmail, forgery, corruption, hate, and lies: one layer of lies laid on another, again and again and again, until the whole body was encrusted and France was almost brought down by the sheer weight of the lies.

I think all of us should be compelled to study the Dreyfus affair. I do not mean that Washington or Sioux Falls, South Dakota, provides a replica of that Mauve Decade scandal in Paris. But we must never forget that men of prejudice and power will halt at nothing when that power is threatened or when political tempers rise. The preservation of political power by any means is a human characteristic that knows no bounds of country or century.

These are the deeper implications of *Vietnam Reconsidered* that were so exhaustively examined in the USC discussions and which are reflected in the materials incorporated in this volume.

---

1. *The Dreyfus Case: A Reassessment* (London, Hart-Davis, 1955).

PART I
THE WAR

THE CITY ON A HILL ON AN ERRAND INTO THE WILDERNESS

William Appleman Williams

George F. Kennan not only provided, in his doctrine of containment, the modern version of the traditional American dogma that ultimately sermonized, cost-accounted, and marched America and Americans—in the name of duty and immortality—into the graveyard of Vietnam, he also told us the essential truth of that dogma. He did this most forcibly by quoting another austere conservative who had also come to understand the dangers of making policy on the assumption that America was "The City on a Hill Destined to Transform the Wilderness." Kennan whispered these words from John Quincy Adams into our soul: "America goes not abroad in search of monsters to destroy. . . . She might become the dictatress of the world; she would no longer be the ruler of her own spirit." [1]

As he informed us in that carefully crafted phrase, "in search of monsters to destroy," Adams understood that the theology of The City on a Hill contains a demonology and a thirst for immortality that are inherently, inevitably destructive. Historian Loren Baritz has documented the bipartisan nature of that outlook, and Henry Nash Smith has made it clear that, from the beginning, the dogma contained a strong and persistent determination to control

---

1. Oration, Fourth of July, 1821.

the economic benefits of transforming the Wilderness into a suburb of the City.[2]

We also know that, beginning long before the American Revolution, American leaders had begun to expand the definition of the Wilderness to include mature but misguided nations. The purpose of The City on a Hill was as much to transform England, for example, as it was to civilize the savages. We must realize, as well, that those mutually reinforcing elements of the doctrine of The City on a Hill were underwritten by an almost euphoric confidence in our military superiority. And all those elements came together in a willingness to intervene and kill people in Vietnam, no later than the winter of 1949–50, during the administration of President Harry S. Truman.

Some of that arrogance of power was subconscious. We had destroyed the first Americans in protracted guerrilla warfare punctuated by occasional set battle pieces. We had wiped out the freedom fighters in the Philippines. We had won two world wars. Some of it was terrifyingly rational. We had the bomb. We were in a position to give reality to the prophecy of The City on a Hill.

There was no problem in defining The Monster To Destroy. During the 1920s, 1930s, and 1940s the Left and the Right in America agreed to define Socialism in terms of the Soviet Union. That legacy of misplaced concreteness made it easy to define Stalinist Russia as The Monster.

And so it was done.

And then there was the fascinating relationship between Truman, the failed small-town haberdasher from Missouri, and his arrogant, frustrated Ivy League secretary of state, Dean G. Acheson. Someday, somebody may delineate the character of American culture by exploring that connection. Here and now we can describe it as a marriage of convenience between The City on a Hill and the Tamed Wilderness. The Wilderness had been subsumed under the City.

We see the essence of that in two unguarded moments. Acheson had a favorite metaphor: America was the locomotive puffing

---

2. Loren Baritz, *City on a Hill: A History of Ideas and Myths in America* (New York, John Wiley, 1964); Henry Nash Smith, *Virgin Land: The American West as Symbol and Myth* (New York, Vintage, 1957).

away to pull the rest of the world into civilization. Truman talked about the hordes of Asians—the Wilderness—threatening to overwhelm civilization. The hordes were Russian. Those images and metaphors (do not forget Kennan's talk about the Soviets as a windup toy) tell us most of what we need to know about why we went to kill people in Vietnam. We were transforming the Wilderness in order to save The City on a Hill. As Adams warned, the City had lost its soul.

It is always intriguing to figure out how economics, ideas, and personalities combine to muck up our lives. And surely intervention in Vietnam did muck up our lives. But we are not talking about economics in the silly sense of short-term dollars in the cashflow account. Whatever else you may say about them, our leaders are more intelligent than that. No, the economics of our intervention in Vietnam had to do with our concern about raw materials and markets, and with our fear that the Japan we rebuilt might play the China card. We were so powerful at the end of World War II that we had to create competitors. Otherwise, the imbalance would destroy capitalism as America defined capitalism. If Japan collapsed, then all hell would break loose. One way or another, Japan had to win World War II. But it could not be allowed to win World War II in China. That left Southeast Asia.

So economics and theology and secular ideology converged in Vietnam.

There were some problems. The demonology of The City on a Hill that defined the Soviet Union as the source of all evil was given a rude shock by Marshal Tito. During the spring and early summer of 1948, he broke with Stalin, sustained his independence, and thereby subverted the neat equation between Stalin and the evil Wilderness. It was a scary moment for Acheson and Truman. Their theology threatened to unravel at the seams.

Acheson considered the possibility that Tito had opened the way to accommodation with China. And surely the Chinese had sent messages to encourage such rationality.[3] Kennan wrote Acheson a long, thoughtful letter suggesting a visceral review of American policy. Acheson put Paul Nitze in charge of the review. Out

---

3. Robert M. Blum, *Drawing the Line: The Origin of the American Containment Policy in East Asia* (New York, W. W. Norton, 1982).

of that came the definitive City on a Hill document—otherwise known as NSC-68 (see Appendix 1 for excerpts). Acheson dismissed other views. And he never moved against Dean Rusk, who—from the beginning unto the end, under Lyndon Baines Johnson—took a militant hard line against any threat to the capitalist City on a Hill in the Wilderness of Vietnam.

Acheson and Truman had trapped themselves. They had sold the Truman Doctrine and the Marshall Plan in Europe by scaring hell out of the American people, by presenting the Soviet Union as evil incarnate. And they had explained the Chinese Revolution as the devious manipulations of Stalin. They had taken the worst of isolationism and internationalism and created the mentality of a fortress American empire.

They had destroyed their own options.

They had no place to go but war.

Military materiel for South Vietnam was loaded and at sea before the outbreak of the war in Korea.

UNITED STATES NATIONAL INTEREST IN VIETNAM

James Thomson

Why did the United States choose to take any sort of a stand in Southeast Asia, given its exceptionally unpromising history, geography, and politics? What was American national interest there? How on earth to define it?

What has surprised me most, both in my years in government and in my later reading of the archives is that the U.S. national interest in Indochina was rarely if ever explicated internally or challenged internally, but instead, regularly asserted as a given and apparently never doubted by those who made the policy from 1950 onward. For example, the second paragraph of an early 1952 National Security Council statement on "U.S. Objectives and Courses of Action with Respect to Southeast Asia" reads as follows: "Communist domination, by whatever means, of all Southeast Asia would seriously endanger in the short term, and critically endanger in the long term, United States security interests."

One pauses at that point to ask, "What are those security interests?" But no answer is offered. The succeeding paragraphs declare that "the loss of any single country in Southeast Asia would lead to Communism in all Southeast Asia, then India, then the Middle East, and finally [of course, magic words], would endanger the stability and security of Europe." A long swim!

Some have suggested that our stake was material, the resources of the region. There is no way to disprove an article of faith, but to those who are revisionists, neo-revisionists, or economic determinists, I can only attest that in my nearly seven years in government, I never saw in writing nor heard in discussion, in the most secret and confidential documents or meetings, any allusion whatsoever to our need for the raw materials or other products of Indochina—or indeed for access to an Indochina market. I never saw an argument for a stake in the region on economic grounds.

Let me suggest a deeper reason. There are phrases in the recent history of American–East Asian relations that are curiously evocative of a long and deeper past. "To win the hearts and minds of Asians," now somewhat out of fashion as a slogan, does in fact evoke a phrase and a strongly felt hope that sustained the American missionary enterprise in its heyday, before and after the turn of the century, namely "China for Christ." Vice-President Hubert Humphrey's proclamation, in 1966, that the Great Society would be brought to all of Asia was reminiscent of Thomas Jefferson's dictum that the American revolution was intended for all mankind. It is not my intention to play games with evangelical rhetoric, but simply to note that our war in Indochina was only the most recent phase of a very lengthy Asian involvement by Americans, stretching all the way back to 1784, right after the close of the American War for Independence, when the first American trading vessel entered the Canton trade.

There have been some interesting continuities in that involvement. A common bond seems to have existed between missionaries and the many secular brethren operating in Asia, particularly in China: namely, the itch to change China, to transform the Chinese to our own image, if possible, and to do good to others. As a result of this itch to do good, the Chinese became prime targets for conversion to our religious offering of Christianity, our political offering of Jeffersonian democracy, and our economic offering of capitalism. I am suggesting that mission and manifest destiny coalesced in our focus on Asia in the first half of this century, in particular, on China.

Prior to World War II, however, the export to Asia of our good works, of our assumed benevolence, was largely in the hands of private individuals and organizations. With Pearl Harbor and American entry into the Pacific war, the United States government itself picked up where the private organizations had left off. In the first years of that war and the Cold War that followed, such organizations as the United Nations Relief and Reconstruction Agency, the Marshall Plan, Point Four, foreign aid, Food for Peace, the Peace Corps, etc., were institutionalized. And they greatly expanded, under secular and governmental auspices, the export of our assumed benevolence, the national itch to do good. I am making no judgment about the evil or good of the enterprise, I am only describing its gigantic enlargement, now underwritten by the state itself, flying its flag, protected by its awesome armaments, and allied to its prestige.

But something else has also happened along the way: the emergence of a new post-Hitler enemy—namely, the Communist revolutionary alternative to our gradualist reformism and its ultimate success in our special Asian preserve, namely, China. The shock of the so-called China loss had many well-known effects on our nation. The one I would stress today is the shift in purpose of America's missionary impulse from China to the Asian periphery, and in particular to Southeast Asia. A century of missionary desire to save and transform China was now beamed in secularized form onto the people of Indochina. And it was done with a sharply intensified sense of urgency, thanks to the perceived Communist threat.

What I am suggesting, then, is that America's sentimental imperialism has been a prime and underreported motivation of presidents and even some secretaries of state in the long and futile effort to deny Indochina to Communism and save it for our way of life. Its motivation runs deep in our history and in our intellectual bloodstream. It has sometimes accomplished great good, but when accompanied with our grandiosity, our military might, and our frustration, it has indeed produced lethal consequences.

The major problem of America's Indochina involvement was not, however, its missionary impulse, but the refusal to understand and acknowledge that the hostilities occurring in Vietnam were fundamentally, for all their complexities, messiness, and longevity, elements of a civil war. Sad to say, it never suited the purposes of the American government to come to this recognition and understanding, to level with the American people on the nature of that war, to level with the Congress, or even to level with itself. Indeed,

at the root of many of the large and small deceptions that characterized America's Vietnam policy over the years, there was that
most fatal flaw of all—namely, collective self-deception. And given
that flaw, there was no way to face and tell the truth that we had,
after all, no real stake or national interest there, had made a bad
mistake, and should simply get out.

VIETNAM AND UNITED STATES NATIONAL SECURITY

Ronald Steel

The American part of the war rested on a very particular definition
of security, one that emerged after the Second World War. It
represented a profound break with the way that American policymakers and the American public had earlier defined security. During the 1920s and the 1930s security was defined narrowly. We
sought to protect our shores and to restrict our political involvement with other nations. We did, of course, involve ourselves economically both in Europe and Asia during the 1920s and 1930s.
But the perception that American security demanded military intervention on a global basis came about after the Second World
War.

Our prewar view of security changed for many reasons. First,
because of the collapse of rival empires: Germany, Japan, Britain,
and France. There were no competitors, and the United States
inherited the Western World as it inherited much of Asia. The
definition of security changed also because there was a rival power,
far weaker than ourselves but nonetheless one that, in its ideological ambitions and territorial sweep, represented an ambiguous challenge and a threat. The vacuum of power that occurred after the
Second World War was unstable. Vacuums require filling, and the
United States was the only power with both the means and the
ambition to fill the perceived vacuum. The new military balance

that emerged after the Second World War combined with an expansive American ideology to give a global framework to security. The ideology of an American mission is a powerful one—a mission to transform, to improve the world, to create it more along the lines which we feel are better for us and better for everyone else.

This combination of factors led to a new definition of security that went far beyond the territory of the United States, far beyond the Western Hemisphere. It went global. The United States had the means to define security globally, and we had elites that felt they had abdicated their responsibilities during the 1930s. They were atoning for Munich and noninvolvement, for nonparticipation in the League. Woodrow Wilson's dream of reorganizing the world was revitalized after the Second World War. And, of course, Soviet expansion into Eastern Europe provided a justification for our outward reach. The containment doctrine thus became the framework for confining the Soviet empire and organizing the world under a more beneficent American direction.

The doctrine of containment was enunciated in terms of Europe and originally confined to Europe. Formally articulated during the time of the Greek civil war, it related directly to the struggle for Germany, the struggle between East and West, the struggle between America and Russia *for* Germany. That struggle for Germany gave rise to a Western alliance, and provided much of the justification for NATO. Not until later, not until Korea in 1950, did containment go global. Only then did the full implication of the Truman Doctrine become known. Truman declared an American obligation to defend free people everywhere against both external and internal threats to their security—in other words, to contain both aggression and revolution. In containment, in this very particular and very expanded definition of containment—including now the determination to control *internal* change—we see the logical justification for American intervention.

As part of the global definition of security, any dramatic change in the status quo is seen as threatening—even a change of forces within a country. The balance itself reflects the status quo, a status quo largely, of course, congenial to the controlling power. Clearly, the United States, even with all its power, could not have intervened everywhere in the world. It could not have intervened in China. At the time of the Communist victory, there was much gnashing of teeth and wringing of hands over China; but there was also the realization that there was very little more the United States could have done to prop up Chiang Kai-shek.

Much of the scapegoating that took place after the fall of China reflected a sense of frustration. The "loss" of China rankled terribly, not just because of the China lobby, although it played a significant part; but because that "loss" reflected the inability of the United States to influence events there. Even the liberals in the Kennedy administration felt frustration over what happened in China. And so Vietnam, when it came along, was almost a return bout. It was seen as another chance, a chance for victory, a chance to recapture a lost opportunity, to turn history around.

Was Vietnam then a crusade, an effort at vindication, or a quagmire? It was all of those. But, most important, it was perceived as a battlefield of symbolic importance. The continuing debate over containment as a guiding principle of foreign policy rests upon this perception of security as ideological and global.

Could we have done it differently? Could we have seen the world in a different light and thus have avoided our intervention in Vietnam? Given the realities of the American power, the ambitions of policymakers, the perception of American interests, the ideological thrust of American policy, the sense of mission in our society, and the need to orchestrate events, it seems to me that something like Vietnam had to happen somewhere. A global definition of security—one that rests on ideological containment—can be challenged or turned around only when it meets an immovable object. This change comes about as a result of defeat, of diminished power, of an inability to control events.

Why did we stay so long? Why did we not recognize defeat earlier? We stayed because we *could* stay; because North Vietnam could not dislodge us. We hung on because policymakers believed that defeat would create a new political reality. An American defeat would establish that we could no longer control events in areas where we had engaged our prestige. Thus, for both psychological and geopolitical reasons, a succession of American administrations believed it necessary to sustain the intervention in Vietnam as long as consensus held at home.

DEVELOPMENT OF A VIETNAM POLICY: 1939–1945

Archimedes L. A. Patti

Not until World War II did the United States show any interest in Vietnam—more accurately, French Indochina. In 1940, Japan, with the acquiescence of the Vichy government of France, sent troops into northern Vietnam. The following year, Japan completed the task of occupying the southern portion of the Indochinese peninsula—threatening British, Dutch, and American interests in Southeast Asia. In response, in July 1941 the United States froze Japanese assets; and Indochina figured prominently in the ensuing negotiations which ended with the Japanese attack on Pearl Harbor.

For both military and political reasons, the United States did not challenge Japanese control of Indochina. The fall of Singapore in February 1942, followed by a catastrophic debacle in Burma, had cut Britain's national pride to the quick. Churchill, a stubborn champion of British primacy in the Southeast Asian colonial sphere, was concerned for the security of India, and he considered Burma a bastion to be held if at all possible. Nonetheless, his priorities were always, and had to be, the survival of Britain and a "Europe-first" strategy.

President Roosevelt sympathized with Churchill's strategy, but still wanted him to take a more effective stand in the Far East. For several years the United States had been committed to support

Chiang Kai-shek in the struggle against Japan's pan-Asiatic ambitions, and China was very hard pressed. Roosevelt feared that if Japan consolidated its efforts in China and gained full military control, China would collapse—with unpredictable strategic consequences.

Despite his misgivings, the president deferred to Churchill's commitment to a "Europe-first" strategy, and Allied planning proceeded on that basis: crushing Germany first, then defeating Japan—and the road to victory over the Japanese did not lead through Indochina. Our military planners assumed that victory in the Pacific would mean the end of Japanese control of Indochina without a necessity for large-scale operations there.

Politically, President Roosevelt made it clear that he did not intend "to get mixed up in any Indochina decisions" or in "any military effort toward the liberation of Indochina from the Japanese." Indochina, he repeatedly insisted, was "a matter for postwar."[1] Yet, during the war, Indochina was a frequent topic of study and discussion by the president, the State Department, and the Joint Chiefs of Staff (JCS). Sometimes this topic arose from French requests for permission to participate in the war against Japan, a euphemism for a French campaign to regain control of its lost colony. Just as frequently, the subject was introduced by the president himself, who held strong views regarding the disposition of Indochina after the war and did not hesitate to express them to such widely differing personalities as his son Elliott, the joint chiefs, the secretary of state, Churchill, Generalissimo Chiang Kai-shek, General Stilwell, officials of the Turkish and Egyptian governments, and Stalin.

Despite the rhetoric, there was no stated policy in the early 1940s regarding America's relations with Indochina as a nation, only as it pertained to American relations with France and Japan in Indochina. President Roosevelt's avowed anti-colonialism notwithstanding, early concern with Indochina was political-military rather than ideological.

After the fall of France in 1940, the Vichy regime hoped to preserve the French empire. Marshal Pétain looked to the British and Americans for support. Only Britain, concerned for its own

---

1. *Foreign Relations of the United States* (1945), 6:293.

holdings in the Far East, responded affirmatively; the United States was not ready to risk a confrontation with Japan over French colonial interests.

Furthermore, American policy toward the French empire was complicated by the presence of two claimants to French sovereignty—Marshal Henri Pétain and Gen. Charles de Gaulle. In September 1941, Great Britain and the Soviet Union recognized de Gaulle as "chief of all the Free French," but the United States refused to support de Gaulle and maintained diplomatic ties with the Vichy regime. A month after the attack on Pearl Harbor, Ambassador Leahy assured Pétain and Darlan of our intention to see France, including the French empire, "reconstituted in the post-war period in accordance with its splendid position in history." And on November 2, 1942, as American troops were preparing to land in North Africa and we sought to enlist French support or, at the least, to ensure that the French would not fire on the American landings, Mr. Robert D. Murphy, American consul general in Algiers, pledged the reestablishment of French sovereignty "throughout all the territory, metropolitan and colonial, which flew the French flag in 1939." Then, just as our American troops hit the beaches, the president himself sent a message to Pétain that "the ultimate and greatest aim [of the American armies] is the liberation of France and its Empire from the Axis yoke."[2] Unfortunately, these pledges did not dissuade the French from resisting the American landings. Instead, Pétain replied: "We are attacked; we shall defend ourselves; this is the order I am giving."[3]

President Roosevelt made no further pledges to restore French sovereignty throughout her empire, and by the Casablanca Conference in January 1943, he was openly voicing his opposition to a French return to Indochina. Whether this was anger over French resistance to the American landings in North Africa or his aversion to colonialism is not clear. Whatever the reason, at Casablanca he confided to his son Elliott that he was not sure "we'd be right to return France her colonies at *all*, ever, without first obtaining in the case of each individual colony some sort of pledge, some

2. Elliott Roosevelt (with Joseph P. Lash), ed., *F.D.R.: His Personal Letters, 1928-1945*, Vol. II (New York, 1950), pp. 1275-76.

3. Robert E. Sherwood, *Roosevelt and Hopkins: An Intimate History* (The Universal Library; New York, Grosset & Dunlap, 1950), p. 645.

sort of statement of just exactly what was planned, in terms of each colony's administration."⁴ Specifically with regard to Indochina, the president asserted, "the native Indochinese, have been so flagrantly downtrodden that they thought to themselves: Anything must be better, than to live under French colonial rule! . . . Don't think for a moment, Elliott, that Americans would be dying in the Pacific tonight, if it hadn't been for the shortsighted greed of the French and the British and the Dutch."⁵ In concluding this discussion with his son, the president pledged that, once the war was won, he would work with all his "might and main to see to it that the United States is not wheedled into the position of accepting any plan that will further the British Empire in *its* imperial ambitions."⁶

On numerous other occasions Roosevelt emphasized that he did not want Indochina returned to France, but expressed a preference for placing it under an international trusteeship. At the Cairo Conference in November 1943, Roosevelt found Chiang Kai-shek receptive to that idea. Several days later at Tehran, and later at Yalta (February 1945), Marshal Stalin was in full accord with the president's idea. But Churchill was strenuously opposed to any action that infringed on French sovereignty over its colonial empire. As Roosevelt put it to Stalin, the British, and particularly Churchill, were against the idea because of the implications of such an arrangement to the British empire. As it developed, Roosevelt never took definite steps for putting his idea into action.

To say that the president's attitude toward Indochina constituted official policy in the 1940s would stretch the point. When I became involved in the Indochina affair, my first concern was to find an official pronouncement of policy; and I found none. Quite by chance, I came across a memorandum of November 1943 from the State Department advisor on political relations, Stanley K. Hornbeck, indicating that "the time has come . . . when it is especially desirable that [we] . . . have as complete as possible a common knowledge of the attitudes, policies, utterances, etc. of the United States, the United Kingdom and the British Dominions,

---

4. Elliott Roosevelt, *As He Saw It* (New York, Duell, Sloan, and Pearce, 1946), p. 114.
5. *Ibid.*, p. 115.
6. *Ibid.*, p. 116.

China, various French groups etc. regarding . . . Indo-China."[7]
Evidently, nothing came of Hornbeck's prodding.

Then on January 3, 1944, Secretary of State Cordell Hull
met with the British ambassador Lord Halifax, who queried him on
the president's views expressed at the Cairo and Tehran confer-
ences regarding placing Indochina under trusteeship. Lord Halifax
wanted to know if "the President's utterances represent final conclusions. . . ." Hull replied that he knew no more about the matter
than the ambassador, adding that in his judgment, "the president
and Mr. Churchill would find it desirable to talk this matter fully,
deliberately and perhaps finally at some future stage."[8] American
policy regarding the return of Indochina to the French was still in
limbo officially.

But military operations kept forcing the issue. The joint
chiefs, the State Department, the White House could not ignore
the president's predilection for unburdening France of Indochina;
and while he lived, the president's attitude in the matter was considered "American policy." In the fall of 1943, that "policy" began
to collide with French colonial interests. The French Committee
of National Liberation requested a large increase in American military aid and petitioned for representation on the Pacific War
Council. It disclosed French intent to use the aid to restore French
sovereignty to all territories of the empire. The program was rejected on both military and political grounds. The JCS saw no purpose
in assisting the French to regain their colonial empire at the expense of the total Allied war effort. The president agreed, but
supported the chiefs' position with a political reason they had not
taken into account: "We should not commit ourselves to the
French to give back to France all her colonies. . . . We should not
let our policy regarding this matter give the appearance of a definite commitment." And in listing the territories he felt should not
be restored to France, he placed Indochina first.

Many similar requests followed. Always, French offers to participate in the Far East war were underscored by one objective, the

---

7. Department of State Memorandum, S. K. Hornbeck to Office of Far
Eastern Affairs, 17 November 1943, No 851G.01/1–1743 EG., Diplomatic Files,
National Archives, Washington, D.C.

8. Cordell Hull, *The Memoirs of Cordell Hull,* Vol. II (New York, Macmil-
lan, 1948), p. 3. 1596.

reconquest of Indochina. These offers were politely declined by the Departments of War and State and, in effect, marked "file and forget." Except for occasional reports from the American Embassy at Chungking of "Annamite" revolutionary activities in southern China, American interest in Indochina remained dormant.

The lack of a clear-cut policy regarding Indochina surfaced once more in mid-1944 when, in July, Maj. Gen. M. E. Béthouart, visiting Washington with General de Gaulle, discussed with Admiral Leahy France's intention to recover Indochina from the Japanese and, of course, asked for American military aid for that purpose. He got nowhere. Instead, Admiral Leahy informed him that "Indochina could not at that time be included within the sphere of interest of the American chiefs of staff." [9]

Rebuffed by the Americans, the French turned to the British, who proved more sympathetic. In July 1944, the French Committee of National Liberation asked the British to use their influence in securing American acceptance of French participation in both regular military operations and clandestine activities in Indochina. The British firmly supported the French proposal for clandestine activities, and for several months strove to obtain American concurrence. In essence, the British wanted the American government to agree to accredit a French military mission to the Southeast Asia Command (SEAC), where it could assist clandestine operations undertaken by the British Special Operations Executive (SOE) or by the American Office of Strategic Services (OSS). The British asked the Americans to accept French participation in the planning of political warfare, with the understanding that it would be limited to areas in which the French had a definite interest. Lastly, the British wanted the Americans to agree to accept a French *Corps Léger d'Intervention* (CLI) of five hundred men, trained to operate exclusively in Indochina against the Japanese lines of communication.

These proposals reopened simmering controversies: French participation in the war against the Japanese; arming the French for retaking their colony; questions of theater boundaries and jurisdiction in Indochina between SEAC and the China Theater; the

---

9. William D. Leahy, *I Was There* (New York, McGraw-Hill, 1950), p. 244.

postwar status of French colonies.

Again we wavered. Our chiefs of staff, urged by OSS, were sympathetic to the British proposal for clandestine activities but objected to everything else. In replying to the British chiefs, the American chiefs so qualified their approval that they actually committed neither themselves nor the American government. But in an aside, they did let the British know that they did not look with disfavor on the establishment of a French military mission in SEAC.

Several weeks later, Lt. Gen. Albert C. Wedemeyer, Commanding General, U.S. Army Forces, China Theater, informed the War Department that General Blaizot, with a French military mission, had arrived at SEAC headquarters at Kandy, Ceylon, and that a British-Dutch-French cabal was working to ensure the recovery of their political and economic prewar position in the Far East. Wedemeyer asked for United States policy.

He got a prompt reply from the White House. The president had already been informed that the French mission had been accorded American approval at SEAC, and he was furious. The president informed Leahy in vigorous terms that he intended to control American policy on Indochina himself:

With regard to this matter, I wish to make it clear that American approval must not be given to any French military mission being accredited to the South East Asia Command; and that no officer of this Government, military or civilian, may make decisions on political questions with the French military or with anyone else.

I would like further to have it made clear that this Government has made no final decisions on the future of Indo-China, and that we expect to be consulted in advance with regard to any arrangements applicable to the future of Southeast Asia. [10]

To all intent and purpose, this *was* "American policy" toward Indochina.

On March 9, 1945, the Japanese overthrew the French administration in Indochina, disarmed and interned the French army, and conducted a mop-up operation against a handful of resisters.

---

10. Message, Wedemeyer to Chennault, WARX 55402, MAPLE 52, 19 March 1945. "Wedemeyer's Papers," National Archives, Washington, D.C.

Despite French claims of "popular resistance" and "extensive *Maquis* operations," the evidence is that there were none. Nonetheless, Maj. A. M. Brossin de Saint-Didier, chief of the French military mission in Washington, made a good case for the "French resistance in Indochina" to the American chiefs of staff. The president relaxed somewhat. He did not object to according General Blaizot a status that would enable him to be of help "in such efforts as we can make towards assisting the French forces now in Indo-China."[11]

The president's intent to assist only "besieged" French underground fighters was quite clear. But the French and, to a lesser degree, the British chose to interpret Roosevelt's humanitarian directive as a loophole to obtain American military aid and to participate in Allied planning and operations in the Far East. In fact, this deviation in the president's policy did not mean that all French possessions should be restored to France after the war. Nor did it herald the approach of vast American armies marching to liberate Indochina. As I was to learn firsthand in Kunming, China, the president instructed Lt. Gen. Wedemeyer to give the French only such aid as would be required in *direct* operations against the Japanese *only*. He urged the general to "watch carefully to prevent British and French political activities in that area." The only Americans entering Indochina under his modified "policy" were members of the OSS whose mission was to gather intelligence and furnish arms to those fighting the Japanese.[12]

The question has been raised why the president and his military advisors decided to give the French underground any help. Aside from humanitarian motives, from the evidence at hand, it seems likely that the president and the joint chiefs were concerned that the British might unilaterally assume military control in Indochina. But it is even more probable that the president was motivated less by military than by political considerations; that his main reason for aiding the resistants was his determination to prevent an Anglo-French coalition from exploiting the situation in Indochina in a manner calculated to restore the *status quo ante bellum* to Southeast Asia. This interpretation is consistent with his many

11. *Ibid.*
12. Memo, LTC Paul L. E. Helliwell (Ch SI OSS CT) to Strategic Services Officer, CT, "OSS Activities in French Indo-China," 10 April 1945 "French Indochina, File No. 93-1, Operations and General Information." CIA Archives.

statements on Indochina and is also supported by his charge to Wedemeyer to prevent British and French political activities in that area.

On April 12, 1945, Roosevelt suddenly died. Nine days before his death he had approved the release of this statement by his secretary of state:

As to territorial trusteeship, it appeared desirable that the governments represented at Yalta, in consultation with the Chinese Government and the French Provisional Government, should endeavor to formulate proposals for submission to the San Francisco Conference for a trusteeship structure as a part of the general organization. This trusteeship structure, it was felt, should be defined to permit the placing under it of the territories taken from the enemy in this war as might be agreed upon at a later date, and also such territories as might voluntarily be placed under trusteeship. [Emphasis in original] [13]

As to the policy Roosevelt would have pursued toward Indochina had he lived, one can only speculate. It would appear, however, that before his death he had abandoned the idea of an international trusteeship. To be sure, he had discussed it with Stalin at Yalta, and they had agreed it was desirable. But further than that they did not go, as the secretary's statement implies.

Several days before the secretary's statement was released, General de Gaulle had issued a declaration published in the *Journal officiel* of March 25, 1945, stating that France had always considered that Indochina was "called to take a special place in the organization of the *Communauté Française* [French Community] and to enjoy therein a liberty in accordance with its state of evolution and its capacities." Therefore, Roosevelt must have realized when he approved the secretary's statement that France would never agree to a trusteeship. And, given the strong backing of the British and the Dutch, the prospect of establishing a trusteeship against the wishes of France was virtually eliminated.

---

13. Department of Defense, *U.S.-Vietnam Relations, 1945-1967,* study prepared by the Department of Defense for the use of the House Committee on Armed Services, 12 vols. (Washington, D.C., United States Government Printing Office, 1971), 8:6.

NATIONALIST-COMMUNIST
STIRRINGS IN VIETNAM: 1944-1946

Robert Shaplen

In those early Saigon days of the mid-forties,[1] it was apparent not only to the handful of Americans who were there but to the more liberal-minded French (a minority including a few dozen lost souls who had in effect been "exiled" by de Gaulle to Indochina after the Resistance in France was over) that a genuine revolutionary condition existed in the country. Unfortunately, American policy on Vietnam was then conducted by the French desk at the State Department, provincially and unimaginatively. There was no recognition of the revolutionary climate for what it was: a legitimate, historic hope of the Vietnamese people to be free of any domination—whether that of their former colonial masters; that of old or new native tyrants or satraps; or, with some important exceptions among the Vietnamese, that of the Communists.

American policymakers mainly failed to evaluate correctly the evolution and significance of the Communist movement in Indochina. Communism in the North, under the leadership of Ho Chi Minh and his small, tight group, was a unique nationalist force that, while owing much to Marxism and Leninism as well as Maoism, was in many ways distinct from the world Communist movement and represented, at least potentially, a Titoist-like con-

---

1. Shaplen made his first trip to Vietnam in June 1946.

stituency of its own. Indeed, it went its own way as did Tito's following in Europe; and if it had been further encouraged by the West, particularly by certain influential Frenchmen and Americans who, for one reason or another, had become *engage*, it could have developed more nearly independent of Moscow and Peking. Had that happened, the tragic course of events in Vietnam during the French and American wars might have been altered if not avoided.

The Communist movement in the South, on the other hand, was far more diffuse and fragmented; it included a number of disruptive and disputatious Trotskyist as well as Stalinist elements; and it never enjoyed the unity of the movement in the North. Overall, it was far weaker. Inevitably, therefore, it became an adjunct of the *Laodong* (workers) party of the North, and despite occasional efforts to develop along its own lines, it never blossomed on its own or seriously established itself independent of Hanoi. Its underground leaders, from the start, were mostly northern or central Vietnamese dispatched to the South.

I have always believed, along with some members of the old OSS who maintained contact with Ho in the jungles of Vietnam and in southern China in the long months before the end of the Second World War (and then afterward for a briefer time in Hanoi), that Ho was sincere in his desire to obtain help from the West, especially from the French, and to steer his own nationalist-Communist course.

The key period was the spring and summer of 1946, when Ho traveled to Fontainebleau in France under the wing of Jean Sainteny, the ranking French diplomat in Hanoi, to flesh out agreements for aid he thought he had obtained in principle. But the French colonials returning to South Vietnam, acting in consort with the old *colon*-minded elements in Paris, vitiated and then destroyed—at the Dalat Conference in central Vietnam—whatever hopes for compromise and support existed, and thereby set the South on its course to disaster.

The noted French scholar Paul Mus was one of the few Frenchmen who later acknowledged that France and the Western World missed a proper opportunity with Ho in 1946. His willingness to deal with the French at the time, before the war broke out, Mus believed, was predicated on Ho's need for French advice, especially for financial and economic advice.

"Marxist doctrine calls for the proletarian state to use, at least temporarily, the accountancy of bourgeois-capitalist countries," Mus told me. Ho knew that Vietnam could not stand on its own feet, either in terms of money or trade, if only because of the corrupt, inbred economy imposed by the powerful Bank of Indochina. While he realized that he could not rely on the colonial French, he understood that his best political approach, initially, was through metropolitan France; and he was determined to play that possibility in his own adroit way. But he was caught between his affection and regard for France—which had given him his Marxist ideology and image as a youth—and his new disillusion of 1946.

"If we had supported him more strongly then," Mus said, "we might have won. . . . We thought we could crush him if it came to war. We did not appreciate how hard he could fight. But we must not forget that he really wanted an agreement with France at the time of Fontainebleau because it would have served him. That part of his motivation afterward died, of course, but we should understand that it existed at the time and that he was truly disappointed."

There probably was little the Americans could have done at this point to change the situation. The "radical" OSS influence, never actually strong enough to guide United States policy, had already been dissipated; and, more sorrowfully, there was no official policy toward Vietnam at the time. Roosevelt had warned all officials to stand clear of the French and to not get involved in Indochina; and after he died, Truman, in his early days, was not yet concerned with the area. In fact, he did not really concern himself until the outbreak of the Korean War, when, at the end of June 1950, he announced that, in addition to sending troops to South Korea, he was accelerating the furnishing of military assistance to the forces of France and the Associated States of Indochina and dispatching a military mission to provide close working relations with those forces. Even in the light of what we later spent ourselves in Vietnam, the figures alone of our earlier involvement are astonishing: American assistance to the French in 1950 was a modest $10 million; by fiscal 1954, it had reached more than $1 billion.

AMERICAN INVOLVEMENT: 1950

George C. Herring

Prior to 1950, the conflict in Indochina remained for the United States a low-priority issue, more important for its European implications than for anything else. As a result of the fall of China to Communism and the intensification of the Cold War, however, the Indochina war came to be perceived as an integral part of the broader struggle between Soviet-dominated Communism and the so-called Free World. More important, in 1950, Vietnam was deemed vital to American security, its defense the key to maintenance of a fragile global balance of power. Thus, in the aftermath of the fall of China, the rationale that would govern American policy in Vietnam for the next fifteen years took root. Commitments to assist the French and later to defend Vietnam with American resources followed logically.

The victory of Mao Tse-tung's Communists in China swept aside the ambivalence and hesitancy that had characterized American policy up to 1949. In December, Red Chinese troops arrived at the Tonkin border, established contact with the Vietminh, and began to furnish material assistance to Ho's forces. The Democratic Republic of Vietnam was among the first governments to recognize the People's Republic of China. Mao quickly reciprocated, and the Soviet Union soon followed suit. The establishment of direct ties between the Vietminh and the major Communist powers appeared to Washington to increase dramatically the threat to Indochina, even raising the possibility of a Chinese sweep across the border. It also provided the clinching evidence the State Department had long sought that Ho's revolution was an instrument of international Communism, making it easier to justify support for France to skeptics at home and abroad. Secretary of State Dean Acheson triumphantly proclaimed, in February 1950, that Soviet recognition removed any "illusions as to the 'nationalist' nature of Ho Chi Minh's aims and reveals Ho in his true colors as the mortal enemy of native independence in Indochina." [1]

Mao's victory, combined with Soviet testing of an atomic device, also provoked a sweeping assessment of America's global Cold War strategy—from which emerged the conclusion that the loss of Indochina would threaten vital U.S. interests. By the end of 1949, the Truman administration considered itself engaged in a mortal, worldwide conflict with the Soviet Union. The "loss" of China was viewed as a major victory for Russia and a "grievous" defeat for the United States. Some American strategists saw the United States facing a situation much like 1941—with Russia taking Germany's place in Europe; and China, Japan's in Asia. Europe was still viewed as the area of preeminent interest, but Asia was deemed vital as a source of raw materials and as an outlet for exports; and its loss to Communism would enormously strengthen the Soviet adversary. In any event, administration strategists reasoned, Communist expansion had reached a point beyond which it must not be permitted to go. Any further "extension of the area under the domination of the Kremlin," NSC-68 warned, would "raise the possibility that no coalition adequate to confront the Kremlin with greater strength could be assembled." [2]

In the dramatically altered strategic context of 1950, Southeast Asia assumed major importance for U.S. policy. China having just fallen, Southeast Asia seemed likely to be the next battleground in the Cold War. The war in Indochina and insurgencies in Burma, Malaya, and Indonesia all sprang from indigenous roots, but their mere existence and their leftist orientation persuaded

---

1. *Department of State Bulletin* (13 February 1950), p. 244.
2. National Security Council 68, 14 April 1950, printed in *Naval War College Review* (May–June, 1975), pp. 51–108. [See Appendix 1.]

American policymakers that Southeast Asia was "the target of a coordinated offensive directed by the Kremlin." Communist victories in Southeast Asia could deny the United States access to oil, rubber, and other vital raw materials. If, after the fall of China, Southeast Asia was also "swept by Communism," the NSC warned, "we shall have suffered a major political rout the repercussions of which will be felt throughout the world. . . ." According to the State Department's policy planning staff, Southeast Asia was the "vital link in the crescent of containment reaching from Japan through Australia to India."[3]

In the calculations of American strategists, Indochina and particularly Vietnam now emerged as the key to Southeast Asia. The French army stood as the only "military bulwark" against Communist expansion in the area, but the French warned that they could not hold the line without American support. Since Indochina was "in the most immediate danger," the State Department concluded, it was "the most strategically important area of Southeast Asia."[4] In an early elaboration of what would later be called the domino theory, Ambassador to France David Bruce warned that if Indochina fell, Burma and Thailand would drop like "over ripe apples"; and the British might have to withdraw from Malaya. The National Security Council agreed that the "balance of Southeast Asia would then be in grave hazard."[5] Thus was born before the Korean War a set of assumptions that would go unchallenged for nearly two decades and would provide the foundation for massive American involvement in Vietnam.

These assumptions were sufficiently compelling to overcome the reservations that surfaced as the United States moved toward direct involvement. Many U.S. officials remained profoundly reluctant to identify with French colonialism. But the fear of a French collapse which might lead to the loss of Southeast Asia

---

3. Quoted in Seigen Miyasato, "The Truman Administration and Indochina: Case Studies in Decision Making," *The Japanese Journal of American Studies*, Vol. 1 (1981), p. 134.

4. Dean Rusk to General James H. Burns, March 7, 1950, U.S. Congress, Subcommittee on Public Buildings and Grounds, *The Pentagon Papers (The Senator Gravel Edition)*. (Boston, Beacon Press, 1971), I, p. 363.

5. Bruce to Secretary of State Dean Acheson 11 December 1949, *Foreign Relations of United States, 1949*, VII, pp. 105–10.

posed risks that were viewed as unacceptable. The United States would then face the grim choice of making a "staggering investment" to recover the losses or of falling back to a "much contracted" line of defense in the Western Pacific. Given these choices, top U.S. policymakers felt they must assist France, and as Acheson put it, "muddle through."[6]

In retrospect, the assumptions upon which U.S. policy was based in 1950—and after—appear misguided. Ho Chi Minh and his cohorts were Communists, to be sure, rigid and doctrinaire in their views and committed to structuring their society along Marxist-Leninist lines. But they were never mere instruments of Moscow. The Soviets did not instigate the revolution, and in fact exerted very little influence until after the United States initiated the bombing in 1965. The Chinese played an important role in the early stages, but traditional Vietnamese suspicions of China—the product of a long history of Chinese imperialism—restricted the closeness of these ties. In any event, by 1950 Ho had captured the standard of Vietnamese nationalism; and by placing ourselves against the strongest force in an otherwise politically fragmented country, we may have ensured our ultimate failure.

The risks of nonintervention seem also to have been exaggerated. We will never know, of course, whether the domino theory would have operated if Vietnam had fallen earlier, but there is good reason to doubt that it would have. Neither the Chinese nor the Soviets had the military power to project their will into insular Southeast Asia, and their influence over the revolutions in the area was in most cases quite limited. It seems highly doubtful that the fall of Vietnam would have triggered a chain reaction which would have resulted in Communist control of Southeast Asia.

---

6. Dean G. Acheson, *Present at the Creation* (New York, Norton, 1969), pp. 673–74.

THE AMERICAN MILITARY IN VIETNAM: 1950s

Murray Fromson

When I arrived in Saigon for the first time, in the early fifties, to cover the withdrawal of the French Foreign Legion, it was with a sense of *déjà vu*. I had come from a tour of duty with the Associated Press in Korea and Japan. One of my first encounters was with a familiar face, the new chief of the U.S. military advisory group in Vietnam, Lt. Gen. "Iron Mike" O'Daniel. Shortly thereafter, there was another familiar face, Lt. Gen. Sam Williams. Both had served as combat officers in Korea. It occurred to me then, and as the result of conversations among Americans at the Majestic Hotel, that, despite warnings from the French, whatever U.S. policy evolved in Indochina would be heavily influenced by the compulsion of our advisors to obtain what was denied them by armistice in Korea—that is, a clear-cut victory over the Chinese Communists. It became an obsession in Washington, repeatedly pronounced, for example, by Secretary of State Dean Rusk, that if we didn't fight the Chinese in Vietnam, we would have to fight them on the beaches of Hawaii.

American soldiers arrived, then guns and helicopters, and then advice on how to use them. The French had done the same thing. But they never left any doubt about who was in charge, whereas America simply supported Diem's strategic hamlet program. American advisors taught the Vietnamese to fight and die;

they dispensed, like missionaries, medical care, food, and agricultural advice. When the Vietcong disrupted the rice harvest in the Mekong Delta, they arranged large shipments of rice from California and Louisiana. The Vietnamese detested it so much that they used it instead of dirt to fill their sandbags.

To the dismay of the professional soldiers, their mission was always tempered by the politics of the moment. The regular soldiers who went to Vietnam in the early days were not evil men. Far from it. They were dedicated and confident of being able to fight a new kind of war. Insurgency, they called it. But they were also politically naive. The lessons learned at Fort Bragg were not always applicable to the realities of Vietnam. They took a stab at being both soldier and politician, only to find as the war dragged on that they had less and less stomach for either.

U.S. soldiers inevitably became trapped in the vortex of U.S. and Vietnamese political decision-making. The advisors assigned to the fledgling army of Vietnam not only had to worry about making better soldiers of the Vietnamese, but also had to cope with the bizarre nature of Vietnamese politics. Variations on a theme, often having little to do with a war, were orchestrated at battalion, division, corps, and sector level, as well as in Saigon. Which Vietnamese officers were trusted by Saigon? Which ones were politically connected? Which ones wanted to fight the VC? Which ones were more interested in the black market or in being feudal warlords? And the ultimate judgment, at least from Saigon's point of view: Which of the commanders were too friendly with the Americans? Which troops were assigned where was often determined by ethnicity, religion, regionalism, who was connected to whom politically—or who was too independent, daring, imaginative, or innovative on the battlefield. Units recruited in the coastal provinces could not be assigned to the Mekong Delta, while those from Saigon were rarely dispatched to the Central Highlands.

For a young American officer, perhaps a few years out of West Point, or for a seasoned combat veteran from Korea or World War II, the labyrinth of Vietnamese politics, at its highest and lowest level, was often stifling and most assuredly incomprehensible. This situation was aggravated by a double-edged frustration. Most of the Americans were unable to communicate with their so-called Vietnamese counterparts. They did not speak Vietnamese well at all; they played at it, using Pidgin English, sign language, and army phrase books. Ultimately, it probably affected how the Vietnamese performed in combat. The other edge of the frustration evolved from what the army called "ticket punching," or the short tour. Officers were rotated into and out of combat after four to six months and then into staff jobs; this meant that the Americans rarely had time to adjust to Vietnam itself or to learn about their Vietnamese counterparts, while the Vietnamese had to adjust to a new American advisor every few months.

The conflicting politics of the White House, of the Pentagon, of the American military in Saigon, and of the Vietnamese affected analysis of the situation and obstructed the reaching of a valid strategy for fighting the war. Question followed question—and the questions betrayed the indecision. Was it to be a war with Americans serving only as noncombatants? A guerrilla war? A conventional large-scale war? How many American troops were needed? No one could decide.

DEVELOPMENT OF A VIETNAM POLICY: 1952-1965

Robert Manning

The development of what passed for an American policy in Southeast Asia began after the end of World War II when the United States, while championing independence for the colonialized Asian nations—India, Burma, Indonesia, and the Philippines—made an exception in the case of France's desire to retain its Indochina colony.

The pro-independence policy was replaced by a policy of neutralism that dashed the Vietnamese hopes for freedom (Ho Chi Minh had already proclaimed, and issued his declaration of, independence) and enabled Paris to reestablish its hegemony over Vietnam, Laos, and Cambodia.

When it became evident that the French might lose their war with the Vietnamese insurgents, and that this would threaten a far more crucial U.S. policy—the maintenance of West European security—the U.S. changed again. She adopted a policy of providing the French with the means to avoid defeat. That made three policies in little more than four years. When *that* policy threatened to crash in the flames of Dien Bien Phu, some American leaders, including Vice-President Richard Nixon and Admiral Arthur Radford, proposed a far more radical policy: direct American intervention, chiefly by air, to save the French at Dien Bien Phu. Secretary of State John Foster Dulles, it is alleged, even talked of using nuclear weapons to achieve this.[1] Admiral Radford has been quoted (by Gen. James Gavin, an opponent of U.S. involvement in Vietnam) as arguing the necessity of intervention to keep Vietnam's seaport potentials in Western hands for a probable war with China.

President Eisenhower sternly forbade direct intervention. Soon came the Geneva Agreement and the *next* U.S. policy: a policy pledging not to upset the Geneva accords by "threat or use of force," but seeking to avoid their intention—one Vietnam united by elections.

The Eisenhower administration saw in the accords a new opportunity. Long frustrated by what the Americans considered France's lack of will, poor military planning, and identification with colonialism, the U.S. thought it could make a fresh start with the new government of Ngo Dinh Diem and build a stable country resistant to Communist encroachment.

Thus came the *next* policy, that of pacification and nation-building, and its justification was something called the domino theory. Under Eisenhower, some $2 billion in American aid went to the Diem regime between 1955 and 1960, and the first American advisors, civilian and military, were introduced into South Vietnam. This American commitment, plus a crisis in neighboring Laos, where Communist forces threatened to prevail over anti-Communist and neutral elements, were inherited from Eisenhower by John Kennedy in 1961.

Kennedy took over when the issue of Communist aggression preoccupied American political debate. The situation in Berlin was deteriorating. Castroism was spreading into much of Latin America; Russia seemed to be infiltrating the Western preserve of Africa. Kennedy's administration got hit by the Bay of Pigs crisis in April, the Laos crisis in May, the truculent summit meeting with Nikita Khrushchev in June, the shock of the Berlin Wall in August, and the resumption of Russian nuclear testing in the atmosphere in September. It was in this superheated atmosphere—when he was calling up 150,000 reservists, making major adjustments in the

---

1. Statement by Georges Bidault, former French Minister of Foreign Affairs, in the film documentary *Hearts and Minds,* directed by Peter Davis (Warner Brothers Pictures, 1975).

defense budget, initiating a national program of fallout shelters for protection against nuclear attack, and orchestrating a new arms buildup to close the alleged missile gap—that President Kennedy undertook his appraisal of the American commitment to Vietnam.

While a cold warrior in his rhetoric ("We will pay any price, bear any burden . . . to assure the survival and success of liberty"), Kennedy was a fairly cautious man, and one made more so by the Bay of Pigs fiasco. He resisted urgings of a task-force proposal that the U.S. declare its intention to intervene, unilaterally if necessary, to save South Vietnam from Communism. He also resisted a JCS recommendation for deployment of sufficient American forces to provide a visible deterrent to further aggression by North Vietnam (and, by implication, China). He did agree to a Defense Department "examination" of the size and composition of forces that would be necessary should the U.S. decide to commit troops to Vietnam. Then, more aid was earmarked for South Vietnam and a four-hundred-man group of Special Forces soldiers was sent to Nha Trang to accelerate ARVN training. Thus began a steady escalation of the number of U.S. "advisors" and the flow of materiel. By the time of John Kennedy's assassination in November 1963, the few hundred American military that Eisenhower sent had grown to more than sixteen thousand U.S. soldiers participating in hundreds of armed confrontations. By the end of 1963, they had flown some seven thousand air missions, lost twenty-three aircraft, and suffered 108 deaths.

By then, South Vietnam's President Diem was also dead, the victim of a military coup exercised with the foreknowledge and at least tacit consent of Washington. It was to be the first of a series of coups that bedeviled efforts to effect stable government there. After eight years of unqualified American support of the Diem regime, less than half of the territory of South Vietnam was under Saigon's control. The Northern-directed National Liberation Front was levying taxes and exerting varying degrees of control in at least part of all but three of South Vietnam's forty-four provinces. The situation was steadily growing worse.

Such was Lyndon Johnson's Vietnam inheritance: a frequently enunciated American commitment to save South Vietnam, an American public poorly informed by their political leaders as to what that commitment might require, and a situation on the ground in South Vietnam which exposed thousands of American soldiers and civilians to injury, captivity, and death.

President Johnson chose to cross the big river. He is widely condemned for having done so, and for the manner of his doing it. It is difficult to believe that he could have easily done otherwise. Johnson did not inherit a clear national policy. He inherited *hubris*—a commitment boldly and frequently stated, and (by the time he took office) already characterized by a sizable American presence. And with Lyndon Johnson, a little *hubris* went a long way.

Looking back, we find few constants in the development of the Vietnam involvement, save for a thread of steady misjudgment and one dominant emotion: fear of Chinese intervention. That imposed a constraint on all major planning, applying limits on the way the Vietnam War was to be fought, forbidding Allied forces to attack either the source of Communist aggression in the North or its avenues of supply and infiltration through Laos and Cambodia.

This in turn imposed constraints at home, causing presidents and their administrations to minimize the nature and size of the American involvement (insofar as size could be minimized as the numbers grew) and deliberately to refrain from drumming up popular support for the war. And, in this one area at least, American leaders, if only subliminally, judged correctly. There was widespread public understanding that America had only limited interests at stake in Vietnam. And without truly realizing it, Americans sensed that, given the distance and the North Vietnamese determination, no amount of American military aid would have allowed South Vietnam to maintain independence for long unless accompanied by a large-scale American occupation. Presidents Kennedy, Johnson, and Nixon were all correct in assuming that no amount of drumbeating and mobilization was going to induce the country to accept that condition.

INTRODUCTION OF AMERICAN COMBAT FORCES: 1965–1969

Lt. Gen. William R. Peers (USA-Ret.)

In mid-1965, the decision was made to send U.S. combat forces to South Vietnam. We should have immediately committed sufficient ground, air, and naval forces so as to end the conflict in the shortest possible time. Such a commitment would have saved countless lives and injuries, avoided the no-win situation in which our forces became involved, and greatly reduced the inner conflict which so divided this nation.

But the U.S. did not do that. American leaders did not mobilize the armed forces, federalize the National Guard, or call reserve units to active service. War industries, the economy, and the population were not mobilized. Nor were funds provided for deploying sufficient combat forces to do the job quickly and get it over with. Instead, Secretary of Defense Robert McNamara made the decision, with the approval of the president, to fight a war of gradualism, a piecemeal kind of war, employing an initial minimum force and adding to it bit by bit as the situation dictated. As a result, it became a Pentagon war, not a people's war, and dragged on for eleven years, much to the disillusionment of the American people.

The army combat units that first came to South Vietnam were in a fairly high state of readiness and were shipped out pretty much in an "as is" condition. These units included the 173d Airborne Brigade, the First Cavalry Division, and the Fourth and Twenty-fifth Infantry Divisions. They all faced problems. The army's orientation toward a war in Europe necessitated rather extensive changes in the types and quantities of equipment. Also, the tour of duty in South Vietnam was set for one year, resulting in the shifting of people in and out of units and the bringing in of frequent replacements—which caused a high degree of personnel turbulence and a lessening of unit cohesion. There were also problems in the command structure. The Commander, U.S. Military Assistance Command, Vietnam, Gen. William Westmoreland, had broad command responsibilities, but he sometimes lacked authority to carry them out. His authority to control troop strength was limited to making requests to Washington; and the daily list of bombing targets had to be approved by the Pentagon, and sometimes even by the president, before it could be implemented. Further, in November 1968, the North Vietnamese army units in the South were running out of food and ammunition; units of squad, platoon, and even company size were surrendering; and victory seemed within our grasp. To the dismay of all, the president called a halt to the bombing in North Vietnam and along the Ho Chi Minh trail. Within a short time, the supplies were again flowing down the trail and we were back to combat as usual.

Our entire operation there was one of counterinsurgency, which could have been fought defensively or offensively. Only an offensive strategy—where you go in and get them out of their redoubts and mountain sanctuaries—allows you to engage them in battle and overcome the insurgency. The Army of the Republic of Vietnam could have done much more of this, but most of their units stayed back in defensive positions near cities. Those ARVN units that did take the offensive—the Rangers and some of the airborne units—did very well. We did take the offensive after the Tet offensive [January–February 1968], quickly leaving the cities and routing the North Vietnamese from the hills and jungles. When I left, in May 1969, I personally felt that we were in a very, very solid condition in terms of counterinsurgency and control of the countryside.

In our system of government, the service departments (Army, Navy, Air Force, and Marines) are not left alone to devise strategy.

But, for the sake of discussion, suppose they had been delegated sole authority for devising a strategy for victory in Vietnam. I am not at all sure what strategy they would have developed, but here are some of the things which I think they undoubtedly would have considered:

1. National mobilization.
2. Early deployment of sufficient combat forces to insure a quick victory.
3. Eliminate the Commander in Chief, Pacific, from the chain of command between the Pentagon and the U.S. military command in South Vietnam.
4. Create a unified command, under a single commander, to control all the forces in South Vietnam (U.S., ARVN, Republic of Korea, etc.).
5. Declare the areas in Cambodia and Laos that were used as sanctuaries by the North Vietnamese as open areas, with NVA units subject to hot pursuit.
6. Inform the North Vietnamese government it must withdraw its military units from South Vietnam and end the flow of combat supplies or face massive retaliation.
7. If the North Vietnamese government failed to comply, establish a naval blockade of all ports, and conduct unrestricted conventional bombardment of all road and rail centers and military industries and installations. If necessary, deploy ground forces across the entire Ho Chi Minh trail.
8. Terminate such applications of force only when positive assurance is forthcoming from the North Vietnamese government that the people of South Vietnam will be granted the right of self-determination.

REASSESSMENT OF AMERICAN POLICY: 1965–1968

John Mueller

Between 1965 and 1968, American policy over the war in Vietnam underwent a major reassessment. In 1965 there was near-consensus: the war was seen as an unfortunate necessity, and the effort to fight the Communists there, and to contain them, was considered vital to American security. By 1968 this consensus had eroded considerably, and there were many, both inside the administration and outside it, who were disillusioned by the war. In that year the administration of President Lyndon Johnson decided to put a ceiling on the number of American troops and to seek to turn the war over to the South Vietnamese, setting in motion the slow process of American disengagement.

In discussing this shattered consensus, commentators have mostly dealt with the cost side of the ledger. Between 1965 and 1968, American troops took over the chief burden of the battle and aggressively tried to carry the war to the enemy.[1] The result was a

---

1. The strategy was one of attrition, an effort to inflict so much punishment on the Communists that they would mellow their efforts in the war. Punishment was effectively meted out, but it appears North Vietnam was virtually unique among combatants in international wars in the last 160 years in its willingness to accept punishment. As a percentage of the prewar population, it accepted twice the battle death rate as the Japanese in World War II, for example. See John E. Mueller, "The Search for the 'Breaking Point' in Vietnam: The Statistics of a Deadly Quarrel," *International Studies Quarterly*, Vol. 24 (December, 1980), pp. 497–519.

substantial increase in Communist casualties, but at the same time, a considerable cost in American lives. As these costs grew, so did disillusionment with the war.[2]

It is the central argument of this paper that the consensus was shattered not only by the increasing *costs* of the war, but also by changing perceptions about the *value* of keeping the Communists from controlling South Vietnam. South Vietnam, which seemed so vital to American security in 1965, was, *using consistent standards,* not nearly so important three years later. By these standards, the war did not start as a mistake, but it soon became one.

At the time of major American escalation in Vietnam in 1965, the strategic picture in Southeast Asia was grim. To the north was a glowering, hostile Communist China, and to the south was a belligerent Indonesia, whose President Sukarno was embarked upon a "confrontationist" policy in the area. Moreover, these two countries, the world's first and fifth most populous, were closely linked. Indonesia had an enormous Communist party closely associated with Peking and had withdrawn from the United Nations to join China in a rival organization—a sort of alliance that was sometimes called the "Peking-Jakarta axis"—and was seen as a major instigator in instability and revolution in the area.[3] Indeed, one National Security Council memorandum from 1964 treats Indonesia as a country that is already all but Communist.[4]

C. L. Sulzberger of the *New York Times* compared the strategic picture to a gigantic nutcracker in which the small nations of Southeast Asia were about to be crunched between two hostile arms.[5] The metaphor may not have been compelling to the dominoes of 1965, but the threat it represented was. The leaders of the dominoes were quick to urge the United States to stay the course. As Malaysia's prime minister put it in 1965, "In our view it is imperative that the United States does not retire from the scene." Leaders in Australia, New Zealand, Cambodia, Singa-

---

2. For an analysis of American public opinion during the period, see John E. Mueller, *War, Presidents and Public Opinion* (New York, Wiley, 1973). Popular support for the war declined as a function of American casualties—the same function as for the Korean War.

3. *Pentagon Papers* (Boston, Beacon, 1971), Vol. 3, p. 267.

4. *Ibid.,* p. 51.

5. "Foreign Affairs: The Nutcracker Suite," *New York Times,* Section E (April 10, 1966), p. 8.

pore, Thailand, and even India concurred.[6]

Bolstered by such pleas, there was a consensus that the policy of containment, formulated to prevent Soviet incursions into Europe, could reasonably be extended to apply to Chinese pressure in Asia, i.e., if the United States did not fight to stop Communism in South Vietnam, it would only have to fight somewhere else later. At the time, most agreed with David Halberstam's assessment of Vietnam: "A strategic country in a key area, it is perhaps one of only five or six nations that is truly vital to U. S. interests"; or with Neil Sheehan's conclusion that: "the fall of Southeast Asia to China or its denial to the West over the next decade because of repercussions of an American defeat in Vietnam would amount to a strategic disaster." [7]

Impelled by such thinking, the United States made a massive commitment of troops and firepower to Vietnam in the summer of 1965. But then something unexpected happened: the arms of the nutcracker broke off.

The most dramatic change was in Indonesia. In the fall of 1965, the Communists, apparently with Sukarno's blessing, launched an effort to eliminate major anti-Communist leaders in the army. The effort failed spectacularly; there was a violent countercoup in which tens of thousands of Communists were killed. By the spring of 1966, the party had been destroyed and the nation's foreign policy had been redirected. Indonesia no longer posed a meaningful threat in the area.[8]

After this foreign policy catastrophe (though not necessarily because of it), China embarked on its bizarre ritual of romantic self-purification known as the Great Proletarian Cultural Revolution. Although still verbally belligerent toward the United States, it mostly focused its energies inward—and toward various confronta-

---

6. Guenter Lewy, *America in Vietnam* (New York, Oxford, 1978), pp. 421–22. See also Neil Sheehan, "Much Is At Stake In Southeast Asian Struggle," *New York Times,* Section E (August 16, 1964), p. 4.

7. David Halberstam, *The Making of a Quagmire* (New York, Random House, 1965), p. 319; Sheehan, *op. cit.* On this consensus, see especially Leslie H. Gelb with Richard K. Betts, *The Irony of Vietnam* (Washington, Brookings, 1979). See also Ian Maitland, "Only the Best and the Brightest?" *Asian Affairs,* Vol. 3 (March–April, 1976), pp. 263–72.

8. For an account, see Robert Shaplen, *Time Out of Hand* (New York, Harper & Row, 1969).

tions with the Soviets on its northern frontier. Its challenge to U.S. global policy diminished considerably.

But by the time these events in Indonesia and China had taken place, the United States had made its massive commitment of ground troops to the war in Vietnam. The war became primarily an American effort; and U.S. prestige, dignity, honor, and credibility had become part of the ante. Some of the most important reasons for the commitment of troops were no longer valid, but now the U.S. was thoroughly enmeshed.[9]

During 1966 and 1967, American policy in Vietnam was increasingly questioned and the administration was continually challenged to explain why Vietnam was so important. Increasingly, the administration found this difficult. The logic of containment remained sound, but the imminent threat from Indonesia and China was no longer there. Accordingly, there was a tendency to fall back on the unsatisfying, question-begging "We are there because we are there" argument: We must fight because we have committed ourselves. It could plausibly be argued that American honor and prestige were at stake, but it was far more difficult to demonstrate a threat to U.S. *security* in the area. Many of those who found Vietnam vital to American interests in 1965 turned to opposition—to Lyndon Johnson's intense displeasure—but this shift often occurred not because these people changed their standards when the going got tough, but because international political conditions had changed so radically.[10]

By 1967 this curious state of affairs had gradually been appreciated within the administration. As Secretary of Defense Robert McNamara observed in a memorandum, "The fact is that the trends in Asia today are running mostly for, not against, our interests (witness Indonesia and the Chinese confusion)."[11]

---

9. As Henry Kissinger observed in 1969, "The commitment of 500,000 Americans has settled the issue of the importance of Viet Nam. For what is involved now is confidence in American promises." "The Viet Nam Negotiations," *Foreign Affairs,* Vol. 47 (January, 1969), pp. 218–19.

10. Johnson's view of the defections from his policy: "When casualties started coming in, why certain folks started looking for the cellar." Interviewed on *Sixty Minutes,* 16 March 1971.

11. *Pentagon Papers* (*New York Times* edition; New York, Bantam Books, 1971), p. 583.

The point was brought home to McNamara's successor, Clark Clifford, when he made a goodwill tour of the dominoes at the end of 1967. The leaders who in 1965 had urged U.S. involvement in Vietnam were now remarkably relaxed about the war and in no hurry to help the U.S. effort there.

"It was strikingly apparent to me," Clifford concluded, "that the other troop-contributing countries *no longer* shared our degree of concern about the war. . . . Was it possible that our assessment of the danger to the stability of Southeast Asia and the Western Pacific was exaggerated? . . . Was it possible that we were continuing to be guided by judgments that might once have had validity but were now obsolete?"[12]

Essentially what had happened was that Vietnam had *ceased* being "vital" to American security and to Southeast Asian stability. As McGeorge Bundy recently observed, although Vietnam seemed "vital" in 1964 and 1965, "at least from the time of the anti-Communist revolution in Indonesia, late in 1965, that adjective was excessive, and so also was our effort."[13] Using constant standards, the war had become an anachronism and a mistake.

---

12. "A Viet Nam Reappraisal," *Foreign Affairs* (July, 1969), pp. 606–607. Emphasis added. The trend toward the "de-vitalization" of Vietnam accelerated after 1968 as detente with the Soviets broadened and as Sino-American relations improved. According to Allen E. Goodman, Henry Kissinger was soon arguing that Vietnam was a conflict "in which the United States had become involved for reasons that were *no longer* as compelling as the need to improve relations with the Soviet Union and China." *The Lost Peace* (Stanford, Calif., Hoover, 1978) p. 84. Emphasis added.

13. "The Americans and the World," in Stephen R. Graubard, ed., *A New America?* (New York, Norton, 1978), p. 293.

THE INTELLIGENCE OF THE CENTRAL INTELLIGENCE AGENCY IN VIETNAM: I

Frank Snepp

Theoretically the CIA was apolitical, outside the realm of policy-making. But seldom did reality conform to the ideal. Often, U.S. intelligence indirectly affected decisions on Vietnam—by reinforcing or undercutting the prejudices of the decision makers, or by limiting their flexibility through error or excess. And then, of course, there was that miscellany of strong-willed CIA officials who simply threw away the rules and made policy themselves. Allen Dulles was one. He believed absolutely in the domino theory and made sure that CIA analyses reflected his bias through the late 1950s. By 1964, agency analysts had officially repudiated the doctrine, at least to the extent of suggesting that Cambodia would be the only regional victim of a Communist takeover in Vietnam and Laos. But by then it was too late. The domino theory had become a basic tenet of U.S. policy in Southeast Asia.

In the meantime, some of Dulles's successors had begun to pursue covert paramilitary operations in the area that likewise had long-range policy implications. William Colby, initially station chief in Saigon and then head of the agency's Far East division, laid the groundwork for the CIA's "secret war" in Laos by dispatching operatives to organize Meo tribesmen into small self-defense units. He also attempted to counter Communist guerrilla tactics in South Vietnam with the first of several "pacification" programs. Village defense units and terrorist squads were organized in the highlands and elsewhere; and a Vietnamese version of the American Special Forces was created, under its own independent command, by CIA bagmen assisted by U.S. Green Berets. For good measure, reconnaissance teams were launched over the beaches into North Vietnam and across the border into southern Laos. None of them ever proved very efficient. But the rest of Colby's brainchildren initially showed more promise—at least, as long as they were held strictly to their limited missions by tight CIA control and State Department supervision. But, beginning in 1962, there occurred a series of events which perverted their objectives and turned them into loose cannons. First, there was meddling by the South Vietnamese government. President Diem and his brother Ngo Dinh Nhu were so impressed with the village defense units, that they took them over, expanded them, and so overextended their reach as to render them ineffective. They also seized control of the Vietnamese Special Forces, converted them into a kind of hip-pocket gestapo, and thereby alienated the regular Vietnamese army command, which rightly concluded it was being upstaged.

As if this weren't bad enough, the U.S. military stepped in to impose its will on the agency's other paramilitary assets. "Operation Switchback," as this exercise was called, had been born of official discontent over the Bay of Pigs fiasco, which had convinced many in Washington that the CIA didn't know how to run paramilitary operations. Maybe they were right. But the U.S. military proved even less adept. Operating on the principle "Big is Better," the Pentagon pressed the CIA to enlarge its secret army in Laos into an offensive force and to involve its irregular units in South Vietnam in conventional military operations outside their pacified enclaves.

By mid-1963, thanks to these changes, Colby's fledgling pacification effort was in shambles. But so was the South Vietnamese government. Curiously, despite all its resources, the CIA had failed to anticipate the coming storm. At the start of the Buddhist riots in Hue, Colby assured his colleagues that Diem could ride out the turbulence. He was dead wrong. Diem, with his brother's encouragement, became increasingly paranoid and eventually sent the Vietnamese Special Forces—the CIA's loose cannon—against

Buddhist pagodas in Saigon and elsewhere. This persuaded a group of hard-liners in the State Department that Diem had to go, if the war was to be won. Colby and CIA Director John McCone emphatically disagreed. They also opposed State Department propaganda designed to justify increased U.S. military involvement in South Vietnam and Laos by exaggerating the extent of North Vietnamese involvement. But in both cases Colby and McCone were overruled. The State Department got its coup in Saigon, and an expanded war effort. In early 1964, with the department's backing, as well as the Pentagon's, President Johnson initiated the secret bombing of Laos and intensified reconnaissance missions against the North. One of these operations now under U.S. military control, precipitated the Tonkin Gulf episode, which in turn rallied congressional support for Johnson's war plans and jogged Hanoi itself into a more aggressive posture. A few weeks later, U.S. intelligence picked up indications that the North Vietnamese were beginning to move regular army units south, as well as fillers and political cadres. With that, Johnson's own case for escalation was cinched, and then followed Rolling Thunder (the bombing of the North) and the U.S. troop buildup in the South.

Here again the CIA found itself overtaken by events and outvoted in policymaking circles. At no point prior to the start of the bombing had the agency done any hypothetical study on its possible effects. Thus, Johnson was left to stumble into one of the most crucial decisions of the war with no intelligence guidance. Afterward, the CIA did manage to recoup—in a manner of speaking. Director McCone warned Johnson that unless the bombing was expanded to every conceivable target in the North, it would not diminish Hanoi's war-making potential or tenacity, and U.S. ground forces would become mired in a conflict they couldn't win. His prognosis was right on the mark, but it did him no good. Such pessimism Johnson didn't want to hear—any more than he wanted the CIA to challenge his domino theory—so he froze McCone out of all major policy decisions. What saved the CIA from political oblivion was Defense Secretary McNamara's own skepticism about the bombing, and his decision in early 1966 to seek independent CIA assessments of its effects.

Under the direction of senior analyst George Carver, the agency turned this mandate into a ticket to partial vindication for its role in the war. With few exceptions, Carver's estimates amounted to unremitting gloom. By the end of the year, McNamara had been infected by them; and so, presumably, had Johnson, for he promptly vetoed proposals for a further escalation of the bombing, except for attacks on Hanoi's petroleum depots. But no sooner had the agency thus burnished its star, than it faltered again, thanks mainly to its new director, Richard Helms. The quintessential team player, Helms slavishly endorsed Pentagon estimates in late 1967, which placed Communist troop strength in South Vietnam at roughly half of what the CIA unofficially projected. The consequences were disastrous. The deflated Pentagon estimate tended to clash with predictions of an impending all-out Communist offensive. After all, how could the Communists mount such an ambitious effort with so few forces in the field? In fact, the informal CIA troop count was right and the Pentagon's was wrong. The Communists sprang "Tet '68" with the very forces the Pentagon refused to acknowledge. Afterward, Helms recanted, and persuaded the U.S. military to revise its figures upward. Armed with the new tally, plus evidence that pacification had been obliterated, CIA analyst George Carver then scored one of the major policy coups of the war: he persuaded the president himself that Hanoi could match the U.S. at the escalation game and that no favorable outcome of the war was in sight. Shortly thereafter, Johnson called a halt to the bombing of the North, ruled out any further U.S. troop increases, and withdrew his candidacy for a second term. In a twinkling, the CIA had helped to turn our Vietnam policy around.

But if it could claim some credit for stopping the "Big War," it stood ready to champion an alternative. In autumn 1968, William Colby briefed U.S. military commanders in Vietnam on a strategy which would come to be known as "accelerated pacification"—the combined use of regular and irregular forces to destroy Communist bases and supply lines, resecure pacified areas, and revive popular support for the government. Already there was machinery in place to handle the last two objectives. Since 1965, the CIA had retrained the territorial forces so mismanaged by the Pentagon, had expanded police units, and established interrogation centers throughout the country. Moreover, former CIA analyst Robert Komer had recently arrived in Saigon to set up an umbrella organization, known as CORDS, to restrain all the loose cannons the CIA had fielded. Though Colby was to become Komer's deputy, and eventually his successor, CORDS was not a CIA front. Rather, it was an ecumenical enterprise, a pooling of talent from all the agencies concerned with pacification. That should have been its greatest asset, but, in fact, the very weight of its massive bureaucracy snapped the lines of command needed to keep it on track. To make matters worse, Komer and Colby tried to beat efficiency into the system with management tools, borrowed from American business, that were totally inappropriate to Vietnam. Quotas and other statistically defined requirements were applied to stimulate progress and to measure it. But the CORDS personnel in the countryside soon discovered it was easier to fabricate progress than to achieve it. As a result, pacification became the Big Lie.

Had no lives been at stake, this wouldn't have mattered much more than so many of the other misfortunes of the war. But one of Colby's creations, the Phoenix program, was very much a life-and-death proposition. Like the CORDS apparatus of which it was a part, Phoenix was a collegial effort. It drew its intelligence from the CIA's interrogation centers and its manpower from the South Vietnamese police and military, and from the terrorist squads now under CORDS' control. Its purpose was to eliminate the Communist political cadre network, *preferably* through capture—since live bodies obviously are far more useful as intelligence sources than dead ones. But from its inception, the program was so fraught with chaos that it was bound to lose its way. Nobody ever bothered adequately to define what constituted a VC political cadre. Moreover, the "neutralization" quotas prescribed by Komer and Colby produced a pressure for quick results that could be more easily met by indiscriminate killing than by careful pursuit and capture. Finally, South Vietnam's preventive detention law and dearth of legal talent resulted in such a backlog of prisoners suspected of VC connections that the court and prison systems simply couldn't accommodate them. Not surprisingly, frustrated police and terror units ultimately decided to take the law into their own hands

Still, for all its ghastly excesses, Phoenix did accomplish its basic purpose. As Hanoi's Premier Pham Van Dong told a journalist following the war's end, Phoenix—plus casualties suffered during the Tet '68 offensive—virtually destroyed the Communist political structure in South Vietnam. Ironically, it had a negative long-term impact on American interest, because it forced the North Vietnamese to pick up the cudgel, to wage the war in the Vietcong's place. It turned the war into a different animal altogether. It became a main-force war, with the North Vietnamese leading the charge, from 1972 to 1975.

When I arrived in Saigon in 1969, the CIA was phasing out the Phoenix program, Vietnamization was getting under way, and the various instruments of CORDS—from the terror units to the CIA-run interrogation centers—were being handed over to the Saigon government. From the available intelligence, it looked as though the moment was right for all this. A captured Communist document, known as Resolution 9, revealed that even Hanoi felt its war effort was faltering. The capture of that document was a major intelligence coup, one that had a profound impact on policy, bolstering our hopes for Vietnamization. But it also had an unfortunate side effect: it made us overoptimistic about Saigon's survivability.

Other factors also contributed to our myopia. With the onset of Vietnamization and the shrinkage of the CIA station in Saigon, the agency became ever more reliant on South Vietnamese government sources for its intelligence—and less and less disposed to question their self-serving optimism—for the last thing the policymakers in Washington wanted was a gloomy assessment from the "front" that might dissuade Congress from voting additional aid. Accordingly, from 1969 till the very end of the war, the CIA contented itself with Saigon's own diagnosis of its political health. And just to make sure that no negative signals reached Washington, the last U.S. ambassador and CIA station chief in Vietnam established a quality-control system for intelligence reporting that amounted to subtle censorship. If you wanted, for instance, to report on a corrupt Saigon official, you had to have an "impeccable" source, and the more scandalous your report, the more "impeccable" your source had to be; otherwise, no distribution. Through just such tomfoolery, we blinded ourselves to the rot that destroyed Saigon's will and capacity to fight.

But it was not merely blinkered reporting that handicapped U.S. intelligence during the last years of the war. Office politics also played a part. In my first year on the front, Station Chief Ted Shackley tried to make himself and his dwindling staff look good by calling on his field officers to step up their recruitment efforts and to begin hiring on as agents anybody and everybody who seemed to have a secret to sell. Two years later, we discovered that our goal had cost us dearly: over a hundred of the "spies" on the CIA's payroll turned out to be clever opportunists whose only source of intelligence was local gossip or newspaper clippings, which they sold to us for exorbitant prices.

To further complicate our lives, both the U.S. military and Henry Kissinger insisted on keeping the agency at arm's length, and largely in the dark, about their own Vietnam machinations. It was through one of our own spies in the Communist command that the CIA first learned the terms of the peace agreement Kissinger negotiated with Le Duc Tho. Since we had no spies within the U.S. military headquarters in Saigon, our knowledge of Gen. Creighton Abrams's plans remained even more limited. Only on the eves of the Son Tay prison raid, the U.S. push into Cambodia in 1970, and the South Vietnamese drive into Laos one year later, were CIA officials informed. One reason for the shutout was Abrams's lingering fury over a CIA kill-plot which had involved and embarrassed the U.S. Special Forces. But there were other causes as well. For one thing, CIA analysts had consistently rejected the military's estimate that COSVN was some kind of giant pillbox on the Cambodian border that could be easily destroyed in one air strike or ground sweep. The agency also had resisted evidence from military sources that the North Vietnamese had established a shipping route into the Cambodian port of Sihanoukville to deliver supplies destined for South Vietnam. Indeed, for years it had been an article of faith in the agency that all NVA supplies flowed south via the Ho Chi Minh trail in Laos. As it happened, the CIA was wrong about this, if not about COSVN. The U.S. incursion into Cambodia turned up irrefutable proof that thousands of tons of North Vietnamese materiel had been landed at Sihanoukville over the years and trucked overland through Cambodia to South Vietnam. The CIA's mistaken judgment on this issue was one of the most disastrous of the war, for it had served as principal rationale for the U.S. bombing of Laos.

The CIA was still reeling in embarrassment over this mistake when it committed yet another. Though nobody forewarned the agency of Lam Son 719—the South Vietnamese foray into southern Laos—the agency was asked in early 1971 to assess North Vietnam's capacity to respond swiftly to such an operation. The agency said North Vietnam would respond slowly. But several months later, when the South Vietnamese did mount their cross-border strike, they were met immediately by three NVA divisions and booted out of Laos. With that, the myth of Vietnamization was exposed for what it was, and Hanoi decided to launch a major offensive the next year to set the stage for a cease-fire on its own terms.

When the U.S. responded to the offensive in 1972 by mining the ports of Hanoi and Haiphong, the CIA, unfortunately, made another miscalculation. While it predicted correctly that the mining would prompt no Soviet intervention, and would have little practical effect (since there were alternate routes of supply, overland, through China), it failed to anticipate Hanoi's psychological response. Contrary to all agency prognoses, the North Vietnamese were devastated—not by the mining per se, but by *Moscow's* seeming indifference to it, and by Soviet failure to cancel the summit talks with the United States. So profound was Hanoi's disillusionment, it soon began backing away from its own tough preconditions for a cease-fire—much to our surprise.

During the two years of the cease-fire war itself, from 1973 to 1975, U.S. intelligence became a slave to U.S. policy. Lest President Thieu be offended or embarrassed, agency operatives were ordered to sever all contact with his non-Communist opposition; and CIA analysts were directed to forgo any investigation into the possibilities for a political accommodation with the Communists, as envisioned by the cease-fire agreement. In Saigon, meanwhile, the U.S. Embassy became a mighty Wurlitzer, churning out propaganda to make the Communists look uncompromising and the Saigon government a paragon of virtue—worthy of our continued support. Indicative of our PR skills was an article, inspired by CIA and embassy briefings, which appeared in *Foreign Affairs* magazine under the by-line of Maynard Parker, now the editor of *Newsweek.* The story argued that the Communists were hard pressed, and that Saigon's chances for long-term survival were good, provided the U.S. Congress continue to dole out the aid. Embarrassingly enough for Mr. Parker, the article's publication very nearly coincided with the final chaotic U.S. evacuation of Saigon.

THE INTELLIGENCE OF THE CENTRAL INTELLIGENCE AGENCY IN VIETNAM: II

Ralph McGehee

I joined the CIA in 1952, as a paramilitary officer, and served overseas in Japan, the Philippines, Taiwan, Thailand (three tours), and Vietnam. During one of my tours in Thailand, I discovered that something was wrong with agency intelligence and that something was very seriously wrong in Vietnam.

I was assigned to northeast Thailand, in early 1967, to develop a program to counter the insurgency that was just beginning there. I developed a very comprehensive interrogation program, in which a twenty-five-man team of interrogators would go into villages known to be under some Communist organization to discover how the Communists organized a revolution. The Thai Communists, we knew, had been trained in Vietnam and had gone to school in North Vietnam. In Thailand, a Masses Mobilization Unit (MMU) of the Thai Communist party would move into a village and sit there for three months assessing the class structure. Who had a problem with the government? Who was poor? At the end of three months, if the MMU thought the village was ready for the next stage, they would identify one man and recruit him into the Communist Liberation Association, whose goals were to establish a more egalitarian society through land reform and to eliminate those people supported by the Americans. This man would recruit two more and a cell would be formed. These three would then be programmed to go out and recruit three more.

Women were brought in to Women's Liberation Associations and youth into Youth Liberation Associations. Over a period of a year—through indoctrination, through talking, and by gradually elevating the propaganda to the themes of basic Marxist class struggle—they were able to recruit and transform the entire village into supporters of the movement. They went from village to village to village, and when they had organized enough villages in a contiguous area, they had what they called a base area. Then they would begin recruiting people as guerrillas, forming a secret government, and setting up a country inside a country.

Meanwhile, the agency was reporting that there were only 2,500 guerrillas in the entire country, that these forces had no support from the people, and that they would come down from the mountains occasionally and force the people to give them money and recruits. I was finding out just the opposite. The people were not only cooperating wholeheartedly with the guerrillas, but they were totally organized, had code names, and were doing it all in secret. My reports were initially graded the highest. But after a few months of reports (including my finding a province that had 2,500 guerrillas alone), I was pulled out of there, told to go home, the program was shut down, and the agency's intelligence went right back to reporting 2,500 Communists in all of Thailand.

With the knowledge I had, I tried, back at headquarters, to say, "Look, you are doing something wrong here; you are reporting these things incorrectly."

The more I agitated, the further away I was moved from positions of authority from where I could do anything about agency policy or practice.

I stayed in the agency even after I found out that there was a problem in Thailand, because I thought Thailand's problem unique. Not until I completed my tour in Vietnam, in late 1970, was I completely convinced that the agency was wrong. At that point, I had a very venal motivation for remaining—I had four children, two in expensive colleges. It would be very difficult to support them if I had left. Also, if I had left at that point, I would have had no way to protest what was going on, no way to call attention to what was happening. As it was, I used every protest channel I could think of. I went through the suggestions awards channel, I went to the inspector general, I went to the grievance officer, I went to the director, William Colby.

Agency intelligence estimates did not include the numbers of recruits the Communists in Vietnam were announcing over their own radio network. Agency people refused to read the works of Mao Tse-tung, Ho Chi Minh, Le Duan, or Nguyen Vo Giap in order to find out how Asian Communists developed revolutions. Finally, I wrote a study on Communist revolutionary practices. I was only able to do that by effecting a series of deceits, foiling the attempts of the leadership to stop me from doing the report.

In late 1974, two reports came across my desk. One stated that thirty percent of the military and government officials of a particular province had deserted the Thieu government to join the Vietcong; the other said that the Vietcong owned a second province, except for the capital city. These reports had been cabled directly to headquarters instead of through the normal route via Saigon, where they were checked before being sent on. When the chief of Station Saigon heard what had happened, he wrote a hasty cable to agency headquarters. Do not, it said, disseminate those reports: they are poorly sourced; they are not accurate; they give a false impression of the war. In fact, these were the only two reports I saw that were accurate at all. Based on these two reports, I wrote an end-of-the-year report saying that the place was coming apart, just deteriorating before our eyes. I knew that nobody would do anything about it—and nobody did. A few months later, the Thieu government collapsed.

THE INTELLIGENCE OF THE CENTRAL INTELLIGENCE AGENCY IN VIETNAM: III

John Stockwell

I was a CIA case officer in South Vietnam from 1973 through 1975. In the winter of 1975, Tom Polgar, the station chief, warned us that he would accept no more reports about the corruption of the South Vietnamese Army. If we sent them in, he said, he would send them back to us. If we persisted, he would put notes in our personnel files. He was saying, in effect, that Washington had decreed that Vietnamization was working and that it would be disloyal to report it was not.

PEACE WITH HONOR

Daniel Ellsberg

There is a good deal of evidence both in what Nixon did and what he said he did (in his memoirs) to formulate the hypothesis that Nixon and Kissinger regarded the political parts of the Paris peace accord as "a scrap of paper," and that they did not expect Thieu to heed them. In other words, they meant to support Thieu, to support the position he took publicly at the time, which was that he would not share power with the Communists. That meant, in turn, that the military cease-fire was not expected, by Nixon and Kissinger, to be maintained by either side. The Communists would continue their pressures when they realized that they were, in fact, being excluded from the political process. In that case, Nixon made specific assurances—nailed down by the dramatic manifestation of his will to carry this out, the December 1972 bombings— that U.S. air power would return to support South Vietnamese troops as needed. And it was assumed that it would shortly be needed, should a major Communist offensive occur. There is strong evidence that Nixon and Kissinger expected to be able to carry out this pledge, and that their complaints that they were not permitted to do so, basically by Congressional action, were sincere.

In other words, what Nixon thought he was signing was an arrangement for a cease-fire that would allow the graceful withdrawal of American troops and provide a change in the American tactical position—one whereby the United States would cease to object formally to the presence of North Vietnamese troops in the South, but would provide whatever air support ARVN needed to hold its ground. That way, U.S. costs, in terms of casualties, could be lowered to an acceptable level.

In short, Nixon's "peace with honor" never contemplated allowing Communist control of Saigon. It contemplated transforming the situation by the threat of major air attack, by escalations demonstrating our resolve, and by a major process of massively equipping the South Vietnamese army and building it up in size. The objective was to maintain, with lower U.S. costs, relatively and indefinitely, a situation in which Saigon and the other major cities had a chief of police who enjoyed the confidence of the CIA, backed up in the suburbs by a massive army paid and equipped by the United States—continued, low cost, stalemate. The North Vietnamese would have been incapable of stopping American air attacks. As Nixon says—and for him it is a complaint, a charge— only Americans could stop him from doing that. And Americans did do that.

DESERTION AS A FORM OF RESISTANCE TO THE VIETNAM WAR

Clancy Sigal

There was a high rate of desertion from the armed forces during the Vietnam War. I remember one year alone when seventy-three thousand soldiers deserted—the equivalent of three full combat divisions with supply units. I am not talking about merely going AWOL, splitting, going over the hill and coming back. I am talking about desertion, an offense for which you could be court-martialed and shot during a legally declared war, which, of course, Vietnam was not.

I got into the desertion business quite by accident. One night in London, in 1968, I got a phone call from a group called Support, a draft counseling center of young Americans: a boy had come in from California with no money, but he had my name on a slip of paper. He was the son of an old UCLA classmate of mine from the *Daily Bruin.* He was running away from the draft, and I was his only contact. I helped settle him in. From that, I developed a natural association with these young American draft counselors; and soon I was sitting in on their sessions, more or less as an official representative of middle age. Eventually, I moved in with them in a kind of resistance commune—the Union of American Exiles in Britain. We were part of an extremely extensive network of anti-war groups in Britain. Almost every village, town, and large city had a grass-roots anti–Vietnam War feeling that extended from the top to the bottom of British society and included opposition to British collusion with America's Vietnam War effort. It included local councilors and mayors, clergymen, union people, and Quakers.

In this draft counseling, one did not have to be very smart to notice the steady trickle of nervous young men, very different from the usual run of draft dodgers. These tended to be secretive; they had obviously phony names and counterfeit passports; they were often wary, freaked out, disoriented, in need of various kinds of practical and psychological help. Usually they were on their way from West Germany, where the American military maintained large installations as part of NATO, to Sweden or Canada or France or Switzerland or Ireland or Spain or any country that would take them in. A great many European governments, though they did not officially declare a policy of asylum, had been moved by the antiwar feelings of their populations to a policy of *de facto* asylum for American military deserters and draft resisters.

I never kidded myself that our operation hurt the Vietnam war effort all that much. In fact, as we learned how to evaluate each man's stress potential, we probably returned quite a lot of them to the military, because there was no way that they would have made it as deserters. Psychologically, to be a deserter is one of the hardest lives possible.

But the deserter movement was part of a resistance culture, part of the resistance to the war inside the military. When I first became active in the resistance movement, I was filled with romantic fantasies from World War I novels. I thought deserters would be nice, clean-cut Harvard-and-Yale-educated ambulance drivers who read poetry and were escaping the war for very deep moral reasons. I soon discovered that they were a much more complicated bunch. The articulate and educated and socially conscious kids that I first visualized were, most often, the draft dodgers and evaders. The deserters, like most soldiers, were, in general, working class—blue collar or farm kids with very few resources and almost no social skills except perhaps a gut instinct for survival.

As a rule, middle-class kids did not have to go and fight the war. They knew about lawyers, psychologists, and college deferments. Most of the deserters I knew never saw a lawyer except perhaps in court, when as teenage civilians they had gotten into some trouble. In fact, many future deserters had, as teenagers, been arrested on minor charges—petty theft, joy-riding with stolen cars—and were more or less shanghaied into serving in the military by judges who had given them a Hobson's choice: the army or jail.

I interviewed many deserters and found that some deserted for explicit antiwar reasons (one had been wounded three times and just did not fancy going back to be wounded a fourth time); some just hated the war from the bottom of their souls and had refused to handle weapons from the very beginning; and some made up their minds within thirty seconds, as soon as they were put on levy for Vietnam. On the other hand, I met many Green Berets and Rangers, whose physical courage could not be questioned. They were not afraid of being killed but of being turned into killers; of being made to kill in a war that hardly anyone believed in. Admittedly, you could not always take their explanations literally. But after you got to know them, you could see that a vague discontent with the war had been germinating for a long time, fed by a network of army resistance papers *(ACT, Fatigue Press, Paper Grenade)* that covered American military bases and "G.I. coffee houses" around the world. In other words, many soldiers deserted for essentially idealistic and antiwar reasons even though they might be inarticulate about them.

We in the underground railway developed a technical vocabulary to distinguish one sort of deserter from another. "RITA" (a resistant in the army), "FRITA" (a friend of a resister in the army), "FUFA" (fed up with the fucking army). We even had a term—baby-sitting—which referred to dealing with recent deserters who were so high, so terrified of a fugitive status, that a counselor had to spend days, sometimes weeks, talking them down.

I was a small part of this international rescue network that involved a cross-section of groups and individuals around the world: Japanese Buddhists, French Catholics, Swedish Lutherans—an extraordinarily large grass-roots movement. Ironically, the Soviets, especially after their experience with four sailors from the aircraft carrier *Intrepid* in 1967, wanted nothing to do with American deserters, whom they found much too hard to handle.

The life of a deserter was extraordinarily difficult, and it took an extraordinary person to make it. He had to have grit, determination, courage, and self-understanding of a high order. In other

words, some of the attributes of the best combat soldier. A disproportionate number were devout Catholics: former seminarians or
altar boys. They came often from very conservative families and
very conservative parts of the country. The trauma for them occurred when they first entered the ranks of the army and found out
about the war for themselves. That turned them. But it was a
terrible separation for them: first separated from their parents and
then separated from the only country that they felt counted. After
going AWOL, they were often, for months or years, on their own,
strangers in strange lands. They did not speak the languages.

Some deserters simply did not make it. They died from tuber-
culosis, drug overdoses, and sometimes of loneliness. Like other
veterans, deserters suffered severe psychic wounds. Many are still
deserting, continuing to go from job to job and from country to
country. They are still running, though no one is chasing them
anymore.

For the deserter, as for many combat veterans, the war was a
rite of passage into adulthood. One way of growing up was to
enlist, and that was also a way of proving one's manhood. But
another way was, once you were inside the army, to resist the war.
At the beginning it might have been an adolescent rebellion, but
what might have begun frivolously grew quickly into something
more serious. Often, for the first time in his life, the deserter had to
start thinking for himself: who he was and what he was actually
about. Through the act of resistance, of desertion, boys became
men; they had to become self-reliant under extreme circumstances, the most extreme circumstances I know outside combat.
Few started with politics of any sort, except perhaps of the most
patriotic kind. They did not read books; they did not attend lec-
tures; their anti-imperialism was self-taught. They were doing the
only thing they could do to fight the war, given their circumstances. Yet, I believe they loved their country. An almost equally
heavy price was to be paid by the young American civilians, the
peace workers, who formed the culture of resistance that the deserters came to depend upon. For example, in our little commune
on Queen Anne Street, there were several serious breakdowns, at
least one permanent, and two suicides. Rest in peace Harry Pincus
and Frank Aller; as far as I am concerned your names deserve to
go on the monument in Washington along with the other war
dead.

HOME FRONT RESISTANCE TO THE VIETNAM WAR

Todd Gitlin
(with thanks to Robert Ross and Jean Cohen)

It's a curious thing. Of all the voices proclaiming these days that the movement against the Vietnam War had an enormous impact, the loudest seem to be those who decry the movement and the impact alike. The so-called conservatives, neo- and paleo- varieties, think that the country was seized in the sixties, more or less, by a "new class" of leftist intellectuals, students, and uppity minorities and women, who not only trashed standards, learning, language, and the family, but broke the back of national security, leveled America's just position in the world, and cost us an achievable and noble victory in Vietnam.

By conspicuous contrast, I have the impression that most of the onetime antiwar activists of the sixties think that the movement accomplished precious little. Most students today, self-protectively, seem to agree that the far-gone sixties were a riotous bust.

I think it is probably truer to say that the movement against the Vietnam War was the most successful movement against a shooting war *in history.*

Nevertheless, much of the leadership of that movement wasn't satisfied to be against the war. It wanted a revolution. And in the process it crippled its capacity to rise to the political occasions that followed. So first I want to speak to the movement's effects on the war. And then I want to say something about the war's impact on the movement, and the movement's impact on itself.

Go back to the years *before* the more lurid images of 1969–71—the NLF flag-waving, window-trashing, and rock-throwing; the bombings and ROTC building torchings; the townhouse explosion that killed three members of the Weather Underground; the rocks thrown at Richard Nixon—back to 1964 and 1965, when the Johnson administration's commitment to the Vietnam War took hold. The September 1964 Tonkin Gulf affair was followed by a *carte blanche* Senate resolution with a grand total of *two* dissenting votes. At Christmas, Students for a Democratic Society (SDS) presumptuously called for a national demonstration against the war in April. In the meantime, the Johnson administration began the systematic bombing of North Vietnam. In April, more than twenty-five thousand marched against the war—the great majority dressed in jackets and ties. Later that month came the first campus teach-ins. That fall (1965), the first coordinated nationwide demonstrations occurred, some of them militant (a few attempts to stop troop trains); there were widely publicized draft-card burnings and national media hysteria about a nonexistent SDS plan to disrupt the draft. Over the course of the next three years, civil rights leaders began denouncing the war; there were attempts to get antiwar measures on the ballot and to carry the war into professional associations; there were the vast mobilizations in Washington, at the Pentagon, and in downtown Oakland; the use of armed troops and riot-equipped police; the first antiwar murmurs—and they were murmurs only—about the need for violence to stop the war; the first activities by the government's *agents provocateurs;* and in August 1968, a few thousand people went out into the Chicago streets under the media spotlights during the Democratic convention.

Suppose that the war had gone on without material public opposition. Suppose there had been passive dissent in the polls but no movement in the streets. Suppose, in other words, Vietnam had been a war like Korea. What would have kept the war from escalating even more intensely, and earlier, with more ordnance, more troops, more death? What opposition would have been mustered?

Concrete evidence of the movement's effects is hard to come by. So much so, in fact, that much of the movement itself usually felt it was accomplishing next to nothing. After all, the successive administrations weren't giving any credit away. And so ensued the movement's desperate cycle of trying to raise the stakes, double or nothing: more fury, eventually more violence—especially when the media dutifully played their parts as amplifiers of the worst and the dumbest of antiwar theater.

David Halberstam reported one instance of the movement's veto power in *The Best and the Brightest:* In late 1966, the military was already urging President Johnson to bomb Hanoi and Haiphong, to block the harbor and destroy the industrial capacity of both cities. Johnson said, "I have one more problem for your computer—will you feed into it how long it will take five hundred thousand angry Americans to climb that White House wall out there and lynch their President if he does something like that?" "Which ended for a time," Halberstam writes, "the plan to bomb Hanoi and Haiphong."[1] And we now know that the Moratorium and Mobilization of fall 1969 stretched out and slowed down Nixon's November 1969 ultimatum: a series of planned escalations— including the bombing of the North Vietnamese dikes and the possible landing of ground troops in the North. All this at a time, memorably, when Nixon let it be known he'd be blithely watching the Redskins game on TV.

The movement, in short, acquired a certain veto power, but had little inkling of it. All it knew was that every day the killing went on, which is in my opinion the main reason why the movement drove itself toward bitter-ended, self-isolating militancy and, by 1972, away from activity altogether.

There's no evidence that the movement directly affected public opinion. Public opinion did turn steadily against the war, but if anything, as the war became steadily less popular, so did the movement against it, maybe even faster. The movement made itself felt mostly by the indirect effects it had on the politics and economics surrounding the war. Although, as time went on, the movement didn't want to think of itself as "merely" reformist, it amounted to a small engine that turned the more potent engines that could, in fact, retard the war.

What happened is that political, corporate, and media elites

1. New York, Random House, p. 641.

grew disillusioned with the war. It wasn't working. First, in the fall of 1967, the *Wall Street Journal* dissented from the war on purely practical grounds. A few months later, in the wake of Tet, Walter Cronkite was saying that the U.S. ought to find a way out—having failed, as he put it, to "defend democracy." Cronkite was far from alone by then. First the McCarthy, then the Kennedy campaign drew antiwar energy into the political mainstream. At the same time, Clark Clifford, Johnson's incoming secretary of defense, lost faith in the war effort and set out to mobilize influential opposition within the political elite that had represented foreign policy consensus since 1945. As the Joint Chiefs of Staff requested 206,000 new troops, and Congress debated, Clifford persuaded Johnson to meet with the informal advisory group later known as the Wise Men: Dean Acheson, George Ball, McGeorge Bundy, C. Douglas Dillon, Cyrus Vance, and others.

Three days later, Johnson refused General Wheeler's troop request, announced a partial bombing halt, and took himself out of the presidential campaign. The Wise Men were wise indeed to see that the war simply cost too much in political and economic terms. Congress sluggishly learned the same lessons. The antiwar movement was instrumental in all of this. Politically, the Wise Men were impressed by the threat to social peace at home. Economically, the dollar was sinking fast, the balance of payments had turned negative, and American gold was draining away. The immediate cause, of course, was that Johnson dared not increase taxes to finance the war, fearing the loss of the political base. To have his war, therefore, he had to go deeply into deficit financing.

Eventually, in ways both direct and indirect, the antiwar movement helped ease the United States out of Vietnam. If the movement had been more powerful and astute, had been able to win more mainstream allies, it could have cut the war still shorter and, perhaps, have thereby weakened the ruthlessly authoritarian tendencies of the victorious revolutionary regimes in Vietnam, Laos, and Cambodia. Even with most of its forces spent, after the McGovern catastrophe in 1972, the movement was still able to keep the Nixon administration from serious thought of going back into Vietnam. As late as 1975, the houses of Congress, belatedly aroused, were able to stop American intervention in Angola; and even today, the ghostly afterimage of the antiwar movement prevents easy recourse to massive direct American military intervention in Central America.

But what happened to the movement itself in the process? The terrible fact is that the movement sloppily squandered an immense amount of its moral authority. Too many leaders, and enough of the rank and file, slid into feeling romantic about the other side. If napalm was evil, the other side was endowed with nobility. If the American flag was now dirt, the NLF flag was clean—and always bait for photo editors, who singled it out from fields of American flags at rallies. If the barbarism of the war could be glibly equated with the deliberate slaughter of millions in the Nazi gas chambers—if the American Christ turned out to look like Antichrist—then by this cramped left-wing logic, the nationalist Communist Antichrist must really be Christ. So, some of the movement mirrored the Great Communicator's jubilant proclamation that Vietnam was a "noble cause," but with the sides reversed.

Many movement people thought they were involved in a revolution, not an antiwar movement. They borrowed their prepackaged imagery from national liberation movements whose suffering and heroism was undeniable but whose political culture had nothing to teach us about how to conduct a modern society. When demonstrators started chanting "Ho, Ho, Ho Chi Minh," this was a moral corrosion that has become all too familiar in the twentieth century: the know-it-alls bringing absolute truth to the benighted masses. It was the left-wing version of "winning hearts and minds." And so, years later, the revolutionists helped return the moral title to conservatives, who are still swollen with it.

It's no simple story why so much of the movement leadership went that route. Dressing up for revolution was easier than wrestling with the unprecedented: the ironies of a radical movement, based on youth and spunk and marginality and educated arrogance, in a society that not only permitted dissent but made it possible to change some history without wholesale bloodshed. The heavily middle-class revolutionists tried to bull past their own isolation—they made themselves Leninists of the will. And others went the Yippie route, with toy machine guns and the glib, dismissive gestures of "kill your parents." The publicity loop, of course, boosted the most flamboyant leaders into celebrity and helped limit the movement's reach into America.

In this maelstrom of images, the movement was massively demoralized. The vast and silent majority was appalled to watch SDS decompose into warring Marxist-Leninist sects. They didn't think revolutionary Vietnam was the promised land. In general, they hated illegitimate authority and they were sentimental about peasants shooting at fighter-bombers with rifles. These Americans wanted to find a different basis for authority—and failed, but succeeded. Movements are compost for later movements, as William Morris once wrote: "Men fight and lose the battle, and the thing they fought for comes about in spite of their defeat, and when it comes out not to be what they meant, other men have to fight for what they meant under another name."

RESISTANCE TO THE RESISTANCE

David Dellinger

The protest that has come to be called the Siege of the Pentagon (October 21 and 22, 1967) began under two slogans: FROM PROTEST TO RESISTANCE and SHUT DOWN THE PENTAGON. These slogans indicated the seriousness of a movement that was not talking about leaving behind legal protests and marches, but of adding something, a resistance movement. And so there was going to be nonviolent civil disobedience, sufficiently separated so that those who wanted to come only for the rally and the march, but not the civil disobedience, could be apart. That action brought out the first massive deployment of U.S. troops to police and restrict an antiwar demonstration.

We needed a third slogan as a means of response to the troops. Some people spoke in terms of snarling at them as fascists and robots and enemies. The organizing committee was up until five in the morning discussing how to respond. We finally decided that the only possible approach was to say to the troops, You are our brothers, join us. You are victims too; we support you; we stand in solidarity with you, stand in solidarity with us.

The Siege of the Pentagon led the government to step up and intensify the plans for COINTELPRO. COINTELPRO began to disrupt the trust that was the movement's greatest strength: the ability to live together in open love and trust and cooperation and dialogue and disagreement, accepting many paths to revolution and many paths to end the war. COINTELPRO also introduced violence.

At the demonstration planned for Chicago at the 1968 Democratic National Convention, Rennie Davis and I were offered, by a veteran, a plan for dropping bombs on the amphitheater. We discovered later, at the trial, that he was employed by the FBI and the Chicago Red Squad. Four years later, in Miami, as I was leaving for the airport, I was told that Rennie Davis and I were scheduled for assassination. When I got to Chicago, there were six Red Star Collectives there, arguing in our innermost circles that we must carry guns for self-defense. When I opposed it as suicidal and a violation of everything we stood for, I was told I would have to be repudiated because I was going to get others killed. They, too, we found out several years later, were organized by the FBI.

The press paid much attention to the violence around the edges of the antiwar movement, but never did a full investigation of government provocation, of government responsibility for that violence.

WORKERS RESIST OVERT RESISTANCE

Paul Schrade

The worst manipulation we suffered, as workers, in the antiwar movement was that done by the media and the White House and the leadership of the American labor movement, all of whom made it seem that the hard hats and the leadership hawks deterred the antiwar movement. People mainly say this because they saw George Meany, the president of the AFL-CIO, hard-lining the war behind the Johnson and Nixon policies—in fact, he was a harder liner than both. A majority of union leadership clearly favored war policies. We saw on television the attack of the hard-hat construction workers on antiwar demonstrators; we heard the attacks by Meany on labor rank and file who were active in the antiwar movement. The AFL-CIO executive council passed a resolution in August 1966, supporting the Johnson policy. Antiwar workers were accused of aiding the Communist enemy of the United States. Meany, in December 1967, attacked the Labor Peace Assembly, the trade union division of the National Committee for a Sane Nuclear Policy (SANE), and said that the meeting, held in Chicago in December 1967, was "planned in Hanoi by a special committee that went there." In 1972, Meany attacked George McGovern as an apologist for the Communist world and proclaimed, for the first time in a national election, labor neutrality.

But if you look under the surface, it is evident that workers were moving against the war at a more rapid rate than people in the middle and upper classes. A study by Harlan Hahn that appeared in the late sixties showed that in all the referenda in all parts of the country at that time, the working-class precincts were leading the other precincts in terms of the need for a pullout from and an end to the war in Vietnam. In 1971, according to a Lou Harris poll, sixty-four percent of the labor union membership was in favor of an early pullout from Vietnam. In California, during that period, fifty-nine percent of union members favored an early pullout. Another poll showed that fifty-three percent of union members disapproved of the hard-hat approach of beating up demonstrators.

We found, however, that it was very difficult to get workers, even those opposed to the war, into the streets for demonstrations. But labor signs were present at all the major demonstrations.

In the Vietnam war, as in all other wars, workers made the greatest sacrifices, but the anti–Vietnam War movement did not succeed in building respect for itself among workers; it did not show full respect for the American worker and the way the American worker feels about political issues.

PART II

THE JOURNALISTS

Editor's Note

The deep schisms born in *Vietnam* between correspondents and the U.S. Government and military live on and feed the fires of the growing "battle of the myth," the struggle for the symbols which will characterize *Vietnam* in history and around which future political controversy will be waged. In fact, the opening rounds of the political controversy have already been fired.

The basic question is: Did press and TV accurately and effectively report the events of *Vietnam* or did government deceit and/ or press bias color and distort the images received by the American public? There is not likely to be an early end to this argument, for it is impregnated with radically divergent conceptions of the function of the press, on the one hand, and the role of the government on the other.

Many in the press believed then, and continue to believe, that the government and the military lied and distorted the picture of what was happening in *Vietnam* and of what U.S. policy really was. On the converse, many government and military spokesmen (and a handful of press supporters) contend that for many reasons the press version was incomplete, confused, distorted, and inconsistent with reality. Some of the most severe critics such as Robert Elegant, himself an old-time Far Eastern correspondent, go so far as to blame the press for the loss of the war.

None of those whose views are here presented are altogether comfortable with the media coverage of the war. All concede that it was not infrequently at fault. The division lies in assessing responsibility for its flaws.

David Halberstam, a *Vietnam* reporter in the early days and a longtime critic of the government, stresses the defects in a U.S. policy which, he believes, was clothed in lies from the start and carried out by stealth, deceit, and hypocrisy. Press reporting from the field in *Vietnam* was impressive, in his view, in its realism and accuracy. In contrast, Washington reporting—political reporting on the war—was heavily colored by political propaganda and failed to match the field reporting for skepticism, challenge, and efforts to penetrate what Winston Churchill once called "the bodyguard of lies" with which truth is surrounded in wartime.

To Seymour Hersh, whose exposé of the My Lai massacre was perhaps the outstanding investigative feat of the Vietnam War, the lying—the government lying—was and continues to be the central factor. He sees little change despite Vietnam and Watergate. If the government insists on lying, he believes, the press has no means to halt it, and government policy will prevail no matter how bold and penetrating the reporting. Nothing basic has been changed. The history of Vietnam was a history of lies and he does not expect this to alter in the future.

Phillip Knightley, the English press critic and correspondent, offers a differing explanation for what he believes were deficiencies in press reporting in Vietnam. The war presented a situation so extraordinary, so without precedent, so complex, as to be beyond the ordinary abilities of the press to understand it or to render it comprehensible to readers and viewers. It was a war without fixed lines, without readily recognizable elements of good and evil; it involved strange psychologies, alien and little-understood cultures. It was too exotic for the journalist.

Moreover, in the opinion of a military observer like Maj. Gen. Winant Sidle, a press officer in Saigon, the correspondents lacked the knowledge and expertise to understand the war. They had not, for the most part, he contends, covered other wars; they knew little about military operations and had no background in the country. And they were young.

Sidle did not address the fact that many of these same criticisms would be laid at the door of the military, few of whom had any experience or knowledge of Southeast Asia, the Indochinese, or the elements of the guerrilla war into which they were thrust. And many of them were young.

George Reedy, a veteran of the LBJ White House, a press spokesman for President Johnson, broadened the factor of ignorance to cover not only the newsmen but the government and military officials dealing with the war and the whole American public. It was not the kind of war the press had been trained to cover, and the levels of ignorance within the government were *equally high. A disaster was predictable.*

To Roger Hilsman, who participated in many of the government's policy discussions, the levels of ignorance inside the government and outside were comparable. Neither side really understood what it or the other was doing.

Peter Arnett, the AP's courageous front-line reporter who saw more combat than many combat GIs, burns with anger at those who criticize press coverage of Vietnam. He assaults their credentials, sees the source of their views in the violent parochialism of the emotion-packed Vietnam days, and blames editors and government alike for suppressing or underplaying many of the more dramatic and revealing dispatches of the war. The efforts of the government and the military, he believes, were directed at suppressing and smothering the truth, not at ferreting it out.

There are quarrels within quarrels in these assessments of the press. Peter Davis feels that the press was changed by Vietnam, that it no longer is a mere extension of government, and that the language of the critics is being employed to distort reality. It was not, he points out, the journalists who killed, who defoliated, who called in air strikes. If blame is to be placed for Vietnam, he lodges it squarely with the military.

Most of the broadcast journalists dispute the contentions of the critics that their coverage played a great role in turning American public opinion against the war in Vietnam. They feel they trailed the evolution of American attitudes rather than shaping it. Not even the dramatic broadcast from Vietnam of Walter Cronkite calling for a negotiated settlement of the war is believed by them to have made a major difference. President Johnson had already reached that conclusion himself.

•BROADCAST•

A TELEVISION WAR?

Lawrence Lichty, Murray Fromson, and John Mueller

LAWRENCE LICHTY:

Between 1965 and 1975, more than ten thousand network evening news pieces from or about Vietnam were broadcast. The television war began with Morley Safer's film story of U.S. Marines burning Vietnamese huts. Viewers saw our soldiers torching a hamlet called Kam Nhe, using cigarette lighters and flamethrowers, advancing from hut to hut, setting fires in thatch while women screamed for them to stop. "The war we lost on television" could be said to have begun on that day. I do not mean to imply that there wasn't television from Vietnam before that. Obviously there was, going back into the fifties. Indeed, the first American correspondent to be shot at was Charles Kuralt.

Much less than fifty percent of all the reporting on Vietnam—not just what was going on in this country, but from Vietnam itself—was actually closely related to battle, the fighting. Aside from the heavy coverage of Tet, probably only six or seven percent of the footage dealt with actual heavy battle.

Tet marked the first extensive and sustained use of satellite from Tokyo. The war was generally not broadcast live or instantaneously. Virtually all the film was shipped via Tokyo or Hong Kong.

MURRAY FROMSON:

Getting to the story often overshadowed the getting of the story. And even with the sheer volume of material broadcast over television, those who watched did not get a complete record or a full history. Television news deals in episodic events.

Hardly a network correspondent in his thirties did not go to Vietnam. Once there, it was often a case of waiting for some action to take place before committing the resources to cover it. Coverage could involve considerable risk to the reporter and crew.

The Vietnam War had a major impact on television. It married picture and sound in every aspect of war coverage, gave birth to the star system in television news (correspondents became almost as identifiable as anchors), and was the subject of the first network color documentary.

It was a war without formal censorship. Had there been, it is conjectural whether Morley Safer's report on the burning of Kam Nhe would have been broadcast as filmed, or broadcast at all. The government's reaction to the broadcast was excessive. After viewing it, Arthur Sylvester, then the deputy secretary of defense for public affairs, called Fred Friendly, the president of CBS News, and asked, "Now that you have spit on the American flag, how do you feel?"

The reaction was hostile in most councils of the White House. I was asked by White House people, "Why are you using a Canadian correspondent [Safer]?" "Why are you using a Vietnamese cameraman?"

JOHN MUELLER:

The Vietnam War was neither peculiar nor unpopular simply because it was shown on television. Television existed during the Korean War and studies made during World War II of the effect of showing people realistic war pictures indicated that showing people realistic war pictures did not change their attitudes toward the war. If you think that the war in Vietnam was a television war, and that people turned against the war because they saw it every night, it is equivalent to saying that the American people are so stupid that they don't know what a war is. People know what wars are; they do not have to have them explained on television. The press did transmit to the American people that there was a war, that it was costly, that people were dying; and it was those articles, rather than television's peculiarly or specially dramatized images, that affected people. Television was not necessarily a major factor in how the war affected people.

THE EFFECT OF THE VIETNAM WAR ON BROADCAST JOURNALISM
A PRODUCER'S PERSPECTIVE

Edward Fouhy

Vietnam was one of a number of factors—though probably the most important factor—in the maturation of network television news. It came at a time when this very new way of presenting the news was struggling through its adolescence.

The first element in the maturation process had come on September 2, 1963, when CBS began the first thirty-minute evening news program. NBC followed a few weeks later. That change gave television producers a geometrically larger canvas upon which to paint their pictures of the news. It was far more than a mere doubling of the time they had available. It changed the way they approached the news. In the days of the fifteen-minute newscast, the approach was rooted in the tradition of the movie newsreel—and indeed, many of the network producers had come from the newsreel shops just up the street on the west side of Manhattan. Their style had been the voice-over: Ed Herlihy or Lowell Thomas in the theater newsreel days, then the anchorman on television—he of the golden tones reading a script based on information sent in by the cameraman on his caption sheet. The rest of the program consisted of rewritten wire stories, also voiced by the anchorman.

By 1963, those early news shows had begun to build an audience; they were attracting far more viewers than the documentaries and news specials the networks had been forced by the FCC to put on the air in the wake of the quiz show scandals. The longer evening news programs gave the business office a way to amortize the expensive documentary-staff salaries, to attract more advertisers, and to slice away for themselves time that many local stations were using for their own profitable programs.

When the documentary producers came to the daily news staffs, they brought their style with them, creating mini-documentaries that filled the extra time on the longer newscasts and introduced two changes in the old newsreel tradition. A reporter and often a producer accompanied the camera crew on nearly every story (i.e., more reporting eyes in the field), and the camera was taken off the tripod—"sticks," in the jargon of the trade—and mounted on the photographer's shoulder (thus it became more mobile, more fluid, and more probing). The addition of the reporter to the camera team and the more fluid style of filming news would have a large impact on the coverage of the war.

As the newscasts were lengthened, there was, in the American South, a story that in some ways would foreshadow for TV newsmen the coverage of the war. The civil rights struggle was in full swing. Many of the reporter-cameraman teams that two years later would be covering Kontum or Con Thien were then covering the racial conflict in Memphis and Meridian. Both stories placed great demands on television news teams. Both demanded physical courage; both demanded enterprise and imagination in order to overcome logistical difficulties; both demanded a high degree of journalistic skepticism. Vietnam was far more complex, of course, but for any network TV newsman, the lessons learned in the South were essential to his success in covering the war.

There was another development, at about this time, that also would have a minor but significant impact on war coverage. Kodak had developed fine-grain, fast color film with a magnetic sound track—an important technical advance over the old black-and-white film with the lower-quality optical sound that had been the industry standard since the early newsreel days. The war film that we remember would not have had nearly so great an impact on public consciousness if those technical advances had not occurred. Color and natural sound give war pictures a totally new dimension. The great World War II and Korean War photographers—Robert

Capa, Margaret Bourke-White, David Douglas Duncan—had worked in black and white. Their pictures were stunningly displayed in *Life* magazine, but no one had seen war pictures like the ones they were to see during the war in Vietnam. (Color film went into widespread use in 1965.)

By 1963, then, network television had new tools to tell its stories, and new people—producers and reporters—who were willing to try new ways to tell them. But the news was in some ways like an adolescent who doesn't understand what his newly mature body can do. That changed when, in November 1963, just two and a half months after the news expansion, President Kennedy was shot. Over the next four days and nights, television became the unifying touchstone for a bewildered and grieving nation. TV newsmen were changed by that experience. It made them far more confident of their ability to use a television camera to cover a breaking news story, and for the first time they saw the reach and impact they could have. All of that was in the background as the war began to escalate in 1965 and the networks assigned full-time resident correspondents to Saigon. The tone of their approach was set by the news executives, and they were men whose attitudes had been shaped by World War II. Indeed, many of them were veterans of that war. At NBC, the producer of the *Huntley-Brinkley Report* was Shad Northshield, who had led an infantry platoon across Europe. His boss was Don Heaney, a former naval aviator. At CBS, news director Gordon Manning was a former naval officer. Les Midgeley, who produced the *CBS Evening News* through much of the Vietnam period, had entered Paris with the liberating forces. And Walter Cronkite was a man who had won his first fame as a correspondent for United Press covering the war in Europe.

Richard Salant, at the time president of CBS News, said Vietnam was approached as an extension of World War II. "That was a war," he said, "in which right and wrong were easily distinguished and in which the American cause was clearly and automatically the virtuous one."

At first, many of the reporters sent out to cover Vietnam were of the same generation. Men like Peter Kalisher and Charles Collingwood were sent to Vietnam from Europe, where they had stayed after World War II. They went to Saigon in the fifties and the early sixties because they could speak French and the war in

Indochina was often seen as a French problem.

Later, when it became an American problem, younger men were sent out. They were ambitious, and, in the way of young men, eager to prove their courage. They also wanted to be on the front line in another war—the one between CBS and NBC for network news supremacy. (That battle was being fought between the two networks then as fiercely as it continues among the three networks today.) So the young men went off to Asia. Many are forgotten now, but others are the leading TV news figures of today. Ted Koppel, Sam Donaldson, Charles Kuralt, Morley Safer, Ed Bradley, Garrick Utley, Dan Rather—all served tours in Vietnam.

Some had served in the Army or Marine Corps in the Cold War days, but none were World War II veterans. They and their cameramen were closer in age, and often in attitude, to the junior officers and civilian advisors than they were to the established commanders and policymakers in Saigon or Washington.

And it was from the junior people that they learned about the war. They couldn't cover it from Saigon as some of their newspaper colleagues could. They had to have pictures—that was what their producers in New York were demanding, and the pictures were in the field. Yes, the producers wanted "bang bang" stories—too much has been made of that—but they wanted other pictures too: the civil assistance platoons, the strategic hamlets, the rice harvest; later, the political campaign. In other words, they sought picture stories of what the briefers in Saigon were selling as evidence of progress being made. But when the correspondents went to the field to get those stories, they found the official optimism in Saigon and Washington wasn't matched by reality in the provinces.

Sometimes this led to clashes between the New York executives and the Saigon bureau. I was in some of those. The men in New York, the World War II generation, were listening to the generals and the ambassadors. The boys in Saigon, as they called their young reporters, were listening to the captains and majors. They saw a different picture. The disparity caused some of the New York people to go to Saigon. Gordon Manning was one of them. He returned to New York, in mid-1967, confident that his Saigon bureau was right. Other senior producers and correspondents went to Vietnam, and they too returned to New York to become advocates for the more pessimistic views of the "boys" in Saigon.

Later, Walter Cronkite came around too. He had been a hawk, seeing the conflict in Cold War terms. He had even flown aboard a Canberra, on a bombing run near Da Nang in 1965. But in a special broadcast after a personal reporting trip to Vietnam in the waning days of the Tet offensive, Cronkite looked into the camera and declared, "To say that we are mired in stalemate seems the only realistic yet unsatisfactory conclusion. The only rational way out will be to negotiate, and not as victors."

I am not persuaded that the Cronkite broadcast had as great an impact on American public opinion as some—including, apparently, Lyndon Johnson—felt it had. Nor did the scores of news specials and documentaries that preceded and followed it, nor the approximately 4,100 filmed reports shown on the network evening news programs during the war years. Of those 4,100 filmed reports only about 10 percent were real "bang bang" stories. Yet those are the ones we recall most vividly.

In terms of money, it was not an expensive war to cover. The usual major expense of foreign news—travel—was very low, for example. Here, the major expense was the purchase of satellite time. But satellite transmission only occurred when there was a major, competitive story breaking.

While Washington did not hesitate to make its opinions known, the far more pernicious pressure on the networks came from the affiliates, many of which are owned by entrepreneurs with fixed and inflexible views. Many of them, particularly those in the South, were great flag-wavers and were extremely critical of many of the young reporters in Vietnam. They brought great pressure on Salant, who, to his credit, passed none of it on to those of us covering the war.

Television news is a medium capable of transmitting small slices of truth. It is not capable, even if the people running it had the will, of changing the course of history. The American experience in Vietnam probably would not have ended much sooner or much later if television had never been invented. Or if the United States had decided to censor the war news.

THE EFFECT OF THE VIETNAM WAR ON BROADCAST JOURNALISM
A CORRESPONDENT'S PERSPECTIVE

Garrick Utley

In late August 1964, an executive at NBC News in New York asked me to step into his office. I had just completed a six-week temporary assignment in South Vietnam (my first major story with NBC News), and management had asked me to return to Saigon as the permanent correspondent.

The executive closed his office door behind him so we could talk in private. I expected to receive details of NBC's coverage plans in Vietnam, or advice on the types of stories in which New York producers were interested. Instead, the NBC man admitted he knew nothing about Asia, that he had to learn fast, and what he really wanted to know were the comparative distances of Hong Kong and Tokyo (where we had full bureaus with camera crews) from Saigon (where we had none). He was surprised to learn that Tokyo was so much farther away than Hong Kong.

I cite this to make the point that this lack of knowledge (at least in television news) had a certain positive aspect in assuring a high quality of reporting from South Vietnam in the mid-1960s. A lack of knowledge of Vietnam in 1964 meant (at least at NBC) an absence of second guessing and the preconceived ideas which producers and editors often direct to their reporters in the field. This was particularly important in selecting the feature or background reports, an area in which producers frequently like to have their say. Today, a network correspondent is rarely out of range of a direct-dial telephone, of an evening news editor reviewing his script and making "helpful" suggestions as to how he can trim his spot to the mandatory minute and a half. In the early television days in South Vietnam, we had no Telex link with NBC New York—let alone telephone contact—and we had a minimum of three to four minutes per report. For television reporters, it was ideal.

Although I returned to Saigon during Tet in 1968, and again for the *dénouement* in 1975, my principal involvement was from July 1964 (just prior to the Tonkin incidents) to December 1965—by which time the American military commitment was expanding rapidly and the story had become the "shooting war" to the exclusion of almost everything else.

In assessing the quality of reporting during this critical period of transition and escalation, I would mention two key factors. First, the freedom of movement journalists enjoyed. This was particularly true for television reporters, whose coverage had been limited under the Diem regime. Television could not begin to do its job until its cameras and reporters could move about the country nor, indeed, until NBC New York provided the camera teams. This happened in 1964.

Freedom of movement meant the freedom to talk with the American advisors in the field. One of my earliest impressions was the difference in talking to an American official in Saigon about U.S. involvement, and discussing the same subject with an American captain or major or an AID official in the Mekong Delta. In both places you might have heard the same facts, but the interpretation of those facts was often strikingly different. The military advisors in those early days offered frank assessments of the strengths and weaknesses of the Vietcong and ARVN forces. As the political climate in Saigon and the military balance of power in the countryside continued to deteriorate in late 1964 and early 1965, I was struck by how few advisors in the field welcomed the prospect of a major American military involvement. Access to this perspective was indispensable to a journalist who otherwise would have been limited to the official American briefings in Saigon, which inevitably reflected official thinking in Washington.

The second factor in assessing the quality of reporting during this period was that the political foundation of the Vietnam story was well laid before the American military escalation began in 1965. The American public had been supplied with over a year of political reporting, from the overthrow of the Diem government through the succession of governments which followed. There could be no doubt of the political conflicts, intrigues, and instability which were endemic in the land and provided the setting for the deepening American involvement. Frequently, in international crises, the United States has found itself involved without the public's having received background information on the forces at work. But in Vietnam, Americans knew (or at least had the opportunity to know) what they were getting into. The dangers, the ground rules had been reported.

When the first Marines came ashore at Da Nang, in 1965, the nature of television coverage in Vietnam changed immediately. It was now a war story. Primarily an American story in a foreign country. Television producers and editors suddenly felt they had expertise on how the story should be covered. It soon became clear that the true reporter for television was the camera rather than the correspondent, who increasingly served as a caption writer for the powerful pictures of men at war.

Ask each correspondent when he first realized that Vietnam was going to be television's first war, and each will give you a different answer. My first awareness came in November 1964, in the Mekong Delta. There had been a number of incidents along the border between South Vietnam and Cambodia (from which Vietcong units were operating), and in one of these clashes an American Special Forces advisor had been captured and then killed. An NBC cameraman and I went to the Special Forces camp near the border and joined an operation of South Vietnamese Regional Force troops with their American Special Forces advisors. Since we had to move through flooded areas, we left our bulky sound camera at the base area and set out with a small silent camera and tape recorder—which could provide ambient sound, but not synchronized sound of people talking. The "objective" of the operation was a small settlement near the Cambodian border which was frequently used by the Vietcong. Indeed, as the South Vietnamese force approached the settlement, there was a brief firefight before the few Vietcong there withdrew into Cambodia. What we found was the typical result of a routine operation, a dozen or so women and old men living in a half-dozen simple homes. A search of the homes produced nothing of a military nature. The end of the mission, though, was not the end of the story.

The South Vietnamese commander was about to order his men to withdraw when the American Special Forces captain (the senior advisor on the operation) said that the homes should be burned. The South Vietnamese commander (speaking through an interpreter) explained that even if the Vietcong passed through the settlement, it was not a Vietcong base; the modest structures were the only homes of these people. The American advisor replied that he understood that, but added that the Vietcong were finding shelter in the settlement and therefore it should be destroyed. The argument went on for about five minutes. It was a candid and precise debate—the essence of the coming American escalation— over whether you had to destroy the settlement (or a country) to save it.

In the end, the South Vietnamese commander prevailed; the homes were not burned. However, we were not able to capture the scene which had just taken place, because we did not have the portable film equipment needed to provide synchronized sound of the debate. We were forced to rely on silent film of the American and South Vietnamese officers talking to each other, with my narration explaining what they were talking about. The facts, the information, were communicated to the viewing audience, but the immediacy, the human emotion and experience of the moment, was not. The incident would have been fine for a print reporter, but clearly the technical limitations were unacceptable for television. In Vietnam, network television was facing logistical and technical problems it not only had never faced before, but problems it was not even aware existed. The awareness came quickly to the television reporters in the field, and soon thereafter to producers and management in New York. The picture of American soldiers at war in Vietnam was incomplete without hearing those soldiers talking, shouting, complaining, and at times screaming in pain. By 1965, we took the picture and the sound together for granted. The ability of the networks, and particularly of the network camera crews, to adapt their equipment to the demands of combat coverage was perhaps the single most important factor in the quality of that coverage.

THE EFFECT OF THE VIETNAM WAR ON BROADCAST JOURNALISM
A DOCUMENTARY FILMMAKER'S PERSPECTIVE

Peter Davis

The war stretched the bounds of tolerance for a participatory role on the part of journalists. In previous wars, from the Civil War to World War II, it was possible for a reporter to be personal and report the agony of the battlefield when the government withheld it—Stephen Crane did that, and in a way Ernie Pyle did that—but it was not possible, as it became in Vietnam, for a reporter to say, All right, I've looked at this, I've listened to what everyone says, and now here's what I think. The best-known journalist who ever went to Vietnam—in fact, he was not merely famous, he was a national figure—Walter Cronkite, could not conceivably have done the kind of reporting as a United Press man in World War II that he did from Vietnam. Cronkite was never what one could describe as antiestablishment, dovish, or even particularly probing in his questioning of the motives or the goals of leaders—but there he was in Vietnam one day, standing up and calling upon his government to get out. He did this rather late in the game, but still it was five more years before we did get out. This would have been unimaginable in any war before Vietnam. No reporter would have done this or been permitted to do it. Hemingway called for an end to World War II before it started, but once it began he was on the team like everyone else.

The fact is, reporters in wartime used to be an extension of the U.S. Government. In World War II and afterward, journalists, like movie stars, frequently made propaganda movies for the government. Newsmen knowingly spread false stories to mislead the enemy and thereby wage war in the press as effectively as on the battlefield. That certainly went on in Vietnam, but there was also another kind of journalist, no longer an extension of his government, who used his full powers of perception and expression to assert his independence. Always before, we journalists had done wars the way we did ball games. The limitations of our craft—deadlines and sensibilities—meant we were always going to be better at telling the score than at penetrating the motives, at separating tragedy from farce. Like other wars, Vietnam was a ball game for most journalists, too, but after a while it became all right to root against the home team.

Sixty years ago an editor said, "The only way to look at a politician is down." We are still learning that one day and forgetting it the next. Vietnam taught us again the necessity for distance between ourselves and government, the necessity of weighing even such apparently innocent phenomena as the jargon of government. Correspondents in World War II picked up the lingo of the Army Air Corps—*kills* and *probables* were all over the papers—and in Vietnam it became body counts and free-fire zones. Very soon, phrases like "search and destroy" or "DMZ" take over our feelings. If you talk about a war the same way as the Air Force, you will soon be thinking about it their way. It seems fairly obvious that when language is held lightly, meaning disappears too.

The second way Vietnam changed journalism, following from the first, is in advancing (and Watergate completed this process) the role of journalist as star. Certain reporters came to take themselves as seriously as the story they were covering. If subjectivity became permissible, the reasoning went, then my feelings and I must be as important as this battle or what this ambassador is telling me or what this guy says at the five o'clock follies. This was inevitable. It was not necessarily bad; frankly, I'd far rather have Morley Safer or David Halberstam in a position of credibility than Westmoreland or Rusk. The self-designated "new journalism" was born before the war, but Vietnam was a perfect place for it to grow. That some journalists became well-known, however, has misled a lot of people, including those in government, to charge them with having power they never had. Peter Arnett could never call in an air strike; the New York *Times* or Los Angeles *Times* could never call one off, or defoliate, or stop torturing, or conduct an assassination program such as Phoenix. The government always had all the power. It also had the power to reach the public whenever it wanted. Presidents could command space and air time far in excess of their opponents or critics. Johnson, who did this best, could have given lessons to the Ringling Brothers. When Sen. William Fulbright at last decided to hold hearings on the origins of the war, LBJ quickly scheduled a three-ring conference in the Pacific among himself, his field commanders, and the South Vietnamese leaders. The headlines came, therefore, not from a stuffy hearing room in Washington but from a sunny holiday island with free drinks and other distractions for the manipulated faithful. The press was more against than for the war from 1967 on, and the majority of Americans felt the same, but the government and the government alone—even with a change in presidency—kept the war going until 1973 in terms of American troops, until 1975 in terms of supporting our surrogate government in Saigon until it lost, and until today, after three *more* presidents, in terms of our implacable hostility toward Hanoi.

THE EFFECT OF THE VIETNAM WAR ON BROADCAST JOURNALISM
A CRITIC'S PERSPECTIVE

Michael Arlen

There is little doubt that Vietnam changed television journalism. Wars are usually bad for people and good for institutions, and television journalism is nothing if not institutional. World War II more or less rescued radio news from news gossips like Walter Winchell and Gabriel Heater and more or less laid down the foundations of two of the great network news organizations. Vietnam, in turn, rescued television news from the likes of *Camel News Caravan* and John Cameron Swayze, and gave us the present majesty of the nightly network news.

I have heard it said also that Vietnam helped television news grow up. I do not doubt that that is true in certain ways, though maybe that is because television news had such a lot of growing up to do. To take a small example, television correspondents no longer cover wars in post-colonial third world countries costumed in those white-hunter safari suits. Nor do they try to report wars by quite so passively passing along as news the pronouncements of the generals and politicians who sponsor those wars.

A certain amount of myth has grown around the television coverage of the Vietnam War: that television kind of stuck it to the home audience with its scenes of bloody combat and kind of stuck it to the military with its relentlessly negative commentary. But I remember something very different. Through most of the war, television very rarely showed us anything of a horrific or bloody or Goyaesque nature on the nightly news—on entertainment programs, yes, but not on the nightly news. In fact, television dutifully passed on the body counts—a distant, alienating kind of announcement—but almost never showed us death, which might have been more meaningful. As for those sad tales that network executives used to tell of Pentagon or administration pressures brought to bear on plucky network executives, the fact is that for most of this undeclared war, almost nothing resembling a flunking grade was given our military by television news, until the final phase when some nervous C-minuses were handed out, though by a television press confident that mainstream America felt pretty much the same way about it.

By the time the war was "winding down," a phrase that one now heard from the same news organizations that had so blithely assisted in winding it up, most reporters had not only shed their safari suits but had discovered, in some cases as a primary reporting tool, the use of irony and skepticism. In other words, if you could not go so far as to report the absence of the emperor's clothes, you could at least suggest, with a solemn and knowing inflection, that the emperor's own view of the clothes situation might be taken with a grain of salt. The phrase déjà vu also made an increasingly frequent appearance, which in itself was somewhat ironic, since the vu that had actually been described back then (déjà) was described quite differently at the time.

And by the end of the war, the whole country, with TV news clinging to the national coattails, had embarked on one of its periodic, sentimental, anti-authoritarian pendulum swings. TV news now gave the cold shoulder to generals and admirals, and rushed off to interview the grunts—and even the Vietnamese whose war it had been all along and to whom both our military and our press were now returning it. In the post-Vietnam world, I have heard it said that this new anti-authoritarian focus marks a new maturity, a new seriousness, but I am wary of it. In some cases, interviewing PFC's can be a refreshing change from interviewing generals, but it strikes me that little meaningful change has taken place. TV journalism, forever seeking an authority outside itself to—so to speak—take the rap for the troublesome ongoing rush of history, has merely switched authority symbols from the once-popular establishment figures to the now-popular man on the street. I am struck, for example, by the narrowness of range of most of the huge current of present-day economic news reporting. Long ago, at the time of the great crash, when the press wanted to tell us the economic story of the country, it went rushing off to J. P. Morgan, who knew a little about it, though his view was somewhat narrow. Now the press goes to Grover's Corner and interviews John Doe, who also knows a little about it but whose view is also somewhat narrow.

In the end, what is most interesting in TV journalism today is the places where it hasn't changed. One place is what we might call the parochial factor, the continued unworldly insistence of television news that complicated international situations, whenever possible, be defined strictly in American terms. Thirty years ago, in Boston, I remember that we used to joke about the parochialism of Hearst's *American* (with its "Hub Man Lands on Omaha Beach" headlines) but the story of our entire Salvador coverage is that nothing really exists there unless an American is involved. An American priest is kidnapped, and everyone runs around for days and days. In fact, recently an entire news story revolved around an American soldier being shot in the leg. At times like that, you feel that network news is reporting on international affairs on the level of an ongoing Mickey Rooney movie—*A Yank at Oxford, A Yank in the RAF, A Yank in the Mekong Delta, A Yank at the Sack of Troy.*

There are two basic reasons for this sort of thing, and I respect one reason more than the other. The reason I don't respect too much is our old friend the chickenhearted news executive who knows that the Yanks play well in Peoria and how the hell do you spell "Agamemnon" anyway? It is not unusual to stick Yanks into things. The other reason is that television news tells stories, whether it means to or not—unlike, for example, print, which can communicate validly, even pleasingly, on other levels. Consider that the real surprise of the Kennedy-Nixon debates was that they produced a story quite independent of the actual content of the debates. In other words, TV news is always searching for figures in the foreground, heroes if you will, or villains. It sometimes makes heroes without meaning to and sometimes sticks them where they do not belong; but once made, these foreground figures redefine our view of history.

When most people ask television news to change, to become more responsible and thoughtful, they are asking it to go against its nature—and its strengths, which are of course considerable. Film is most naturally a medium of narrative. A narrative on film, whether fictional or nonfictional, inevitably composes itself into scenes. I said "composes itself" intentionally, because television news, like all other film narrative, is dominated not merely by what the camera sees but by what the camera takes pleasure in. We remember so-called news events not merely as events or even as filmed records, but in terms of certain scenes. The Iranians with their fists raised outside the American embassy in Tehran defined not only the hostage crisis, but what in former times one might call the whole Iranian question. Those scenes of F-4 napalm strikes and choppers landing on hillsides and Westmoreland forever inspecting the ARVN defined the Vietnam question for many years. Israeli jets, and Arafat kissing babies, recently defined the Beirut question.

As a television critic, I probably took too easy an aim at all that "bang bang" footage. Of course, it was often trivial or misleading; of course, it did not speak to my wider sense of the war's complexity. But I think the interesting point, and the point I missed then, is that the really telling scenes on the news were the scenes the cameras made sense of and took pleasure in. I realize now that, though cameras are owned and operated by men and women who can pick them up and supposedly lug them around anywhere, the cameras see differently from those men and women and with a different logic, certainly with a logic different from print journalism. A film narrative makes a different impact than other narratives. I do not think that can ever be changed, except superficially. My point is that we should not expect it to change. Of course, superficial change is not all that bad; God knows we could afford to lose some of the sillier stuff; we could use more people to aim their cameras at unlikely places and see if the cameras do not find something to please them there. But I suspect that if there is an important challenge in television journalism, it is only in part a challenge to the people who own the cameras; the much greater part of the challenge is to the rest of us, the audience, who consistently confuse the camera eye with the human eye, who of course love the cameras—all those cameras everywhere—in the fashion of lovers in the early stage of an infatuation who, alas, expect the love object to do, somehow, absolutely everything.

THE ROLE OF JOURNALISTS IN VIETNAM
A FEATURE WRITER'S PERSPECTIVE

Phillip Knightley

As more and more Americans arrived in Vietnam and the United States involvement became more open, the reporting changed. Increasing numbers of reporters thought that the war was unjust, and they sought out stories to support this view. I see nothing ethically wrong with this sort of subjective journalism, providing the correspondent does not resort to lies and invention to make his case and does not attempt to disguise his stance. And, to balance those correspondents who wrote what the war was doing to innocent civilians, there were others who wrote stirring stories about American heroism and the praiseworthiness of American war aims.[1]

The significant point about the flush of stories in this period, attacking U.S. involvement, is not that they were written—that was inevitable—but that the United States provided the access and the freedom that enabled them to be written. Other democracies would have been much less tolerant. Look how Britain managed the news during the Falklands campaign.[2] Or, perhaps more to the

---

1. See, for example, Jim Lucas, *Dateline Vietnam* (New York, Award Books, 1967); and Frank Harvey, *Air War Vietnam* (New York, Bantam, 1967).
2. See Phillip Knightley, "The Falklands: How Britannia Ruled the News," *Columbia Journalism Review* (September–October, 1982).

point, consider an encounter that correspondent Murray Sayle had with an Israeli press officer when, in 1967, he switched from reporting Vietnam to the Six-Day War. "Just a word of warning," the Israeli press officer said. "You're not in Vietnam now. You can't do or write anything you like here. Here you do what we say. Okay?"[3]

True, a lot of Vietnam stories and photographs ran into problems in the United States because they were considered "too tough for American readers" (Martha Gellhorn's series of articles on hospitals and orphanages), or "too harrowing for the American market" (Philip Jones-Griffith's pictures). But you cannot suppress a good story indefinitely, and all the good Vietnam stories *were* published somewhere, sooner or later.

Nevertheless, half of all Americans, according to Gallup, had no idea what the war in Vietnam was all about. The reporting of Tet, with its emphasis on the ability of the enemy—fourteen years after the first American commitment to South Vietnam—to penetrate the grounds of the United States Embassy, suggested that whatever it was about it was a war the United States appeared to be losing. Yet, most correspondents got Tet wrong. As a whole it was such a military disaster for the Vietcong that they never really recovered. How could this misreporting have happened?

A war correspondent is in a different psychological position from any other reporter because he cannot avoid sharing some of the risk taken by the people he is writing about. A reporter covering the proceedings in a police court runs no danger of the judge suddenly saying, "The press is also convicted and is hereby sentenced to eighteen months in the state penitentiary." The war correspondent's involvement makes it difficult for a genuinely concerned correspondent to take a lofty *j'accuse* position. He knows that both sides die in wars; both are brave and cowardly; both are kind, both cruel, both equally capable of atrocities. (The overall proportions no doubt vary, but how do you discover what the proportions are while the war is still on?)

So the honest correspondent sticks to what he himself has seen, and is careful not to edit his material to make one side do all

---

3. Robert Elegant, "How to Lose a War: Reflections of a Foreign Correspondent," *Encounter* (August, 1981), p. 83.

the nasty things and the other do all the good. But in a war with no easily identifiable enemy, no simply explained cause, no clearly designated villain, no front line—in a war with complicated political issues and in which the correspondent had regularly to try to make sense out of a whirl of experience and ghastly sights—this did not work. No one correspondent could hope to get a broad, general experience of it; all that most correspondents succeeded in doing was obtaining a limited, spotty experience.

It was a complex war, equally difficult to understand and convey in all its ramifications. One indication of this was the proliferation of symbols or images of the war offered by correspondents as substitutes for explanation, and grasped by the readers and viewers as substitutes for understanding. The Marines raising the flag on Iwo Jima remains the lasting image of World War II. In Vietnam, we have the soldier with the Zippo lighter, General Loan shooting the man in the checked shirt, the Vietcong with black tape across his eyes, the Vietnamese woman swimming a river with a child on her back, the Vietnamese child with napalm burns running down a road, the children dying at My Lai, and the famous quotation, "We had to destroy this village in order to save it." The lesson must be: Beware of too many symbols; they represent the easy way out.

Now, if it was impossible to convey all the ramifications of Vietnam to the public, then what we are facing is not a failure on the part of the correspondents but a flaw in the very nature of journalism. We have had the arrogance to believe that there was nothing in the tide of human affairs that journalism could not select, encompass, analyze, and explain; no event, no matter its magnitude or complexity, that could not successfully be subjected to the journalistic process. We now have to consider the possibility that we were wrong; that there are happenings of such dimensions—and I submit that Vietnam was one—that journalism alone is unable to present or explain adequately.

That is the bad news. The good news is that in any assessment of the quality of story that the correspondents *were* able to tell, the basic constitutional guarantees of the United States worked. There were hiccups. Some stories did not get the emphasis they deserved; others were overplayed; there was pressure and government lying. But to pretend that this was unique to Vietnam is to ignore reality. In the end, the story as the correspondents saw it came out, warts and all. Do not forget that the first step that led to the uncovering of My Lai was, as in so many stories, that most elementary act in the democratic process: an ordinary citizen writing to his congressman.

As to the effects of these stories, I find myself undecided. You can accept one of two versions. The first is that the reporting toppled a president, destroyed a major American policy, lost the war, tilted the global balance of power, and is directly responsible for the sad state of Southeast Asia today. If that is true, then so be it. Either one believes in a free press or one does not. If you tinker with the concept, if you try to achieve a three-quarter-free press, or a half-free press, you risk destroying it. Because governments will always find reasons why, on just this one occasion, the press should surrender some of its freedom in the national interest.

The other version is that the first view is an exaggeration, and that the reporting from Vietnam, mainly because of the flaw in journalism discussed above, did not have the influence attributed to it; that journalists failed to convey the war's significance to the public. But—and this cannot be emphasized too strongly—this was not because the correspondents did not try, or because of any conspiracy of distortion. It was because Vietnam was such a complex tragedy that the reporters, like everyone else, were overwhelmed by it.

THE ROLE OF JOURNALISTS IN VIETNAM

AN ARMY GENERAL'S PERSPECTIVE

Maj. Gen. Winant Sidle (USA-Ret.)

In a study of Vietnam news reporting done by the American Society of Newspaper Editors (ASNE), the quality of the press corps in Vietnam—and hence the reporting—was characterized as not sufficiently professional as a whole. The reasons cited included: too many inexpert free-lancers and stringers; too many short tours; too many reporters trying to make a name for themselves.

These are valid conclusions, and I would add the following based on my experience there: there were too many reporters. We had 649 accredited in-country at the end of March 1968. That's far too many, especially when most of them stayed in Saigon. Only approximately seventy-five to eighty regularly went into the field.

There were too many inexperienced reporters. This ties in with ASNE's "too short tour" criticism. I was surprised that so many of the media sent over young reporters with no appropriate background. One newcomer, representing a major U.S. newspaper, asked me at the end of his initial briefing, "What's a battalion?" He proved to be so ignorant about military and political matters that he was fired at the end of a year. But during that year, think of what his many thousands of readers "learned" about Vietnam! Some of the young reporters who stayed a year or longer eventually became quite good, but the American people suffered while these gentlemen did their on-the-job training.

There were too many reporters unwilling to check stories before filing. Some were lazy; some believed we wouldn't give them facts; some felt it was unnecessary to check. We all know that not checking out stories invariably leads to mistakes and low-quality reporting.

There was too much stateside editing of stories sent in from the field. There were many examples of fair stories edited by ignorant, biased editors into slanted inaccuracy. I remember one story in a major news magazine which reported three rather poorly conducted ARVN operations. It was converted into a vitriolic, inaccurate downgrading of the entire South Vietnam military. When I asked the reporter about it and he showed me the copy of what he had sent in, I found little relationship between what he had written and what was printed. His comment was, "There is a bunch of kids back there who don't know the score." When I came back to the States in late 1969, I arranged a meeting with the group of four news magazine editors who normally handled Vietnam copy. The oldest was twenty-eight; the others were under twenty-five. None had any military background, none had spent more than a few days in Vietnam. All, however, were firmly convinced they knew everything about everything going on in Vietnam. This does *not* lead to quality coverage.

My last point is, perhaps, the most important. The quality of reporting from Vietnam suffered from advocacy journalism. Too many reporters, especially the younger ones, arrived firmly convinced that the war was unjust, immoral, or whatever, and that the U.S. should not be there. This trend became more noticeable after Tet. These advocacy journalists seemed to think that Americans are incapable of reaching sound, reasoned opinions based on plain old factual, complete, and objective reporting. So the reporter tried to convince his audiences via his *news* coverage that his opinions should be their opinions.

I must add that, while I thought the overall reporting in Vietnam left much to be desired from a quality standpoint, there was a lot of good reporting done by the true professionals. They tried to tell the story as it was really happening. Unfortunately, they were considerably outnumbered by the non-pros.

Perhaps Dan Henkin, assistant secretary of defense for public affairs during part of my tour in Vietnam, had the answer. He liked

to point out that the Baseball Writers Association had more stringent rules for the assignment of reporters than did the U.S. media.
To be the official scorer of a baseball game, a writer had to have
five years' experience in covering baseball. To be eligible to vote
for membership in the Baseball Hall of Fame required ten years'
experience. Had our media used similar rules for the assignment of
reporters to Vietnam, I believe reporting of the war would have
been much more objective. And this might well have changed the
entire outcome.

THE ROLE OF JOURNALISTS IN VIETNAM

A REPORTER'S PERSPECTIVE

David Halberstam

Hearing General Sidle last night left me with a melancholy feeling that the debate over Vietnam reporting, even ten years later, had not progressed. His critique was woefully incomplete. He said there had been too many short-term reporters there, but the Department of Defense was constantly flying in reporters from home-town papers because they were more malleable than the resident correspondents like Peter Arnett; he said that *Newsweek* and *Time* wrote softer in Saigon and had it made tough in New York, a canard of the first order; and above all he challenged reporters for failing to verify stories when the most constant use of misinformation and lack of verification went on day after day in the "five o'clock follies" [press briefings sponsored by Military Assistance Command, Vietnam (MACV)]. There, reports from Vietnamese officers, never substantiated or witnessed by American officers, would be passed on, and would thereupon come out as "American sources said." Each day, then, there would be a positive story coming out of the briefing. Even though some reporter might have sat there and torn the flesh off an American briefing officer, he or the others could still go back and write the story they were programmed to write about how we had once again defeated the Vietcong and the NVA, thus negating or effectively neutralizing the story that Peter Arnett or Horst Faas would be doing that day.

We need a far larger context to see what journalists did in Vietnam and why it caused so much contention and pain. The war was an extension, finally, of a policy conceived in lies and fear—the fear not that Vietnam would be lost to Communism but the fear that if that happened the Democrats would lose Washington to the Republicans—a misconception of the other side, and an unwillingness to understand what the French Indochina war had done to nationalism. Reporters faced a situation in which our highest political officers, for example our secretary of state, still believed that there was no split between the Chinese and the Russians, a president systematically upping the ante without admitting that he was—saying it was a small war while going on to a big war—and the highest levels of military officers and the secretary of defense lying. No wonder, then, that we who were the reporters in Vietnam came under such criticism and found ourselves, again and again, challenging the alleged norms being set by Washington. There was no comparable tough-minded reporting coming from our colleagues in Washington. In fact, the government quite skillfully used the meat-grinder journalistic style of *Time* and *Newsweek* to offset the reporting coming out of the field. So there we were, in an odd way, the single group trying to sort out the projected aims from the realities.

Since the people who started that war and made the combat commitment completely and absolutely misassessed the strength, vitality, resilience, and historical dynamism of the other side, since they largely misassessed the comparable strengths of their ally, since they did not understand the dynamic of the French Indochina war and what that had done, there was from day one a flaw in American policy. The basic hope, that American technology could do it through bombing, was quickly shown to be unrealistic. The policy of a small war, won by technology, on the cheap, was proven, in fact, false from day one. The other side came into the country very quickly; the bombing failed to interdict them; and those of us who were the reporters there caught the shit for the failure of reality to match American hopes. And that made us different from war reporters in the past. And there is to this day, in this room, bitter division among us, none of it pleasant, old enmities not yet settled. In terms of our assumptions of our duties, it is not so much an ideological as a generational divide between those who go back to the loyalties engendered by World War II and Korea, and who had a simpler and more traditional view of what a reporter does and what his loyalty is to the flag, right or wrong; and the generation to which I, and Peter Arnett, and Morley Safer belong, who found that duty more conflicted and who found that the ideals of democracy made it harder to automatically salute the flag each night. That made us controversial. Were we going to be loyal first and foremost to the ideals of American democracy, or were we going to be loyal to—in the immortal words of so many American officials—"the team"? It was not fun; it was often very painful. During the fall of 1963, I was twenty-eight years old, and I went to the Mekong Delta with a man named Richard Tregaskis; he had been a classic war correspondent of World War II, a hero of mine, who had written a book, *Guadalcanal Diary,* that I had greatly admired as a boy. We had spent what I thought were an entirely pleasant two days in the Mekong Delta. I had introduced him to treasured sources of mine. On the way back to Saigon, he turned to me and in a very soft voice said to me, "If I were doing what you are doing, I would be ashamed of myself." We traveled the rest of the way in stony silence; my face, I am sure, was ashen. The attacks which were to come from higher officials, even from the president of the United States, never shook me and upset me so much as that harsh condemnation from a man whom I had once thought I so admired.

I am enormously proud of the military reporting we did. I am not nearly so proud of my political reporting. I don't think it was nearly so profound. I think I have always been criticized for the wrong thing: I have always been criticized for being too pessimistic. In truth, I was not pessimistic enough. Our military sources were very good, and a good reporter can always find good sources. Our political sources—the people in the embassy—were not nearly so good. The McCarthy era had wiped out a generation of state department people, just ravaged it. It wiped out not only the old Asia hands, but the next generation coming after them who might have served in Vietnam, who might have phrased some of these things in a historical way, given us younger reporters a sense of their expertise. They were gone; there was a vacuum there; and thus we as reporters and we as a nation were weaker for it.

It was relatively easy, in 1962, to ascertain that the war was not going well and the reasons why. Slowly, and only by late 1963, did we begin to understand that the failings of Diem were not so much causes as symptoms of a leadership that had stayed on the sidelines during the French Indochina war. The painful lesson, one we had to learn ourselves, was that there was a great deal of replay of the postwar China situation—of a feudal society coming apart and being challenged by a more modern, nationalistic one.

DIFFICULTIES OF COVERING A WAR LIKE VIETNAM: I

Robert Scheer

First, it is historical: the assumption is that the war started when the first group of correspondents went, or when television became interested, or when U.S. troops went. The idea that there had been thousands of years of history of that country, that it had been occupied by Chinese, French, Japanese—that there had been a long struggle against these groups—frequently goes unmentioned. There is a perverse assumption that all of history begins when it is important to American ambitions, goals, and interests. Second, the part of history that is taken seriously is the war game, the shooting, the firing, the stuff that works on television, rather than the underlying, more serious factors that might have caused all this to happen. Third, there is a very limited ability to question the assumptions of the government that represents you.

We had not noticed Vietnam until our government noticed it—so that everything that happened before 1950 was totally uninteresting to us. That there had been a movement led by Communists against the French and the Japanese; that the Communists in fact had a position of some significance in that country; that the French tried to turn back the clock in 1945; that the fighting then continued until 1954—those facts didn't interest us until the Korean War. Because of the Korean War, because of our view of the international Communist conspiracy and its timetable for the takeover of the world, and our view of America's Cold War struggle with the Soviets, we discovered Vietnam. So even though the French were the colonialists, even though the French had an abysmal history in that country, we came to the aid of the French. And our media covered that resurgence of French colonialism as if it were a chapter in the fight for freedom. Because it was the Cold War, because it was a fight against godless Communism, therefore it had to be supported. The United States Government made the French return possible.

When the French gave up the ghost, media coverage basically turned off Vietnam. The Geneva Conference was meeting; there would be elections; and the assumption was that the country would be unified under Ho Chi Minh and that we would be diverted elsewhere. At that point a great deal of media manipulation occurred. There were a great many scare stories, and the creation of a George Washington figure in the form of Ngo Dinh Diem, notably in *Look, Reader's Digest, Time,* and *Newsweek.* The U.S. Government totally ignored the Geneva accords, the matter of elections, the political solution that had been developed for that country—and at the same time invented Diem and created a government for him. And the media basically celebrated that government. The period between 1954 and 1961 is the period of the miracle of South Vietnam.

I personally did not learn much about Vietnam by going there; I learned much more in the stacks of the library of the University of California. Quite by accident, I came across a brown package that had been donated to the university by the widow of a man who had been involved in what was called the Michigan State Project. She did not know what she had; she had just donated these papers. I discovered, when I opened the package, that "the miracle" had been an invention of public relations, done by Michigan State University people working for the CIA. So the great democratic constitution that was written in Vietnam, all of the national trappings—every single aspect involved in the selling of this anti-Communist alternative—had been, in fact, a creation of our own government. That was a story that was not reported by the American media at all, which was too busy focusing on the celebration of Diem's miracle, which collapsed in 1961.

The press missed many things during the pre-1961 period,

and by 1961 the die of American involvement had been cast. The idea that neutralism could be a force in that part of the world, or the third world generally, was not taken seriously. Communism as anything but an extension of Soviet power was simply a foreign notion to the American media. Connected with this was the refusal to see Communism as having a nationalist component, or to see divisions among national Communisms. The Sino-Soviet dispute had visibly begun before we sent combat troops to Vietnam. And all during the sixties we were in this absolutely absurd position of justifying this war on Vietnam in global terms when the whole underpinning of that global analysis had dropped out and no one had noticed.

Another idea that was ignored by the media, particularly during this early period, was that there could be bad guys on our side. The assumption during the fifties and sixties was that we were virtuous in the world, and that if we supported the French, they must be virtuous; if we were in Vietnam, it must be a virtuous cause. The media never challenged that stereotype. The media were and still are incapable of challenging the moral stereotypes of their own government, and the idea that we are the repositories of all virtue and *they* are the repositories of all evil, was at the root of the problems of reporting the Vietnam War.

Finally, it gets to the question of the political attitudes of media people. I think that the best reporters are Trotskyists, even after they have become neo-conservatives. They are profoundly political people who want to deal with big ideas, want to deal with history, want to do library research, want to think about major questions in provocative ways, and, being Trotskyists, there is never a government in the world for which they have to apologize. I commend that as a stance. When you are talking about international events, when you are talking about intervention in another people's history, you have to get historical, you have to read about it, you have to care about it, you have to be sensitive to its complexities. But you also have to get involved with the big political and economic questions that are supposed to be behind it. The war in Vietnam could never have been sustained for twenty-four hours if this country had really focused on the basic assumptions of that war. Because the assumptions had evaporated before we committed half a million troops.

DIFFICULTIES OF COVERING A WAR LIKE VIETNAM: II

George Reedy

1. *The war in Vietnam was not the kind of war which the press is organized to cover.*

The daily press—print or electronic—is inherently event-oriented, and it may be impossible to recast it into another form. This means that journalists cover wars in terms of what is regarded as a *significant pattern* of events such as troop movements, battles, major destruction of property and lives, occupation of key territories, and surrender of armies. For World War I, World War II, and even Korea (where there were front lines) this pattern held, and journalistic performance could be judged by its success or failure in supplying answers to the questions implicit in the formula.

In Vietnam, the so-called significant pattern had very little significance. Mass troop movements and battles were a rarity, slaughter and property destruction were not determining factors; territories could be conquered for the moment but not occupied; and armies did not surrender but merely scattered. There was not even a front line to be drawn on a map and displayed on television. The situation was particularly difficult for television crews, but even print journalists found themselves baffled in attempting to explain what was happening. Fundamentally, the war was a struggle for allegiance rather than for strategic position—and this is not readily portrayed in the traditional block paragraphs of journalism or in the kind of film that electronics reporters can gather by accompanying a convoy.

2. *The American public was not prepared to understand the reporting from Vietnam regardless of its quality.*

Although editors are fond of describing the "educational" features of the press, newspapers and news telecasts are educational only if the word is broadened to include all life experience. A more defensible thesis is that the press exists to supply facts to a public which is already educated to comprehend the facts and use them to make prudent decisions. For this reason, what is often regarded as uneven reporting by journalists may well reflect, instead, uneven education of the public.

There are very few areas in the world that were as mysterious to the American people before 1965 as Southeast Asia. Traditionally, the citizens running our country have looked east (because our ancestors came largely from Europe) and west (because of the impulse that sent so many missionaries to China). But our knowledge of anything to the south was very sketchy. In my own case, I would have had difficulty even locating Vietnam on a map until I found myself actually walking down the streets of Saigon in 1962.

What this means is that the press was faced with a triple task: first, educating itself on Vietnam; second, educating the American public on Vietnam; third; supplying the citizens of this country with the facts of the war. The burden was too much. Individual journalists did what I consider to be a remarkable job in educating themselves about a part of the world where they had to start from scratch. But the vast complex we term "the press"—the network of wire services, editors, and publicists who are responsible for the total product that reaches the readers—did not really catch up with the correspondents in the field. The media had paid virtually no attention to Southeast Asia prior to the Vietnam conflict, and as institutions, they were not prepared to cope with the totally new situation that was presented.

To make matters even worse, the discussion publications—which normally provide the public with the depth of understanding that the daily press cannot achieve—were as poorly prepared as the orthodox journalists. They could take positive or negative stands on American policy, but the reasoning behind their positions was no more solid than the mental processes exercised by a cable editor on the New York desk of one of the wire services.

3. *The United States lacked spokesmen who were both authoritative and knowledgeable to spark and lead public debate.*

There are a few prestigious journalists who play a role in initiating and fostering public debate. But their influence is limited to a few communications centers in the United States—and even in those centers, their tendency is to reflect the views of policymaking officials. For the majority of Americans, debate conducted through the news media means the reporting to the public of the thoughts and counterthoughts of public men and women who are regarded as either authoritative or knowledgeable or both. This system was quite adequate during the three previous wars when pro and con spokesmen who belonged in both categories were readily available.

Vietnam, however, was an area in which the sources for conducting public debate were wholly inadequate. The number of high-level American diplomats and army officers who had served tours in Southeast Asia was negligible. American businessmen had dealt with that part of the world largely through their counterparts in England and France. The few academics who had some experience were not generally known, and only a handful of journalists had paid any attention—even perfunctory—to Saigon and Hanoi. This left the conduct of public debate in the beginning to the American officials who became *authoritative* (but not necessarily knowledgeable) simply because they were in charge of United States operations.

As the war went on, antiwar spokesmen achieved a degree of prominence, but their authority rested solely upon their ability to articulate the resentments of draftees and college students threatened with the draft. In many respects, they were even less knowledgeable about Vietnam than the pro-war leaders, though history may well decide that they were on the right side of the argument. At no time during the war years could one discern a public debate that promised to yield that kind of conclusion which a nation must reach in order to sustain itself through a debilitating war.

The important question is whether the press changed public attitudes toward the war. To this, there can be no certain answer. My personal judgment is that press attitudes toward the war changed at the same time that public attitudes changed—and that the basic cause for the change was the introduction of draftees into the fighting after the 1964 election. Very few people noticed that anything was going on as long as the fighters were professional soldiers. It was when "the boy next door" was killed in a rice paddy in a part of the world whose existence had previously been unknown that Americans began to register opposition. The impetus for dissent came from the returning veterans and the prospective draftees—not from daily journals, magazines, and newscasts.

DIFFICULTIES OF COVERING A WAR LIKE VIETNAM: III

Roger Hilsman

The press frequently does not understand what forces are at work (which can also be said of policymakers). I think most people who have studied Vietnam deeply would agree that the principal force at work was not "worldwide Communism" but an anti-colonialist, nationalist movement feeding on social discontent in the South, whose leaders happened, by a quirk of history, to be members of the Communist party. But I can think of few reporters who wrote the story that way at the time. In the early days, people like David Halberstam were trying to influence policy all right, but they argued that supporting Ngo Dinh Diem was a mistake and not the best way to defeat the Vietcong. Later, the doves stressed the "immorality" of the American adventure, and often that the people did not really support the South Vietnam government. But few gave a thorough analysis of why. And, of course, the same is true of the policymakers. There were some who saw the deeper forces, but after Kennedy's death, they lost out to the hawks.

One question—for which I have no answer—is, "What can the press do to understand what is really happening?" And the question can be broadened to include not only policymakers but every one of us, scholars included. A "cautionary tale" concerns the Buddhist crisis. When the Buddhists started burning themselves with gasoline, and parading and demonstrating, we on the policy side asked everyone we could think of to tell us just exactly the extent of the political power of the Buddhists. The Vietnam experts in the foreign service didn't know. Neither did the CIA specialists. We contacted the academic specialists in the universities, and they didn't know. We actually found an American Buddhist working in the United States Information Agency who was a vice-president of the international Buddhist society. He was able to tell us the views of all the major Vietnamese Buddhist notables on such questions as how many angels could stand on the head of a pin—but he was nonplussed when it came to their political power.

I personally glimpsed the dim beginnings of wisdom when I found out that neither the Vietcong nor Ngo Dinh Diem had a clue to the answer. But true wisdom did not come until I found out that the Buddhists themselves didn't have even an inkling of their political power. They bit on the issue of being denied the right to carry Buddhist flags in a parade on Buddha's birthday when the Catholics had been allowed to carry flags in a parade celebrating Diem's brother's twenty-fifth anniversary of being the bishop of Hue. They tasted political blood, and they bit harder. Pretty soon they were carrying signs in English—although none of them could speak a word—and they came to know which TV crews to phone when a self-immolation was scheduled, and how much time to give them to get to the appointed place and set up their cameras.

Another question for which I have no answer is where to draw the line between the genuine need of policymakers for secrecy and the genuine need of members of the press to report what is going on. The need of policymakers for secrecy rarely has anything to do with national security or information getting to the enemy. The need exists because policy arises from negotiations and bargaining among a wide variety of power centers within the government, and because that kind of politicking cannot be done in public. The best "cautionary tale" I can think of goes back to the Constitutional Convention in Philadelphia in 1789. The first resolution passed by the framers of the Constitution was that their proceedings should be entirely secret. As practicing politicians, they knew that if the proceedings were public, anything they said would be used against them by opponents at home. Changes of mind, even speculative ruminations, would be dangerous. Worse, concessions would be almost impossible once a delegate or delegation had taken a public stand. Utopians might want "open covenants, openly arrived at," but politicians wanted open covenants arrived at in utmost secrecy—because otherwise no covenants would ever be arrived at. The same is true of all policymakers working on any major policy.

The genuine need of the press to report what is going on is not just to sell papers or win high Nielsen ratings. If we are to maintain a democratic society, people must be able to have a say in policy decisions. Obviously, they will have a say only if they know what is going on. And it is equally obvious that the press is the only vehicle by which ordinary people can find out what is going on.

On this point, "cautionary tales" are easier to find. An obvious example from the Vietnam experience is the secret bombing of Cambodia. Because the policymakers were able to keep the bombing secret, everyone outside of government—and many inside—were unable to voice an objection to the policy.

But the line is impossible to draw with any precision. Two "cautionary tales" spring to mind. One was the Bay of Pigs, and the other was the Cuban Missile Crisis. The press in the form of the New York Times found out about both in advance; and on both occasions Kennedy asked them not to publish. Later he said that he wished they had published all they knew in the first case. (He was glad that they had not published in the second.)

My own view is that if they had published the full story of the Bay of Pigs in advance Kennedy would have blamed their disclosure for the failure—and everyone, including Kennedy, would have believed the charge. If they had published on the Missile Crisis, he would have done the same—and everybody would have believed it, too. "Whether the policy was right or wrong," people would say, "who elected the New York Times to make our national decisions?"

The decision to publish something about the past—such as the Pentagon Papers—is not such a problem. It is publishing about planned policies that poses the difficulty.

Again, my view is that there is no answer in any general sense. It has to be on a case-by-case basis. To publish is to bring others into the making of policy. Sometimes doing so will help, and sometimes it will only wreck things and merely ensure that the policy being developed will be stillborn. Whether this is a good thing or a bad thing depends upon whether the policy was good or bad.

So, in the end, I doubt if Vietnam has taught us very much about the role of the press in the policymaking process or the relationship between the press and the policymakers.

DIFFICULTIES OF COVERING A WAR LIKE VIETNAM: IV

William Tuohy

I think that the best reporters, over the course of the years, pointed out the weaknesses of Saigon regimes, the difficulties facing American combat troops, the corruption and waste, the wrenching burden on refugees and villagers, and at the same time, the determination and ruthlessness of the Vietcong and North Vietnamese. But, of course, no one reporter could do all these subjects justice all the time.

It was difficult for a member of a small bureau—to take a hypothetical example—to examine the effects of the Tet offensive on a Delta village, while at the same time the Marines were fighting to regain the citadel at Hue or were under siege at Khe Sanh. These were the events that captured the world's attention.

In retrospect, what now seems to me a serious journalistic weakness was the need to switch suddenly from an in-depth examination of some facet of Vietnam and jump on a plane or helicopter for the latest hot spot that was garnering headlines and editorial interest.

There was always a running disagreement between most of the media and government officials on how well the war, pacification, and Vietnamization were going—with the reporters, in from the field, generally taking the much more negative view. But assessments *were* difficult to make under the circumstances. And there were always disagreements over the success or failure of various programs and operations.

THE CIA AS A SOURCE

Keyes Beech and Frank Snepp

KEYES BEECH:

My relations with the CIA were solidly based on self-interest. The CIA was in the information-gathering business and so was I. Since their resources were infinitely greater than mine, I wanted to tap their information bank. A reporter needs all the help he can get. Looking back on Vietnam, one of my professional regrets is that I was never able to develop credible Communist sources. But then I was never enthusiastic about their revolution.

There are different opinions on what relations, if any, a correspondent should have with the CIA. My own firmly held opinion is that the foreign correspondent who *doesn't* have CIA sources isn't doing his job.

There are risks, of course. One is that a reporter will become so dependent on the CIA that he will be susceptible to manipulation in what he writes; that he will, wittingly or unwittingly, become a CIA stooge. It is possible that I was on occasion "used" by the CIA without my knowledge. There were a few occasions when I suspected someone was trying to "use" me—and I reacted rather violently. But the practice is not confined to the intelligence community. Officials are always trying to use reporters to further their own or their country's interests, which are not necessarily shameful and may sometimes even be honorable.

In any event, during more than three decades of reporting from Asia, I learned to trust the CIA more than any other overseas agency of the U.S. government. CIA political reporting was generally superior to that of the embassy political section, if only because the CIA was not bound to tailor its reporting to fit a policy line.

Thanks to a frustrated CIA official in Bangkok, who wanted to direct Washington's attention to his own needs when Vietnam was getting all the play, I was able to predict a Chinese-backed Communist insurgency in Thailand long before it happened.

Thanks to a CIA official in Saigon, whose intelligence was so good that he had only to look at his Rolex—or maybe it was a Seiko—to read the future, I was sometimes able to predict, down to the day and hour, when the Communists would launch their next offensive.

Thanks to the same official, I was able to report that certain documents indicating that the 1971 election was rigged in favor of President Nguyen Van Thieu were indeed authentic. I still don't know why he told me. Certainly it was against the U.S. interest for such information to get out.

Thanks to a bright young CIA analyst, I was able to predict, a full two weeks before it happened, the fall of Saigon and how it would happen. His scenario was so uncannily accurate that it could have come only from an agent or agents in the Communist high command.

Here I would like to make one vital point. No reporter should ever allow himself to become a captive of his source, just as a good intelligence officer never wholly relies on one source. As with all generalizations, there are exceptions. There are times when a reporter has to make a value judgment, which is to ask himself, "Is this s.o.b. telling me the truth?"

Another vital point. This is an *outsider's* view of the CIA role in Vietnam, not an insider's view. Perhaps those here who *were* on the inside will have a different view.

FRANK SNEPP:

We were always trying to cultivate journalistic contacts. We tried to develop a confidence, a rapport, so that when we were ready to drop a disinformation bomb on him, he would be receptive. In fairness to the press, when a CIA agent was assigned to do this, it was almost impossible for the journalist to double-check the information. For instance, I would give out information on Communist infiltration from North Vietnam. And I would say to a journalist, It is so and so. The journalist then might go to the British ambassador to double-check the information, but the British ambassador has also received his information from my briefings. When we hand out information, or disinformation, or half-truths, it is generally information which is so obscure or so exclusively within the CIA's province that a journalist cannot double-check and he has to make a judgment. He has to say to himself, "Do I go with it or not? Do I trust this agent?" And if you have done your job as an agent well and developed a rapport, he does trust you and you get your disinformation printed.

THE LAST YEARS AND THE AFTERMATH

Peter Arnett

Our generation of reporters opened a Pandora's box in Vietnam. We chose to write about what we saw with our own eyes and heard with our own ears, rather than practice the selective reportage that enthusiastically enhanced national objectives in previous wars. Why? Maybe the civil rights struggle fed our social consciences, or maybe the Ivy League colleges were finally giving their best and brightest to journalism. I, myself, was a rather naive colonial when I first went to Saigon in 1962—to be inspired by the single-minded gutsiness, physical and intellectual, that my young American colleagues exhibited. Our efforts shook up the system. But do not let our Pulitzers, our best-sellers, our ratings fool you. Vietnam tainted us, as it did all who ventured there. Tune into your average press bull-session. On leaving Vietnam, after his tour was over, my distinguished colleague Horst Faas commented, "We'll never sit around and talk about the good old days in Vietnam. There were no good old days." How right he was.

What has become of us? A few veteran Vietnam reporters might command healthy lecture fees. But, for example, in the management of the mighty Associated Press—which was once totally populated by World War II veterans, and which had three hundred reporters in Vietnam over the years—there is not one Vietnam-experienced man in management. Chance? Of course not. The conservative AP tolerated our dispatches and our pictures. It didn't necessarily like them.

And for every Vietnam reporter who is at the top of his profession today, how many, because of Vietnam stress, dropped out of the news business, or were pushed out, or took their own lives—case histories not too different from those on file at any Veterans Administration office. I'm not complaining: we opened our own Pandora's box and have to live with the animosities that came flying out. I'm sure this very night some diligent lecturer from Accuracy in Media, armed with my colleague Peter Braestrup's book *Big Story,* is trying to convince a Rotary Club somewhere that the American press not only lost the Vietnam War but is on its way to collapsing the whole Republic.

But that all came later. In late 1968, after seven years of covering the war, I remember touring the countryside, writing about the cease-fire that seemed to be evolving from the Paris peace talks. It was all wishful thinking: the new leadership (Nixon, Kissinger, Gen. Creighton Abrams) embarked upon a daring strategy to pacify the countryside while withdrawing American troops.

This new team, however, was far less apprehensive of the press than its predecessors. Barry Zorthian's successors (as heads of the Joint United States Public Affairs Office in Saigon) were not blamed for every negative dispatch that winged its way to the United States. And General Abrams solved the press problem by totally ignoring us. The story by Horst Faas and me about Company A, the unit that refused to fight, rang bells in U.S. newspapers but did not bring the muttered threats from MACV that might have been uttered a couple of years earlier. There were many more stories like Company A, and a willingness by the military to help us cover them. On one occasion, we heard that some units intended acknowledging a major antiwar rally in Washington in 1970. We were flown to the American Division to join a unit that was wearing black armbands to show their support for the antiwar movement.

By 1969, and later—with both Lyndon Baines Johnson and William Westmoreland gone from the scene—much of the pressure was off everybody. There were officers coming back to Vietnam on their third tour, coming back reluctantly. Neither they nor the GIs were trying to hide the obvious fact that they didn't want to be the last Americans to die in Vietnam. More and more, we were chronicling the disintegration of the U.S. Army—the fragging of officers, the mutinies, the drug use.

Ironically, it was not the authorities that tried to interfere in my reporting in those years, it was my own Associated Press. I rode with the tanks into Cambodia in 1970, and in the wake of the Kent State massacre, I filed a story from the Snoul rubber plantation about U.S. troops looting a town of jewelry and radios, and putting stores to the torch. The AP killed my story—and my pictures— fearing that distribution of such material might further inflame the campuses.

I left Vietnam for permanent residence in the U.S. soon after, and returned to Vietnam each year until the fall of Saigon in 1975. By now the South Vietnamese government was actively involving itself with the foreign press, after years of total indifference. This was to culminate, in 1975, with the murder of an *Agence France Presse* reporter at Saigon's police headquarters, a murder that has never been investigated even though the Vietnamese involved are now living in the United States. With the war declining in significance in the early 1970s, politics became the centerpoint of news coverage—few newsmen wanted to be the last to die in Vietnam, either. And the Vietnamese people were finally discovered as news subjects, mainly by Gloria Emerson, whose dispatches were the first I ever saw that captured the humanity of a people engulfed for years in war. As far as the Associated Press was concerned, Vietnam was basically a GI hometown story. When the GIs left in 1974, the AP bureau was trimmed from a high of twenty to just one reporter—George Esper. George covered the story single-handedly until the collapse of the Central Highlands, early in 1975, brought us all rushing back.

My own analyses of the war from 1970 on suggested that, with American troops pulling out, the South Vietnamese must inevitably lose. After all, the North Vietnamese had built up their army to fight an American force. With the Americans gone, the NVA must be superior to what was left. In 1973 I wrote yet another series reflecting this view, but it was published in only a few newspapers. The strongest reaction came from Thieu's press office. I was threatened with expulsion, while being asked, "Is the military situation really so bad for us here?"

I watched Saigon fall less than two years later. I had no sense of vindication that in the end events had proved us right. No, I was overwhelmed by a deep melancholy. What historians would see as inevitable had taken so bloodily and painfully long to resolve.

THE PRESS AND
THE GOVERNMENT: I

Barry Zorthian

To generalize about virtually anything in Vietnam is most often misleading and frequently dangerous. The war extended through many phases and many administrations; the press—and throughout these comments I use the word to include audio-visual media as well—contained many outlets, many forms, and many viewpoints. To talk about "the government" is as inaccurate as to talk about "the press." There was no monolithic institution or control in either category. But what comments I do make about "the press" in these remarks apply to the major media, the national media, certainly not to the dozens of "non-journalists" who were present.

Now, having cautioned against the practice, let me pose some general conclusions. But in doing so, let me set my own limitations: I speak of 1964–68; I speak of Vietnam; I speak of the coverage of South Vietnam and the operations, programs, and actions there; I speak not of the Diem period or the post-Johnson administrations in the U.S., not of debate or dispute about the war in the United States, not of coverage of Hanoi, not as to whether we should have been in Vietnam, not even of the morality of war.

• More often than not, the press was more accurate in covering the situation in Vietnam than the official government public reports—at least up until Tet. And yet, far too often at key points, on critical issues, there were stories that contained inaccuracies, distortions, and misinterpretations.

• More often than not, the U.S. public was well served by the performance of the briefing authorities, military and civilian. And I base this judgment not just on the on-record briefings but also on the voluminous backgrounding and on the extended and constant access the media had to government sources. And again I say, this is not to mean that there were no flaws in the government's performance and no need for improvements.

• More often than not, the press covered military operations better than the political aspects; the American presence better than the Vietnamese; the individual GI better than the big picture.

• Far too infrequently, in fact virtually never, did reporters transmit accurately the policies and objectives of the National Liberation Front and the government of Hanoi.

• Reporters were used: That is, they were given information with the motive of seeing a particular story appear in print—by the government, by the critics, by the South Vietnamese, by the VC, by Hanoi, and by each other.

• As the number of U.S. troops increased, the press did not switch from political analysis to an emphasis on battle coverage. But the press did let its growing opposition and criticism of the war begin to show up in the nature and tilt of its coverage—not more often than not, but in far too many cases.

What are the lessons of all this? Certainly Vietnam was a failure in terms of government communication to its electorate. I would suggest that perhaps it was not an overwhelming success in terms of communication by the media, either. How can the two sides do better in the future?

For the government:

• Expect and anticipate an open war with full exposure to the media—to a pervasive, probing, skeptical media.
• Develop a government doctrine in dealing with the press based on a concept of an independent press and as open a govern-

ment as is possible. Make such a doctrine part of the training of your military and civilian officials—particularly the foreign service and the military officer corps.

• Provide full and candid information to the electorate on your actions and judgments. Maximum candor with minimum security is a principle well worth observing.

• Develop a better method of collecting information on military operations to meet the needs of the press and, beyond it, of the electorate.

• Learn from the press. Use its observations as a source of information, as a check on your own channels. The added input can be extremely useful.

And for the press:

• Reexamine the current institutional characteristics of the media. The pressures of time, competitiveness, volume and dramatic impact distort and intensify coverage to a degree that obfuscates rather than informs or clarifies.

• Place more stress on qualifications. The media have a need to spend more time and resources in developing qualifications of their personnel for complex and difficult assignments—time spent learning language, culture, history, politics, mores, even the nature and conduct of war, if that is what is involved.

• Don't generalize from the particular. (And for the government, don't dispute the particular on the basis of the general.)

• Be skeptical indeed of the government's public posture. But be equally skeptical of all your sources. Look for the motivation—even from the critics, certainly from the other side, and most of all from any of the actors on stage to whom you do not have access.

• Discriminate and limit the authority of your sources to the extent of their expertise. The president and the private both spoke in Vietnam—and the press solicited and sometimes gave equal weight to both.

• Beware of the home office and its pressure for competitive copy. Beware of the herd instinct and your peer pressures. Beware of your own biases and sympathies. Save your opinion for product labeled as such. Keep your reporting to reporting.

• And finally, when you think you see everything clearly, when you feel you have all the answers, when everything makes sense, when you begin to speak in absolutes and feel you are the sole guardian of truth and morality, run, don't walk, to another country. The time for reassignment has come.

THE PRESS AND THE GOVERNMENT: II

Seymour Hersh

I do not think the press is very relevant at all. I think that the Pentagon Papers and the Vietnam War showed us that there is not much the press can do when the government decides to lie. Many reporters try hard; many do not. The history of Vietnam is a history of lies, a history of evasions. And even though the press is doing a great job of reporting in Central America, we just do not know what is going on. We learned about all the horrors of the Nixon administration only after the 1972 election. Probably George Mc-Govern has the greatest gripe against the press; he probably wonders what all this hoopla about its power is about. We are not that relevant. If the government decides it wants to lie to us, where is the press? I do not think it is anywhere. I do not think we have learned an awful lot; I think a lot of us try hard and want to do well, but the fact that the government has such awesome power renders the press powerless.

For all of the work that has been done, all the wonderful reporting that has been done, these things happened; they can still happen; the government still can get away with it. At some very basic level, nothing we have done in Vietnam or in Watergate has really changed the attitude of the people running the government, the absolute certitude they have that a lie they tell can go down, the absolute ability they have to look at a foreign policy event and commit our children to it without ever once saying, Who is going to die? How many people are going to die because of this? How many deaths will it cause?

•PRESS CONTROVERSIES•

Editor's Note

The principal indictment of the press in Vietnam has been made by Robert Elegant, himself a sometime correspondent in Saigon and long resident in the Far East. Now a writer of works of fiction, Elegant in 1971 stated his case on the pages of the British magazine Encounter.

What he had to say was very simple: the United States and its South Vietnamese allies won the war, but the press lost it for them. It is his belief that the correspondents in Vietnam—that is, basically, the Americans—wrote "for each other," for the adulation of their peers; that they came to Vietnam as bitter critics of the war or quickly so became; that they knew nothing of Vietnam, did not possess the language, and that their dispatches created such an atmosphere of pessimism that no effort by the American military could possibly have succeeded. The pen proved more mighty than the sword.

The Elegant indictment is cast, for the most part, in generalities, and while he often speaks of "cases," he does not present names, dates, or places. In general, he sets up a dichotomy between the "old hands" like himself and the Johnny-come-latelies who arrived in Saigon and were off and running toward putting their names in headlines and their faces on the evening news.

The harshness of Elegant's language, his sweeping allegations, his accusation of what amounts to treason and treachery on the part of unnamed American correspondents inevitably aroused violent responses among his erstwhile colleagues. Some of the older generation, like Keyes Beech, the distinguished Chicago Daily News *correspondent who spent as many years or more than Elegant in the Orient, defended Elegant in part, finding virtue in his contrast of the old Asia hands and the young hands. Beech believes that the press, and particularly television, played a part in establishing American attitudes inimical to successful pursuit of the war.*

Morley Safer responded in blazing terms to Elegant, seeing in

*Elegant's picture of a TV reporter handing his Zippo lighter to a
Marine to torch an "empty" Vietnam village in a "practice exercise" a distortion of Safer's famous footage of a genuine incident of
a Marine unit burning a peaceful village in an exercise that was
anything but a training mission.*

*Safer saw in Elegant's rhetoric a deliberate attempt to brand
the press with responsibility for losing Vietnam and the Cold War
by use of what he called "Soviet-style" journalism.*

*The problem of the war, in Safer's view, was that it lacked a
"moral, intellectual, and strategic core."*

*The controversy over the press took its sharpest form in de-
bate about the Tet offensive of January–February 1968 which
immediately preceded Lyndon Johnson's decision to call a bombing halt, enter into negotiations with Hanoi, and relinquish a quest
for a second term as president.*

*The weight of the indictment of the press in Tet is borne by
Peter Braestrup, a former correspondent of the New York Times
and the Washington Post, a former Marine who was himself present in Saigon at the time of Tet.*

*It is Braestrup's contention that the press panicked at the Tet
offensive, misreported its intensity, severity, and consequences,
thus stimulating LBJ to refuse requests for massive troop increments (206,000 men) and start down the long, long trail toward
the Nixon-Kissinger truce of 1973 and the final victory of North
Vietnam in 1975.*

*For the most part, it should be noted, the participants in this
controversy seize upon Tet as though it were the only factor in
American attitudes, ignoring the fact that opposition against the
war had steadily mounted within LBJ's own administration—first
with the by-now-retired defense secretary, Robert McNamara, and
secondly with the rapidly escalating efforts by the new defense
secretary, Clark Clifford, to get LBJ to bring the war to an end.
Nor do the participants pay heed to the actual reports which were
sent back to Washington by government and military representatives at the time of Tet from Saigon, nor to the panicky statements
made by high U.S. officials on the ground in Saigon at that time.*

*The argument, in a word, has moved forward in a kind of
detachment from reality, focusing on allegations of cowardice or
stress demonstrated by the correspondents and on their failure to*

understand that, in the long view, Tet cost Hanoi most of its infrastructure in South Vietnam.

General Sidle joins in criticism of the press, although he admits the military lacked credibility and that its credibility was further strained at the time of Tet by its own mistakes—such as reporting the recapture of Hue, which continued to be held by the North Vietnamese, and by other blunders.

The case for the correspondents on the scene is presented by John Laurence of CBS, who reveals that he and other correspondents had ample warning of the impending "surprise" attack from one of the better U.S. commanders, Lt. Gen. Frederick Weyand, and made arrangements accordingly. They brought in extra men, redeployed their staffs, and prepared for a big blow. Tet was a shock to them, as it was to the U.S. military and diplomats, particularly when the Vietnamese assaulted the U.S. Embassy in Saigon. But they gritted their teeth, did their job, and covered the story.

HOW TO LOSE A WAR

REFLECTIONS OF A FOREIGN CORRESPONDENT

Robert Elegant[1]

In the early 1960s, when the Vietnam War became a big story, most foreign correspondents assigned to cover the story wrote primarily to win the approbation of the crowd, above all their own crowd. As a result, in my view, the self-proving system of reporting they created became ever further detached from political and military realities because it instinctively concentrated on its own self-justification. The American press, naturally dominant in an "American war," somehow felt obliged to be less objective than partisan, to take sides, for it was inspired by the *engagé* "investigative" reporting that burgeoned in the U.S. in these impassioned years. The press was instinctively "agin the government"—and, at least reflexively, for Saigon's enemies.

During the latter half of the fifteen-year American involvement in Vietnam, the media became the primary battlefield. Illusory events reported *by* the press as well as real events *within* the press corps were more decisive than the clash of arms or the contention of ideologies. For the first time in modern history, the

---

1. Robert Elegant was not a participant at the conference, since he was not invited, but his presence was strongly felt; no fewer than five journalists noted or took issue with the remarks he made in the article, excerpted above, which appeared in *Encounter* (August 1981), pp. 73–90. The emphases are his.

outcome of a war was determined not on the battlefield but on the printed page and, above all, on the television screen. Looking back coolly, I believe it can be said (surprising as it may still sound) that South Vietnamese and American forces actually won the limited military struggle. They virtually crushed the Vietcong in the South, the "native" guerrillas who were directed, reinforced, and equipped from Hanoi; and thereafter they threw back the invasion by regular North Vietnamese divisions. Nonetheless, the war was finally lost to the invaders *after* the U.S. disengagement because the political pressures built up by the media had made it quite impossible for Washington to maintain even the minimal material and moral support that would have enabled the Saigon regime to continue effective resistance.

Since I am considering causes rather than effects, the demoralization of the West, particularly of the United States, that preceded and followed the fall of South Vietnam is beyond the scope of this article. It is, however, interesting to wonder whether Angola, Afghanistan, and Iran would have occurred *if* Saigon had not fallen amid nearly universal odium—that is to say, *if* the "Vietnam syndrome," for which the press (in my view) was largely responsible, had not afflicted the Carter administration and paralyzed American will. On the credit side, largely despite the press, the People's Republic of China would almost certainly not have purged itself of the Maoist doctrine of "worldwide liberation through people's war" and, later, would not have come to blows with Hanoi if the defense of South Vietnam had not been maintained for so long.

THE BROTHERHOOD

"You could be hard about it and deny that there was a brotherhood working there, but what else could you call it?" This is a question that Michael Herr asked in his *Dispatches (1977)*, a personally honest, but basically deceptive book.

But. . . . all you ever talked about was the war, and they could come to seem like two different wars at the same time. Because who but another correspondent could talk the kind of mythical war you wanted to hear described?

I have added the emphasis: for in the words "mythical" and "wanted," the essential truth is laid bare. In my own personal experience, most correspondents *wanted* to talk chiefly to other correspondents to confirm their own *mythical* vision of the war. Even newcomers were precommitted, as the American jargon has it, to the collective position most of their colleagues had already taken. What I can only call surrealistic reporting constantly fed on itself, and did not diminish thereby but swelled into ever more grotesque shapes. I found the process equally reprehensible for being in no small part unwilling.

John le Carré (whose extravagant encomium adorns the cover of the Pan edition of *Dispatches:* "The best book I have ever read on men and war in our times") is, I feel, too clever a writer to believe he painted an even proximately accurate picture of Southeast Asia in *The Honourable Schoolboy* (1972). But he brilliantly depicted the press corps and the correspondents' Asia, an encapsulated, self-defining world whirling in its own eccentric orbit. Correspondents, briefly set down in the brutally alienating milieu called Vietnam, turned to each other for professional sustenance and emotional comfort. After all, there was nowhere else to turn, certainly not to stark reality, which was both elusive and repellent.

Most correspondents were isolated from the Vietnamese by ignorance of their language and culture, as well as by a measure of race estrangement. Most were isolated from the quixotic American Army establishment, itself often as confused as they themselves were, by their moralistic attitudes and their political prejudices. It was inevitable, in the circumstances, that they came to write, in the first instance, for each other.

To be sure, the approbation of his own crowd gave a certain fullness to the correspondent's life in exile that reached beyond the irksome routine of reporting and writing. The disapprobation of his peers could transform him into a bitterly defensive misanthrope. . . . Even the experienced correspondents, to whom Asia was "home" rather than a hostile temporary environment, formed their own little self-defensive world within the larger world of the newcomers.

It was no wonder that correspondents writing to win the approbation of other correspondents in that insidiously collegial atmosphere produced reporting that was remarkably homogeneous. After each other, correspondents wrote to win the approbation of their editors, who controlled their professional lives and who were closely linked with the intellectual community at home. The consensus of that third circle, the domestic intelligentsia, derived largely from correspondents' reports and in turn served to determine the nature of those reports. If dispatches did not accord with that consensus, approbation was withheld. Only in the last instance did correspondents address themselves to the general public, the mass of lay readers and viewers.

THE CLOUD OF UNKNOWING

It was my impression that most correspondents were, in one respect, very much like the ambitious soldiers they derided. A tour in Vietnam was almost essential to promotion for a U.S. Regular Army officer; and a combat command was the best road to rapid advancement. Covering the biggest continuing story in the world was not absolutely essential to a correspondent's rise, but it was an invaluable cachet. Quick careers were made by spectacular reporting of the obvious fact that men, women, and children were being killed; fame or at least notoriety rewarded the correspondent who became part of the action—rather than a mere observer—by influencing events directly.

Journalists, particularly those serving in television, were therefore, like soldiers, "rotated" to Vietnam. Few were given time to develop the knowledge, and indeed the intellectual instincts, necessary to report the war in the round. Only a few remained "in country" for years, though the experienced Far Eastern correspondents visited regularly from Hong Kong, Singapore, and Tokyo. Not surprisingly, one found that most reporting veered farther and farther from the fundamental political, economic, and military realities of the war, for these were usually *not* spectacular. Reporting Vietnam became a closed, self-generating system sustained largely by the acclaim the participants lavished on each other in almost equal measure to the opprobrium they heaped on "the Establishment," a fashionable and vulnerable target.

[Elegant criticizes reporters then for competing in the "beastliness" of the images they presented, covering American massacres more thoroughly than Vietcong or North Vietnamese atrocities, not treating American restraint as news, not covering ARVN thoroughly, and losing perspective on official truth. (Since Washington lied consistently, Hanoi must be a font of truth.) He criticizes them now for failing to look back critically, for failing to acknowledge Hanoi's "proudly trumpeted" gratitude to them, and for not dwelling "upon the glaring inconsistency between the expectations they raised of peaceful, prosperous development after Saigon's collapse and the present postwar circumstances in Indochina." He then suggests "The Reasons Why."]

Beyond the pressures exerted upon them, most correspondents—serving six-month to two-year tours—were woefully ignorant of the setting of the conflict. Some strove diligently to remedy that crippling deficiency by reading widely and interviewing avidly. Many lacked the time or the inclination to do so—or any real awareness of how crippling their ignorance was to them professionally. Most, as I have noted, knew little about war in general from either experience or study—and less about the theory or practice of guerrilla war. They were untutored not only in the languages, but also in the history, culture, ethnography, and economics of Indochina, let alone of China and Asia. Since so many were also untroubled by acquaintance with Marxist theory or practice and were hazy about the international balance of power, they were incapable of covering effectively a conflict involving all those elements.

Not even the "old hands" were necessarily well qualified to cover the conflict—Who could have been? Arthur Waley? [2]—but, considering our divergent backgrounds and political convictions, the old hands' general agreement about the nature of the war was remarkable. Most deplored the ineffectiveness and the corruption of successive South Vietnamese governments, but judged native (i.e., Southern) disaffection incapable of mounting an armed rebellion without direction, reinforcement, and weapons from the North. Most concurred with the thesis Robert Shaplen advanced in *The Lost Revolution* (1966), agreeing that ineffectual leadership had failed to foster latent nationalistic and reformist enthusiasm in the South, by default ceding those dynamic forces to the North. We did not deceive ourselves that the South enjoyed even marginally good government; but we believed that Northern rule

---

2. Translator of Chinese and Japanese literary classics, who died in 1966.

would be much worse for the mass of the people. We knew that the North and the South, though not necessarily two separate countries, were distinct entities because of the strong regional feelings of the Vietnamese. Although most of us had opposed major American involvement, we saw no way the United States could withdraw unilaterally.

Needless to say, even we old hands were not always accurate in our reporting or correct in our judgments. Reacting against the spate of negative reports, I myself tended to emphasize the positive aspects, sometimes excessively. No more than the newcomers were the old hands immune to irritation at the duplicity of the American establishment, though we were not so dependent upon press officers. That irritation undoubtedly affected our reporting; so did smoldering anger (which sometimes flared into fury) at the Vietnamese, who were always difficult, often unavailable, regularly evasive, and routinely deceitful. But the old hands knew they had to live and work with the Vietnamese, and they understood the insecurity that haunted Saigon officials. After generations of colonial rule and internal conflict, no Vietnamese really trusted any other Vietnamese except those within his immediate family (and them neither invariably nor wholly). The newcomers either could not or would not understand what moved the Vietnamese or why they so often seemed to be behaving so badly.

HOW TO LOSE A WAR
A RESPONSE FROM AN "OLD ASIA HAND"

Keyes Beech[1]

Let's suppose that all the correspondents covering the Vietnam War had been required to serve in at least one Communist country as a precondition for their assignment. Would their reporting have been different?

I suspect that if forced to choose between a Communist dictatorship and a military dictatorship—and it was Chairman Mao who said there was no third road—they would have chosen the military dictatorship. At the very least, there might have been more balance in their reporting.

Even when the wicked South Vietnamese regime was at its worst, I did not see refugees setting out to sea in leaky boats, many of them to drown or to be robbed and see their women raped by pirates. That came only after "liberation."

My point then and now was this: If the Communists could be defeated or held to a draw, there was hope for a change for the better. If the Communists won, there wasn't going to be any second chance. . . .

If I may speak for some other tired "old Asia hands"—and I do with some trepidation—I think they felt the same way. For the vast majority of American correspondents, Vietnam was their first

---

1. Excerpted from a letter to *Encounter* (January, 1983), p. 94.

war. It was also their first experience outside the United States. To most of them, Vietnam still is "Asia."

They can hardly be blamed for this. But after thirty-three years in Asia, including the better part of a decade in Vietnam, I knew that war was hell long before I got to Saigon. My education in Communism began at the 1940 American Newspaper Guild convention in Detroit and received added touches in Korea, China, Indochina, and Indonesia. I confess to a prejudice against it.

Bob Elegant has been a friend of mine for about thirty years—but a friend with whom I frequently and violently disagree. His premise that the outcome of the Vietnam War was determined not on the battlefield but by the media—especially television—will be hotly debated.

I don't think I would go quite that far; but the media helped lose the war. Oh yes, they did, not because of any massive conspiracy but because of the way the war was reported. What often seems to be forgotten is that the war was lost in the U.S., not in Vietnam. American troops never lost a battle; but they never won the war.

Besides, Elegant has Hanoi on his side. Visitors to that miserable, impoverished capital often hear their Vietnamese hosts complain about the hostile press treatment they now receive in comparison to the good old days.

HOW TO LOSE A WAR
A RESPONSE FROM A PRINT HISTORIAN
Phillip Knightley

Since the end of the war in Vietnam, there has been a reassessment of the role that press and television played in the Communist victory. During the fighting, correspondents learned to live with accusations that their reporting was helping the enemy.[1] But the postwar conclusion goes much further. It is eloquently summed up by Robert Elegant, a long-serving Asia expert and a former Vietnam correspondent himself. Elegant accuses the correspondents not merely of *contributing* to the Communist victory but of being *directly responsible* for it: "For the *first* time in modern history the outcome of a war was determined not on the battlefield but on the printed page and, above all, on the television screen."[2] He goes further. This did not occur by accident: ". . . never before Vietnam had the collective *policy* of the media—no less stringent a term will serve—sought by graphic and unremitting distortion, the victory of the enemies of the correspondents' own side."[3] As a result, says

---

1. See, for example, William Small of CBS, quoted in Edward J. Epstein, *News From Nowhere* (New York, Random House, 1973), p. 9; John Mecklin, *Mission in Torment* (New York, Doubleday, 1965), p. xii; David Duncan, quoted in Phillip Knightley, *The First Casualty* (New York, Harcourt Brace & Jovanovich, 1975) p. 360; Joseph Alsop, *ibid.,* p. 384; Marine officer, *ibid.,* p. 373.

2. "How to Lose a War: Reflections of a Foreign Correspondent," *Encounter* (August, 1981) p. 73.

3. *Ibid.,* p. 89.

Elegant, the correspondents tilted the global balance of power and made the "Vietnam syndrome" (the likening of any other U.S. foreign enterprise to Vietnam) such a powerful incantation as to make it virtually impossible for the West to conduct an effective foreign policy.

Elegant's catalog of accusations against his fellow correspondents is long and detailed: they lacked intellectual instincts, they were untutored not only in the languages but the history, culture, ethnography, and economics of Indochina; they wrote for the approbation of each other and for their editors; they invented stories; they wrote about unconfirmed atrocities and set up others for the television cameras; they deceived themselves as to the true nature of the enemy; they wanted to disbelieve the avowed motives of the United States, etc. These are a serious set of charges.

If Elegant's case stands up, then an examination of the quality of the reporting is over before it can begin. But Elegant's case, although containing some important observations about the nature of journalism, is, I submit, essentially wrong. If we go back to those early days of the 1961–63 period, the resident press corps in Saigon consisted of Malcolm Browne for the Associated Press, Ray Herndon and then Mert Perry for the UPI, Jerry Rose of *Time,* François Sully of *Newsweek,* Rakshat Puri of the *Hindustan Times,* Simon Michaud and Jean Burfin of *Agence France Presse,* Françoise Nivolon of *Le Figaro,* Nick Turner and then Peter Smark of Reuters and John Stirling of the *Times* of London.

None of these men was an intellectual pygmy or ignorant of Indochina. Rose had been assistant professor of English at Hue and later worked for the Vietnamese government on refugee resettlement. Puri knew all of Asia well, and although his work is little known in the West, was one of the most competent correspondents ever to work in Indochina. Browne, Turner, and Herndon were married to Vietnamese women, and all had some knowledge of the language. They lived in Saigon in apartments or houses (not in hotel bars), they had deep roots in Vietnam, and they thought of themselves not as *war* correspondents but as *Vietnam* correspondents. Browne has said that they were all "emotionally involved up to our necks."[4] (His father-in-law had been murdered by the Viet-

---

4. Letter to the author, 13 September 1976.

minh.) But they strived for objectivity, and the agency men in particular saw their role in traditional agency terms: they filed what they saw and what they believed to be true. So Browne, for example, while accepting that there were American atrocities, never filed a story on an atrocity by an American serviceman because in two years in the field with American units he never saw one.

And at this stage of the war, none of these correspondents nor those who were soon to join them—David Halberstam, Charles Mohr, Neil Sheehan—were against American involvement in Vietnam and they wanted the United States to win. They were against the *way* in which the war was being fought, and they were against the corrupt government of Diem. This is where the so-called "press mess" had its origins. The Diem government did not like what the correspondents were writing and it did its best to stop them from continuing. There was censorship and intimidation. Browne and Peter Arnett were beaten up and charged with attacking the South Vietnamese secret police, and could well have been shot had not President Kennedy intervened personally on their behalf.

At government level, South Vietnam complained to Washington and Washington did its best to persuade the American correspondents to present a more sympathetic picture of the Diem regime and of the progress of the war. It wanted the correspondents to play up Diem's successes against the Vietcong and to play down American military involvement. The correspondents refused to do this because it did not accord with what they were seeing with their own eyes. So, the pained exhortations to "get on side" and "get with the team" were, in effect, pleas not to get on side with the USA—the correspondents were already there—but to get on side with Diem.

Some editors and publishers in the United States to whom the pleas were also addressed preferred to believe Washington rather than their own man on the spot and now began to send out correspondents to write Diem's line. A stream of famous names—Joseph Alsop, Marguerite Higgins, Kenneth Crawford—went to Vietnam and duly decided that the war was going well and that Diem was democracy's white hope.

It is ironic, then, that the "fashionable" story of Vietnam in the early sixties was not the one that Elegant accuses the correspondents in Vietnam of writing. The fashionable story of the sixties, the one that got the cover treatment, the one that earned the correspondent the approbation of his editor, was the Washington line. Those correspondents indicted by Elegant were, at considerable risk to life and reputation, writing the *un*fashionable story, the one with the *un*palatable facts.[5]

Whether this story got over to the American reader is another matter. At that stage, the level of interest in Vietnam was low. Rose had been the first American correspondent to witness and photograph a South Vietnamese atrocity—the use of "dingaling" electric shock torture on a Vietcong suspect, in some cases with the knowledge and perhaps acquiescence of American advisors. *Time* had used the story. Browne had photographed a South Vietnamese militia soldier choking a farmer to death with a stick across his throat and then the final tableau—the widow cradling her dead husband's head. The story and the photographs were available to thousands of subscribing newspapers in the United States and were used by many.

The readers' reaction in the United States was—as far as it is possible to measure such things—minimal. Rose, now dead, told his colleagues at the time that his story had produced little sense of outrage among *Time* readers, and Browne received only two or three letters from Americans who thought that what had happened to the farmer was horrible. So we have to face this possibility: stories and photographs of cruelty—providing the cruelty is by one foreigner upon another, so that the reader has no one with whom he can quickly identify—may entertain rather than appal.

Now, reporting like this might not have got over the Vietnam story to the readers; it certainly got over to the Vietnamese and American governments. They reacted to it on what we can now see was a false assumption at that time—that the story was also getting over to the American public. With hindsight, instead of running a high-powered public relations exercise to alter the way the correspondents were reporting Vietnam, the American government might have achieved more by ignoring them. (Diem, of course, could not. Non-democratic regimes must control the press

---

5. See for example, François Sully, "Vietnam: The Unpleasant Truth," *Newsweek* (August 2, 1962), pp. 40–41.

as a matter of policy, and if they fail to be seen to be doing so, their entire structure is put at risk.)

So the picture we have of the early reporting in Vietnam is that of a core of skilled, intelligent, and involved correspondents working under extremely difficult circumstances, trying to get over to a not-yet-aroused American public the war as they saw it. (In fact, Puri has said that their main difficulty was to convince their editors and readers that there *was* a war.) Almost to a man they supported the American involvement and wanted victory over the Vietcong. None of them wanted to hinder the war effort or to see the war lost to prove that they were right. But they questioned the nature of the South Vietnamese regime, its ability to carry on the war, the skill of the American advisors, and the need for the lies told to them by U.S. officials in the Mission and the United States Information Service—a picture somewhat different from that painted by Elegant.

HOW TO LOSE A WAR
A RESPONSE FROM A BROADCASTER

Morley Safer

Robert Elegant, formerly of *Newsweek* and lately a successful writer of fiction, wrote in *Encounter* a year and a half ago that the war was won by the combined American–South Vietnamese forces, but was lost because of political pressures, built up by the media, that prevented Washington's giving further support to the Saigon government. He goes further and states that the press and broadcasting helped, one way or another, to bring tens of millions of people under grinding totalitarian rule, and that, because our [reporters'] responsibility in tilting the global balance of power is too great to acknowledge, we absolve ourselves by blaming exclusively Johnson, Nixon, and Kissinger.

So Mr. Elegant accuses us of not only losing Vietnam, but the Cold War as well. Maybe Jimmy Hoffa and Judge Crater, too. Our purpose in all this, he says, was for the praise of fellows: we were members of a club out there, and the club wrote and spoke with one voice.

The *Encounter* piece is seventeen vituperative pages long. It claims to quote correspondents who, since the war, have come to Mr. Elegant confessing their sins, saying they knew they were spreading lies, disillusion, and disinformation; and admitting that the devil of ambition and approval by colleagues made them do it. He offers no names.

He saves his big artillery for television. He offers a quotation, a "hard-documented instance." I quote exactly: "A burning village was news even though it was a deserted village used in a Marine training exercise, even though the television correspondent handed his Zippo lighter to a noncommissioned officer with the suggestion that he set fire to an abandoned house."

Hard-documented instance. No date. No village named. No network named. No correspondent named. No Marine corps unit named. Hard. Documented.

I recommend the Elegant piece as a primer in journalism— Soviet style: meat-ax the critics of a policy by questioning their patriotism, by accusing them of being in the thrall of petit bourgeois ambition; generate enough smoke; and hope that no one examines the piece closely enough to notice that there are no facts, only scapegoats.

The latest "old Asia hand" to take up this cause is the venerable Keyes Beech of the Los Angeles *Times*. In *Encounter* last month, Mr. Beech pulls the pin on his squib when he tells us that "a" correspondent—unnamed, of course—confessed to him ("saw the light," in Mr. Beech's words) about the nature of his coverage of the Vietnam War. It was the later experience in Cuba and China, says Beech, that made this slightly apocryphal correspondent understand how wrong he had been about Vietnam. The Beech letter to *Encounter* is truly remarkable—even less subtle, if that is possible, than Mr. Elegant's article. Mr. Beech says plainly that American reporters should go out and seek truth, but only within the context of serving American foreign policy. Since, for the most part, American foreign policy is even more elusive than the truth, this would make for some fairly fancy dancing—footwork that perhaps only a seasoned Marxist or a seventeenth-century Jesuit or certain old Asia hands are capable of performing. The essence of this journalistic version of *Das Kapital* is that since the other side is an even bigger liar than our side, then our side must be supported without qualification.

Mr. Beech, speaking for what he describes as, "other tired old Asia hands," states that for the vast majority of people who covered the war, it was their first war and their first experience outside the United States. He states this as if he has taken some kind of Roper poll. My earliest editors taught me to not use phrases like "vast majority" unless we had numbers to back them up. I would like to know who bothered to calculate such meaningless statistics, or even if they exist at all. Maybe a survey should be done of Mr. Beech's old Asia hands to find out how much time they spent questioning the official Saigon version of the truth, how much time they spent as the hacks of government handouts writing pieces at the bidding of MACV, how much time they spent to put a positive face to a war no one had his heart in. This might be old Asia handism. It sure ain't journalism.

Mr. Beech and Mr. Elegant, and no doubt others, and former and current military and state department people as well, would have had us cover the war blinkered by ideology—not even ideology but a vague, indefinable idea that once Americans are joined in battle, all rational and traditional rules of journalism no longer apply. There is no question that as a story, and as a war, Vietnam was a special case. It is not my intention to give you a potted history of both. Only to try to describe the pressures, sometimes the dilemma, of covering the war.

From the beginning, on the questionable night of August 4, 1964, when Congress approved the Gulf of Tonkin resolution, the official fudging—perhaps even the lying—began. The war, such as it was then, was being reported only by old Asia hands. Even so, there were enough doubts at the time to make for a general unease; for questions to be asked that produced only half-truths. None of Mr. Beech's peacenik reporters were yet out there in any numbers demoralizing America. America was being demoralized single-handedly by Lyndon Johnson.

The Tonkin incident was followed by the Vietcong infiltration of the American compound at Pleiku and the blowing up of an officers' quarters in Quinhon. Those two events led to the major commitment of regular American units to a major war in Vietnam—and a parallel commitment of American reporters. Some months after Quinhon and Pleiku, I asked the gallant general, scholar, and diplomat Maxwell Taylor how important those two Vietcong actions were in leading to the escalation that sent Americans by the division to Vietnam. He said, rather wearily, "If Quinhon and Pleiku hadn't happened, we would have had to create them." One can fairly conclude that the president's determination to hang the coonskin on the wall had reached something approaching an obsession; and good soldiers and decent diplomats were obliged to share that obsession or get out. Most chose to share it and to use whatever means necessary to fulfill a policy that had been thought through about as carefully as the Children's Crusade.

Did this mean that every military and civilian briefing authority lied, all the time? Not exactly. But you were a fool to report what they told you without checking it very carefully. Those of us who were based more or less permanently in Vietnam quickly became disillusioned by the so-called five o'clock follies. Those afternoon briefings' only significant use was for gathering basic facts: arrivals of units, the inevitable body count, losses, North Vietnamese and Vietcong troop strength. I would be less than honest if I did not mention one further use. Those briefings provided sport of a kind: to tweak the briefer or dazzle your friends and competitors with more up-to-date information than anyone else had—and occasionally to publicly embarrass MACV. It was not difficult. The Saigon version of events was almost always at variance with what actually happened in the field, witnessed by a correspondent or described by an officer or civilian representative who gave you unfiltered information. This kind of adversary relationship is to be expected, and is, generally speaking, quite healthy.

A main criticism of the press in Vietnam, and particularly of the broadcast journalists, was the heavy emphasis on combat reporting. While some of the criticism may be justified, most of it will not wash. This was, after all, a war. Sixty thousand Americans and hundreds of thousands of Vietnamese were killed in battles. The military and civilian establishments in Saigon and Washington were obsessed by those numbers; the so-called body count was the only standard of success. Those numbers, and particularly enemy troop strength, were manipulated mercilessly. Prior to the commitment of new American units, enemy troop strength would rise; when it was necessary to demonstrate success in Washington, enemy troop strength would dramatically fall. The numbers in Vietnam were like the emperor's clothes. Unlike that fable, however, most people—most reporters, anyway—saw through the numbers.

I offer one example as proof. On August 20, 1967, Gen. Creighton Abrams, General Westmoreland's deputy, cabled the joint chiefs, with the approval of General Westmoreland, that MACV wished to reduce the enemy numbers by a hundred and twenty to a hundred and thirty thousand troops. But how do you wipe out one-fourth of the enemy? It's easy. The secret weapon is the press handout. Just take them off the books. General Abrams, in his cable, is worried that if the higher figure is released, the newsmen will immediately seize on the point and draw "the erroneous and gloomy conclusion as to the meaning of the increase." His cable goes on to tell the joint chiefs that Joe Fried of the New York *Daily News* has learned of the true intelligence estimate and that Barry Zorthian and General Sidle are trying to persuade him that the figures are wrong.

On that same subject, in reviewing the draft of a press briefing that General Westmoreland was to give in October 1967 announcing lower enemy numbers, Paul Walsh of the CIA writes in an internal memo, "General Westmoreland's statement is one of the greatest snow jobs since Potemkin constructed his village," and goes on to say that such number-juggling can only lead to greater credibility problems. He ends with a plea that the CIA disassociate itself from MACV on intelligence estimates. Statements like Westmoreland's, he writes, "give us all the justification we need to go straight again."

Finally, Col. Gaines Hawkins (USA-Ret.), whose tour of duty in Vietnam covered 1966 and 1967, and whose job it was to analyze intelligence and estimate enemy forces, writes fifteen years later that General Westmoreland and MACV were, in 1967, announcing publicly that American troops were facing three hundred thousand Vietcong and North Vietnamese. The true estimate— the one MACV would not accept—was five hundred thousand. General Westmoreland expressed concern, writes Colonel Hawkins, that people might be led to believe there had been no progress in the war if the truth were published.

The assumption in Vietnam back in the sixties was that reporters who would not get on the team were anti-American, pro-Vietnamese, at worst leftist, at best pacifist. Maybe that was true of some; I would not know who they are. I think most of the reporters in Vietnam smelled something terribly rotten about this war from day one of their tours—that it lacked a moral or intellectual or strategic core. This had nothing to do with ideology, with the feeling that the other side was more humane. Its own awful corruption was clear to anyone who bothered to inquire. What was equally clear was that in the American intervention, no purpose was being served by the waste of material, the waste of a country, and, above all, the waste of life. Vietnam has a cruel history of self-inflicted wounds and of inflicting even deeper wounds on strangers who intervene.

The press was not especially antiwar. It did, justifiably, have many questions about the Vietnam War.

In the Second World War, Winston Churchill, discussing the deceptions and trickery the Allies were using to keep the secrets of D Day, said, "In wartime, truth is so precious that she should always be attended by a bodyguard of lies." The lies were designed to beguile and confuse Hitler and the German high command. In Vietnam there was a bodyguard of lies as well. But from whom was it keeping the truth?

THE TET OFFENSIVE
ANOTHER PRESS CONTROVERSY: I

Maj. Gen. Winant Sidle (USA-Ret.)

My strong belief is that, although there was much sound and objective news reporting throughout the war, there was even more reporting that did not meet these criteria. This was especially true of Tet.

It is necessary to summarize, briefly, the action at Tet. The offensive included attacks of some sort on more than 150 towns and cities and on numerous military installations. However, by February 2, just *four days* later, the enemy had been cleared from almost everywhere. Fighting continued in a few parts of Saigon, and Hue had fallen, but elsewhere mopping up was the order of the day. By February 5, when Hanoi was proclaiming impending victory, the only real fighting going on was in the Hue area and at Khe Sanh; the latter began on January 20, not at Tet. Shellings continued for several weeks, especially on February 18, when forty-five cities and towns were rocketed, but these were accompanied by only four ground attacks, all unsuccessful. Hue was recaptured in late March, but the offensive was over by February 5 as far as the country-wide effort was concerned.

The massive attack cost the enemy dearly. Vietcong infrastructure members exposed themselves and were killed or captured. Vietcong units were decimated, and as Don Oberdorfer wrote in his book *Tet* (1971), the VC "lost the best of a generation of resistance fighters." Further, the lack of public support of the VC during Tet was a serious blow to North Vietnam's claim to moral and political ascendancy in the South.

Therefore, Tet was a smashing victory for U.S./ARVN forces and a grievous military setback for the enemy. Why, then, was Tet a smashing psychological victory for the enemy in the United States?

I would say there were two reasons. First, the sheer size and scope of the attacks exceeded anyone's expectations. Although we had known something big might happen at Tet, and had told the press in Saigon on a background basis beginning in December; and although it had been mentioned publicly in speeches by both General Wheeler and General Westmoreland, there is no question that the American public and many of our leaders were taken by surprise.

Second, and I feel this is the more important reason, many, probably most, of the Saigon press corps seemed to go into shock—at least for the first few days—with the result that reporters seemed to have a desire to believe the worst; and this produced disaster-type reporting. This is not hard to understand. After all, many of us at MACV were shocked too, especially by the enemy's ability to penetrate Saigon. Several of us, including me, had to run a roadblock to get to MACV headquarters on the first morning. That was a shock. But, there was no trouble getting to the five o'clock follies over the same streets that night or at any time thereafter.

However, although the offensive quickly turned out to be an overwhelming military victory for us, the overall reporting continued to treat the matter as a disaster. As we announced on February 4, all of the nearly two hundred attacks of various sorts that occurred at the start of the offensive had been repulsed by that date—except that fighting was still going on in four locations: Hue, a few areas in the greater Saigon area, Phan Thiet, and Da Lat.

But the media reports gave the impression that the offensive was still going strong long after February 4. It was as if reporters either just didn't want to let go of the story or simply could not believe in the quick military defeat of the offensive. With respect to the latter, our spotty credibility was obviously a factor, not helped by our erroneous early report of the recapture of Hue. But, it also may well have been a carry-over of the media's readiness to believe the worst, resulting from the initial shock from the original attacks.

Therefore, the initial shock to America of the offensive itself was compounded and continued beyond reason by the reporting. The calm, professional, factual reports that should have followed the first few days never materialized. In retrospect, there appeared to be a conspiracy never to admit that the original coverage was greatly overblown.

THE TET OFFENSIVE
ANOTHER PRESS CONTROVERSY: II

Peter Braestrup

In the end, Tet represented a severe military setback for Hanoi. But that was not the way the 1968 Tet offensive came across in the news media, then or later. To varying degrees—and in various ways—the dominant themes in the press, and especially on television, added up to this message in February–March 1968: "Disaster in South Vietnam."

Why did this malfunction—of a magnitude rare in the annals of American crisis journalism—take place? And what were the consequences?

Tet was an extreme case. At no other time in the war, not during Hanoi's more powerful 1972 Easter offensive, not during the final 1975 debacle, did the U.S. press and TV suffer from the same high fevers. Tet's peculiar circumstances—surprise, melodrama unprecedented in the war, White House ambiguity—impacted to a rare degree on the peculiar habits, susceptibilities, manpower limitations, and technological constraints of newspapers, news magazines, wire services, and TV news. Long before Tet, with the commitment of U.S. battalions to South Vietnam in March 1965, the war had become a "hometown story" in the U.S. media, especially on TV; coverage of the South Vietnamese ally and the Vietnamese Communist foe was far more intermittent. The coverage reflected the usual journalistic ethnocentrity, but an attentive reader of the U.S. big-league newspapers, in my view, was not left ignorant as to the war's costs, cruelties, and contradictions.

In crisis, first reports are always partly wrong, and instant analysis by reporters or TV anchormen represents the hasty reactions of the half-informed. Tet abounds with examples. But the failure to convey the changing realities on the ground in February–March 1968 was perhaps the media's greatest sin. As the fog of war lifted and the Communist tide ebbed, the managers of the press and especially of TV put the accent on *more* melodrama rather than on trying to update the inevitably melodramatic first impressions—urban destruction, enemy omnipresence, allied confusion—of the Tet surprise. After four weeks, *Time* the *New York Times* and the Washington *Post* began to publish a few such recovery stories, but rarely on page 1. Other publications and TV waited even longer. Disaster, real or impending, was a "story"; recovery was not.

The melodrama of Khe Sanh, for example, preoccupied newsmen and their bosses to the exclusion of much else in Vietnam. It was, in reality, a fairly low-intensity siege, only twelve miles from the nearest U.S. forces; and U.S. bombers dumped 100,000 tons of bombs ("five Hiroshimas") to discourage the North Vietnamese besiegers.

But to the eyes of the American reader or viewer, all perspective was lost; Lyndon Johnson's own "leaked" worries about a repeat of the famed 1954 French disaster of Dien Bien Phu only fanned media anticipation of the same climax at Khe Sanh. The siege accounted for twenty-five percent of all weekday network evening news shows during the Tet period, and slightly smaller chunks of newspaper front pages; *Newsweek* put the "Agony of Khe Sanh" on its cover on March 18 (after Communist troops, in fact, had started to withdraw). Khe Sanh was an aberration, an uncharacteristic battle with little military impact on a long war; yet Walter Cronkite and others made it a "microcosm" of the whole war, even as the allies elsewhere began to recover from the Tet onslaught, repair the urban damage, and recapture the battlefield initiative.

The "disaster" occurred not in Vietnam but in Lyndon Johnson's Washington. The Tet surprise led to a political crisis that led to LBJ's own "abdication," the entrance of Robert F. Kennedy into the Democratic race, and as it turned out, to eventual U.S. disengagement from the war.

Why did the crisis take place? Many a pundit has claimed that Tet, exposing the folly of U.S. intervention, suddenly turned the public against the war and forced LBJ to reject "military victory." This analysis is simplistic, as will be seen below. So is the "hawk" critique—that LBJ deliberately threw in the towel in the midst of enemy defeat. So is the complaint by Johnson administration alumni that the media treatment of Tet "created" the crisis in Washington.

The story of the Tet crisis in Washington is complex, and not totally clear, particularly with regard to LBJ's own motives, reactions, and expectations.

But it must be seen in context. Before Tet, Lyndon Johnson was *already* in trouble on Capitol Hill. His popularity was sagging, and the Democratic party was split on the war, which had gone on for three years at the cost of sixteen thousand U.S. battle dead. And, as the TV correspondents were fond of saying, there was "no end in sight." Indeed, the administration's limited-war policy promised no quick end—only losses and a hope that Hanoi would "compromise." In late 1967, the administration launched a last big propaganda effort, including a much-publicized speech by Gen. William C. Westmoreland, the Vietnam commander, to shore up public opinion with assurances that "progress" was being made on the battlefield.

Implicitly, President Johnson promised the press, politicians, and public that no bad news was in store. Although he had clear warnings from Westmoreland of an impending major enemy effort, he did not warn the U.S. public. He barely mentioned Vietnam in his State of the Union address, which held out the prospects of "peace." The Tet surprise found Washington in the middle of another "crisis"—the January 23 seizure by the North Koreans of the *USS Pueblo,* a Navy spy ship. In short, Washington was caught badly off guard by the big bad news from Vietnam.

The Tet surprise—and the attention thereto—forced LBJ to confront the old contradictions of his Vietnam policy. Both the Pentagon hawks and the more visible doves sought to exploit the Tet surprise to revive old demands for changes (i.e., another bombing halt for the doves, a reserves call-up for the hawks). LBJ hunkered down and sought to buy time. He left the explanation of Tet to subordinates. In effect, the president left a vacuum that others—senators, pundits, news managers, critics—hastened to fill.

Washington newsmen conveyed the White House's "siege" atmosphere, and partial echoes of the administration's inner debate over a 206,000-troop increase. But neither newsmen nor their sources understood that LBJ at Tet, as earlier in the war, always resisted the massive reserves call-up sought by the joint chiefs— unless such was needed to ward off catastrophe in Vietnam. LBJ saw such mobilization as fatal to his beloved Great Society programs. In early February he may have wavered a bit, but Westmoreland soon told him that the allies were going on the offensive without additional troops. Thus reassured, LBJ apparently cast about for ways to quiet the opposition at home and to enable him to pursue his middle-of-the-road war policy as before.

In public, for two months, Johnson gave local sermons but no nationwide TV address—until March 31. Then he announced his decision not to seek reelection, another temporary, partial bombing pause, and another offer to Hanoi to talk peace. He did not rule out further U.S. escalation, but he spoke of greater efforts by the South Vietnamese. In effect, he again sought to buy time. But, to his surprise, Hanoi accepted the offer to talk; and thereafter, "peace with honor," not "winning," emerged as the chief U.S. hope.

Did the press and television—through their impact on public opinion—alter the course of the war?

Such claims—made by both critics and champions of the media—are impossible to substantiate. (No empirical data exist to link news coverage with changes in public opinion.) We now know, thanks to Herbert Schandler's *The Unmaking of a President* (1971) and other studies, that the White House was shaken not only by the Tet shock but by its portrayal on TV—and so (as a result?) was the rest of political and journalistic Washington. Yet, as measured by pollsters, *public* support for the war effort itself remained remarkably steady (i.e., continued a slow decline from 1965) in February–March 1968, even as LBJ's popularity hit a new low. Scholarly studies have shown that among Democrats who voted for "peace candidate" Eugene McCarthy in the March 12 New Hampshire primary, *anti-Johnson hawks outnumbered anti-Johnson doves by more than three to two!* Yet the primary results were interpreted by politicians and much of the media as an antiwar protest; Robert F. Kennedy entered the race against LBJ a few days later on a "dove" platform (which called for negotiations, not withdrawal).

My own hunch is that the media's generalized portrait of "disaster" in South Vietnam affected political Washington far more than it did the general public. As Oberdorfer suggests, the "disaster" portrait may have prompted many congressmen, pundits, and "opinion leaders," long uneasy about the war policy, to put themselves on record against it. But I would also suggest that election-year politics, and *Lyndon Johnson's own indecisive behavior,* did more to aggravate the Washington crisis than did all the alarms of the media.

In my view, the election-year pressures—and the underlying contradictions of the Johnson administration's ambiguous, costly "guns and butter" war policy—would have forced a New Look sometime in 1968, even if the major media had come closer to the realities of February–March. The Johnson administration was running out of time; it had tried to fight a war at the lowest possible cost, and now the cost was getting too high.

However, one can speculate that if the press and television had portrayed the battlefield with more cold light and less black fog, the politicians might have reacted more calmly. The Washington hawks and doves and Robert Kennedy would not have had a "disaster" to exploit; LBJ might have felt less cornered, less impelled to try (once again) to pacify all factions in Washington, more willing to wait for the dust to settle and for Hanoi to make an offer.

In any event, the February–March 1968 crisis and LBJ's climactic speech did not end the war, which went on for five more years. They merely made it more difficult for LBJ and his successor to deal from a position of strength with Hanoi in negotiating an end to it.

The ultimate responsibility—for candor and coherence before the crisis and for firm leadership and coherence in crisis—lay not with the media but with the president. By failing to meet this responsibility, Lyndon Johnson made the Tet crisis in Washington and his own humiliation, in large measure, a self-inflicted wound.

THE TET OFFENSIVE
ANOTHER PRESS CONTROVERSY: III

John Laurence

It is claimed that journalists in Vietnam were ill-equipped to cover the war: they were inexperienced, immature or irresponsible. They are accused now of being "shaken," "shocked," and "shook up" by the Tet offensive in 1968; of then dramatizing their reports because of personal fear and foreboding. It is being said that they lived and worked in such an incestuous journalistic atmosphere that they wrote stories simply for the approbation of their peers in the press corps. Worst of all, perhaps, they stand accused of seeking out what's described as the "melodrama" of the war and of reporting it in "emotive" terms, exploiting the widespread misery and suffering for their own personal benefits.

This kind of criticism seems to me an overreaction to the truth of the time, retribution of the most malicious kind, arising now in part from old hostilities that originated in the wartime relationships between the U.S. Mission and individual reporters, and finding expression now in statements such as: "An acorn fell on the reporters' heads in Saigon [at Tet], and they cried out—like Chicken Little—'The sky is falling.'" As a matter of fact, on the eve of the Tet offensive, Ho Chi Minh sent an inspirational message to his troops, saying, "The mountains of Annam are moving!" Mountains, acorns—we didn't believe a bit of it.

Let's go back a bit, to January 11, 1968, to the time just

before the big attack, and perhaps we may all be able to gain some insight into the way it actually was. Fifteen years ago last month, I was sitting in the comfortable office of an American three-star general just outside Saigon listening to a briefing. It was one of those relatively quiet days in the war, as I recall. The heavy fighting of the previous fall had tapered off along the DMZ and, in the Central Highlands, the siege of Khe Sanh had not yet begun in all its fury. The official word from Washington and Saigon was that the war was going well for our side; the Vietcong and North Vietnamese were seriously hurting; and the pacification program was making measurable progress in the countryside.

Lt. Gen. Frederick Weyand had invited a few reporters up to his headquarters at Long Binh where he commanded American field forces in the III Corps Tactical Zone, the area around Saigon. It was a pleasant day; the office was air-conditioned; the armchairs were made of soft leather. The general spoke in his easy California drawl. Weyand was worried. The enemy, he said, "has gone through a tremendous reorganization" in the past two months. The VC were now maneuvering in "mass formations" of 150- to 600-man units, "puffed up in strength" with North Vietnamese replacements and new weapons. The general showed us on his map where three or four VC main-force battalions had moved to within twenty miles of Saigon. Enemy prisoners and documents had been captured, he said, and they indicated that a major Communist offensive was coming soon, probably against Saigon, either just before or right after the national holidays at Tet. "Psychologically," Weyand said, "these attacks have a considerable effect on the people. They indicate that we do not have the power to protect them from the VC." Then he confided to us that he was shifting some thirty American battalions into a defensive ring around the capital.

Well, that was strong stuff, especially as it came from a general who was regarded as intelligent and honest.

I went back to the CBS bureau in Saigon and told my colleagues what Weyand had said. And since he had also warned of major enemy concentrations throughout the country, we decided to reorganize and redeploy, somewhat like the military. Senior correspondent Robert Schakne, who had covered Korea and other wars, became acting bureau chief. Three correspondents and camera crews went to Da Nang to stake out I Corps in the North. Camera stringers were alerted around the country to stand by. Scheduled Rest-and-Recreation was postponed, and staffers who were on leave outside Vietnam were cabled to get back as soon as possible. The head office in New York was advised that the Saigon bureau was going on a stepped-up "war footing."

CBS also sent in considerable help. Veteran Vietnam hands Murray Fromson and Peter Kalischer, both of whom had covered the Korean War, came in to reinforce; Bernard Kalb, with long experience in Southeast Asia, arrived. The same was true at the other networks and some of the newspapers. At NBC, for example, seasoned Vietnam correspondents Garrick Utley, David Burrington, and Ron Nessen returned after Tet, adding to a staff which included Wilson Hall and Howard Tuckner, two other veterans. Even Walter Cronkite, who distinguished himself in World War II, came back.

Looking back, I don't recall any of the CBS reporters or crews being shocked or shaken by the attacks. We were certainly surprised by the *scope* of the offensive, because it was unprecedented for that war, but the Weyand briefing had prepared us for what came, and no one, in the weeks and months ahead, cracked under the pressure of the long hours and the danger. I was not taking notes on the behavior of my colleagues at the time, but I recall that the men and women of the American press corps went about the job of trying to get the story in a professional, hardworking, and dedicated way. And—with one or two minor exceptions—they maintained the old tradition of "grace under pressure." It wasn't always easy.

Nine years later, a book called *Big Story*[1] appeared, a bitter indictment of the press corps at Tet written by Peter Braestrup, a former correspondent who was there at the time. After six years of research and writing, the author concluded that the American press in Vietnam overreacted to the Tet offensive, misinterpreted what was a significant military defeat for Hanoi and the NLF, focused instead on the drama of human suffering in Saigon, Hue, and Khe Sanh, and sent back the message to the American public:

---

1. All page references are to the Anchor Books edition (Garden City, N.Y.), 1978.

"DISASTER IN VIETNAM!" "Rarely has contemporary crisis journalism turned out, in retrospect, to have veered so widely from reality," the author wrote (p. 508).

To the book's credit, it should be stated that it includes a prodigious and praiseworthy job of research. But the evidence presented does not necessarily support the conclusions. In fact, an opposite case can be made for the quality of press coverage at Tet. Instead, what we are presented is a military historian's view of events, including much military analysis, petty in many of its criticisms and written with the cold, clinical detachment of hindsight—without acknowledging that stories written in the tumult of breaking events and pressing deadlines produce, understandably, the kind of journalism that should be regarded only as "the first rough draft of history."

Perhaps it might be instructive to examine the author's bias. Peter Braestrup holds formidable credentials: a graduate of Yale, Marine Corps service in Korea, a Nieman fellow at Harvard, a reporter for the *New York Times* and the Washington *Post*. Of himself in Vietnam he wrote, "I was perhaps less shocked by war's waste and destruction than were my colleagues experiencing these for the first time; I was probably also more interested in such military matters as logistics, 'foxhole strength,' enemy tactics, and allied deployments than they were" (p. xvi).

But it was not because of lack of experience with the savagery of war that the other reporters saw the Tet offensive in a light different from Mr. Braestrup's. Indeed, many of them had as much or more experience than he. The MACV statistics he cites in his argument—that reporters were inexperienced in Vietnam—are used in a misleading context and do not take into account the many veterans who returned to Vietnam after the offensive began.

As I've suggested, the reporters who covered the Tet offensive were uniformly steady under combat pressure. They took casualties alongside the people they were covering. Yet, *Big Story* claims repeatedly that journalists were "shocked" and "unsettled" by the dangers of combat, and that their personal reactions crept into their copy. "Some of the exaggeration," it claims, "was also doubtless a subjective reaction to the Tet surprise, and to the greater degree of personal risk involved in reporting combat operations thereafter" (p. 144). Yet, the only evidence offered in support of this claim is the behavior of one rattled reporter, and the *author's* own reactions. He describes himself as experiencing "shock" (p. 138), being "shaken" (p. 150), and that "the new sense of danger shook up many newsmen," including himself (p. 177). But, without citing examples of other reporters who were "shocked" and "shaken," as he suggests, Mr. Braestrup leaves the reader to conclude that he has projected his own emotional reactions to the risks of getting the story onto his colleagues.

One chapter of *Big Story* is devoted to a critical analysis of the coverage of the attack on the U.S. Embassy. Because the Associated Press reported—incorrectly—that the Vietcong had occupied part of the Embassy building, Mr. Braestrup concludes that "the immediate result was gross exaggeration of what really happened" (p. 91). But at the time of the battle, both an American Military Police captain and a sergeant at the scene told reporters that the VC *were* in the building (p. 82). The reporters got it wrong because the MPs had it wrong, and the AP duly corrected its mistake within one twelve-hour cycle. It was unfortunate, understandable, and human. But Mr. Braestrup argues that "the wires . . . let the drama run away with them" (p. 109), and "the embassy fight became the whole Tet offensive on TV and in the newspapers during that offensive's second day. . . ." (p. 110).

The point is that reporters' work can only be as accurate as their sources of information, and in Vietnam, it should be remembered, the major source of information originated from official American and Vietnamese sources. How well, I wonder, would coverage of the Tet offensive compare, for example, with similar crisis journalism at Three Mile Island? Or the U.S. Embassy takeover in Tehran? Or the 1973 Middle East War? Reporters do not create stories from a vacuum. They reflect what their sources of information tell them and what they manage to observe on their own.

PART III

THE LEGACY

•THE VETERANS•

Editor's Note

In America the effects of Vietnam were nowhere more concentrated than on the men who fought the war—the ordinary Americans plucked from assembly line, gas pump, or the educational process and whirled across six thousand miles into an alien, unknown land; then on the 365th day whirled back and dropped into the "real world" possibly thirty-six or forty-eight hours out of the range of the enemy mortars in the "boondocks."

It was a traumatic experience, an experience inflicting even more indelible wounds when the fighting men found themselves landed in a country which, to their view, was hostile, savage, unthinking, and incapable and unwilling to understand who they were, where they had been, and what they had done.

They encountered what many of them felt—rightly—was a conspiracy of silence about the deeper questions of the war. It was a conspiracy which they joined, feeling that if they wore their army fatigues or mentioned their service, they might be greeted with hostile comments such as "baby-killer" or "candy-ass." So they thought.

They joined the conspiracy of silence which settled down over the whole society after the Paris protocols were signed by Henry Kissinger in February 1973. It has only been very recently, almost literally since the unveiling of the Vietnam War memorial in Washington in November 1982, that they have begun to come out of the closet.

The cold indifference and outright hostility with which the country greeted the men who fought in its behalf was unprecedented in the history of the United States. It contributed and continues to contribute to a legacy of deep ills associated with Vietnam.

To none of these ills has much public heed been given—not to the veterans, not to the impact upon their health inflicted by Agent Orange, almost nothing at all to the savage consequences of the war to the Vietnamese and their country. Not even to those Vietnamese who by luck, daring, and bribery managed to make their way to the United States, there to be absorbed almost invisibly in the remoter areas of the country—in southern California or northern Oregon or rural upstate New York—into small, forgotten refugee colonies, grimly trying to get a footing in the harsh and alien soil of that country which, increasingly, they blame for their plight.

Nor, of course, has much heed been given to the consequences of the war in Southeast Asia, to that domino which our policymakers were so certain would topple the whole continent if it fell. Not even the fact that the war's end brought to Southeast Asia extraordinary, almost unbelievable, Communist presence in the form of Soviet bases and strong Chinese Communist intervention has stirred the sluggish political and policy muscles of a Washington long since having reached the determination that there is no political mileage to be acquired by mentioning the word Vietnam, a calm so sluggish that President Reagan did not even visit the Vietnam memorial for six months after it was dedicated.

But this may change as the Vietnam veterans move out onto the political and public stage with their embarrassing questions as to why their government will not accept responsibility for inflicting Agent Orange upon their unwitting bodies, especially since the same government quit dumping it onto the feckless South Vietnamese population in 1969 when it became convinced of its hazards to health due to that only-too-familiar ingredient—dioxin.

The silence of the veterans seems permanently broken, for as George Swiers asserts here, "if we do not speak of [Vietnam] others will surely rewrite the script."

"Each of the body bags, all of the mass graves," he observes, "will be reopened and their contents abracadabra-ed into a noble cause."

The "noble cause" to which Swiers refers has, to be certain, already surfaced in the rhetoric of presidents like Nixon and Reagan.

There are deep concerns among the veterans—why did so heavy a percentage of those who fought and died in Vietnam come from the working class and lower-income ranks in the USA, the "caste system," as Gloria Emerson calls it; why the disproportionate casualties—more Hispanics killed than any others, 20 percent, although they constituted only 7 percent of the combat troops in Vietnam, and 20 percent black casualties; why did 300,000 of the "bad" discharges out of 800,000 go to blacks and Chicanos; why the bias of the Veterans Administration toward Korean and World War II veterans; why was Lyndon Johnson's GI Bill for Vietnam stingy, lacking the generosity of the World War II provisions?

All these questions are on the agenda, and the others which seeped through American society—the stereotype on television of the Vietnam veterans as crazies, criminals, wild men, rapists; the fact that the Vietnam veterans averaged only eighteen years old against the twenty-seven-year-old average of World War II.

Underlying these and other issues appears clear evidence of the guilt which Americans feel over the war, and a stealthy process of trying to shift its burden over to the men who fought rather than to those who made them fight; to the combat soldier, not the generals or the men in the White House.

All of this has compounded the conspiracy of silence into which, it has become apparent, the military has joined, locking up its Vietnam experience within deep-sealed security chests never to be opened. Whatever lessons there are have been confined to burn-bags quickly hauled away to the incinerators.

VIETNAM VETERANS SPEAK
AN INTRODUCTION

Gloria Emerson

Most of the soldiers had a one-year tour of duty in Vietnam. And one of the most wrenching experiences, even for a civilian, was being sent straight back to the United States when the tour was over. In some cases, this meant that you could be in a fire base in the jungle on Tuesday and home by Saturday, with no time to defuse. So huge an adjustment simply could not be made. I know one veteran who, that first year back, used to stand in his family's kitchen and eat peaches out of a can with a knife. His mother said it was disgusting and would he stop?

Vietnam illuminated nothing quite so clearly as the American caste system. Watching who was fighting the war was to be aware of a caste system that is almost ironclad. It was the working class who got caught and who died. They were the surplus. They were the children we could afford to lose, the acceptable casualties. When they came back, the very country that was so willing to kill them, to waste them, was hardly willing to help them. The GI Bill for Vietnam veterans was in no way comparable to the benefits extended to veterans of other wars. I was appalled at veterans' hospitals and the treatment veterans received. I went to one in Chicago to see how a twenty-four-year-old blind veteran was being treated, and I was taken to a wallet-stitching class.

The poverty of our culture is so profound that what what Americans see today is a stereotype of the crazy, wacko, freaked-out psychotic, created by script writers who know nothing. I sometimes think there is a conspiracy to show the weaknesses and the grief, not the strengths, of Vietnam veterans. Because we see the Vietnam veteran as kind of a crazy, inadequate, second-rate, feeble, advanced neurasthenic, we never have to face Vietnam. Or face what was required of him. We can keep our distance.

HISPANICS AND THE VIETNAM WAR

Ruben Treviso

History's accounting of the Vietnam War must reflect what I believe to be the most important lesson of that war: it was fought by the poor of this nation. The war in Vietnam was fought by minorities and by the poor who chose not to escape duty to country. It was fought by those individuals whose class in society made them most vulnerable to be sent to Vietnam. We must not forget the poor and minority communities in Vietnam, for they were the ones that fought the war.

That is why there are cities and towns in the Southwest, on the eastern seaboard, and in Puerto Rico that were depleted of their young, draft-eligible Hispanic men during the Vietnam War. In the over fifteen-year saga of our involvement in Vietnam, the Hispanic community suffered the highest ratio of casualties of any community in this nation. The Hispanic casualty figures throughout this country's history have always been exceedingly high, but in Vietnam they were glaring:

• *One out of every two* Hispanics who went to Vietnam served in a combat unit

• *One out of every five* Hispanics who went to Vietnam was killed in action

• *One out of every three* Hispanics who went to Vietnam was wounded in action

• *10 percent* of Hispanic veterans who have been examined at the VA hospital in Brentwood, California, have experienced episodes of momentary paralysis.

This disproportionate number of Hispanics on the casualty lists was the result of insensitive systems and bureaucracies that drafted, recruited, trained, and sent Americans to Vietnam. Besides being insensitive, these systems were unfair and unrepresentative of the communities they were established to serve. The draft boards chose those individuals who were most vulnerable, those who were not deferred for one reason or another. Unlike middle America, many of the poor and minorities did not have money for frivolous-type deferments. Within the Hispanic community, men were drafted at double and triple their proportional representation in the population. An example is the state of New Mexico. By U.S. Census count, Hispanics made up 27 percent of the population in New Mexico in 1970 but supplied 69 percent of all those drafted—and accounted for 44 percent of combat deaths. This was primarily due to the inability of many Hispanics to receive deferments and the under-representation of Hispanics on local draft boards.

Today, the All Volunteer Force (the nation's armed forces—without a draft) is becoming increasingly minority in membership, 41 percent now, and projected to reach 50 percent by 1985; minorities represent 30 percent of the enlisted ranks and 5.5 percent of the officer corps; in 1971, there were ninety-eight Hispanic women officers in the U.S. Army; there are 102 today.

It was not until 1979 that the Department of the Army began to keep data on Hispanics separate from "other minorities." As of now, in the army, the count is 32.5 percent blacks and 4.3 percent Hispanics. But Hispanics are probably badly undercounted. The data the armed forces use to determine the number of Hispanics is based on self-identification. It is accurate only to the extent that Latinos correctly indicate and mark themselves as of Hispanic/Latino origin. According to Maj. Don Rojas, "Many feel it's an advantage not to speak with an accent or advertise their culture to anyone." In a random survey conducted by Lt. Col. Ray Dennison, of the Marine Corps Office of Equal Opportunity, approximately 25 percent of the Hispanics who were questioned indicated that they had not identified themselves as Hispanics.

A manpower expert at the Department of the Army observes, "Hispanics, for some reason, do not mark themselves as Hispanics. At home they're told that to be identified as a minority is a disadvantage both inside and outside of the service." Instead of the reported 4.4 percent of Hispanics in the army, he estimates, "it is really about 7 percent Hispanic . . . and unless the unemployment rate is turned around quite a bit, they'll be going up to 12 or 13 percent in the next two or three years."

"SONG OF NAPALM" AND OTHER POEMS

Bruce Weigl

SONG OF NAPALM
for my wife

After the storm, after the rain stopped pounding,
We stood in the doorway watching horses
Walk off lazily across the pasture's hill.
We stared through the black screen,
Our vision altered by the distance
So I thought I saw a mist
Kicked up around their hooves when they faded
Like cut-out horses
Away from us.
The grass was never more blue in that light, more
Scarlet; beyond the pasture
Trees scraped their voices into the wind, branches
Criss-crossed the sky like barbed-wire
But you said they were only branches.

"Song of Napalm" originally appeared in *TriQuarterly Review* (Fall 1982); "Girl at the Chu Lai Laundry" originally appeared in *The Black Warrior Review* (Spring 1981); "Burning Shit at An Khe" originally appeared in *Quarterly West* No. 16.

Okay. The storm stopped pounding.
I am trying to say this straight: for once
I was sane enough to pause and breathe
Outside my wild plans and after the hard rain
I turned my back on the old curses. I believed
They swung finally away from me . . .

But still the branches are wire
And thunder is the pounding mortar,
Still I close my eyes and see the girl
Running from her village, napalm
Stuck to her dress like jelly,
Her hands reaching for the no one
Who waits in waves of heat before her.

So I can keep on living,
So I can stay here beside you,
I try to imagine she runs down the road and wings
Beat inside her until she rises
Above the stinking jungle and her pain
Eases, and your pain, and mine.
But the lie swings back again.
The lie works only as long as it takes to speak
And the girl runs only as far
As the napalm allows
Until her burning tendons and crackling
Muscles draw her up
Into that final position
Burning bodies so perfectly assume. Nothing
Can change that; she is burned behind my eyes
And not your good love and not the rain-swept air
And not the jungle green
Pasture unfolding before us can deny it.

GIRL AT THE CHU LAI LAUNDRY

All this time I had forgotten.
My miserable platoon was moving out
One day in the way and I had my clothes in the laundry.
I ran the two dirt miles,
Convoy already forming behind me. I hit
The block of small hooches and saw her
Twist out the black rope of her hair in the sun.
She did not look up at me,
Not even when I called to her for my clothes.
She said I couldn't have them,
They were wet. . . .

Who would've thought the world stops
Turning in the war, the tropical heat like hate
And your platoon moves out without you,
Your wet clothes piled
At the feet of the girl at the laundry,
Beautiful with her facts.

BURNING SHIT AT AN KHE

Into that pit
        I had to climb down
With a rake and matches; eventually,
        You had to do something
Because it just kept piling up
        And it wasn't our country, it wasn't
Our air sick with the thick smoke
        So another soldier and I
Lifted the shelter off its blocks
        To expose the home-made toilets:
Fifty-five gallon drums cut in half
        With crude wood seats that splintered.

We soaked the piles with fuel oil
  And lit the stuff
And tried to keep the fire burning.
  To take my first turn
I paid some kid
  A care package of booze from home.
I'd walked past the burning once
  And gagged the whole heart of myself—
It smelled like the world
  Was on fire
But when my turn came again
  There was no one
So I stuffed cotton up my nose
  And marched up that hill. We poured
And poured until it burned and black
  Smoke curdled
But the fire went out. . . .
  Heavy artillery
Hammered the evening away in the distance,
  Vietnamese laundry women watched
From a safe place, laughing.
  I'd grunted out eight months
Of jungle and thought I had a grip on things
  But we flipped the coin and I lost
And climbed down into my fellow soldiers'
  Shit and began to sink and didn't stop
Until I was deep to my knees. Liftships
  Cut the air above me, the hacking
Blast of their blades
  Ripped dust in swirls so every time
I tried to light a match
  It died
And it all came down on me,
  The stink and the heat and the worthlessness
Until I slipped and climbed
  Out of that hole and ran
Past the olive drab
  Tents and trucks and clothes and everything
Green as far from the shit
  As the fading light allowed. . . .

Only now I can't fly.
    I lay down in it
And finger paint the words of who I am
    Across my chest
Until I'm covered and there's only one smell,
    One word.

SONG FOR THE LOST PRIVATE

The night we were to meet in the hotel
In the forbidden Cholon district
You never showed
So I drank myself into a filthy
Room with a bar girl
Who had terrible scars
She ran her fingers over
As we bartered for the night.

But drunk I couldn't do anything with her, angry
I threw the mattress to the street
And stood out on the balcony naked,
Cursing your name.
She thought I was crazy and tried to give the money back.
I don't know how to say I tried again.
I saw myself in the mirror and couldn't move.
She crushed the paper money in her fist
And curled in sleep away from me
So I felt cruel, cold. . . . Small arms fire
Cracked in the market place below.
I thought I heard you call back my name
But white flares lit the sky
Casting empty streets in clean light
And the firing stopped.
I couldn't sleep so I touched her
Small shoulders, traced the curve of her spine,
Traced the scars,
The miles we were all from home.

AGENT ORANGE AND THE EFFECTS OF THE HERBICIDE PROGRAM

George Ewalt, Jr.

When I was in Vietnam, the land was in the early stages of dying. Even so, I have never seen land that had the deep, lush green color of Vietnam. Even though we were dirty and smelled from living in the bush, we could not help but be impressed with the land.

During my tour in Vietnam, we were never informed of the herbicide program that has come to be known as Agent Orange. We drank the water from the streams and rivers and bathed in it. My tour was over on February 24, 1968, during the Tet offensive. We devastated the land, the trees, the rivers, and the people. The final result was that Vietnam was turned into an ashtray. We will always live with what we killed in Vietnam.

After returning from Vietnam, I was reassigned to Fort Hood, Texas, and was discharged on September 13, 1968. I turned twenty-one the next day. After leaving both Vietnam and the army, my feelings were completely destroyed or burned-out. The only feeling that I had was that I had survived something horrible. I thought that I was finally safe, and did not know that Vietnam's aftermath would still get me. I believe that the army knew that the herbicides would not only punish the Vietnamese but also us, the survivors.

The stated purpose of the herbicide program was to destroy the vegetation, thus making it difficult for the enemy to ambush our troops and those of our allies. Another purpose was to deny their forces much-needed food supplies.

The herbicide program began in 1965 with the use of Agents Pink and Purple. The herbicides were given names of color due to the color bands on the outside of the barrels that they were shipped in.

In 1965, Agents Pink and Purple were replaced by Agents Orange, Blue, and White. Agent Orange was a mixture of 2-4-5-T—which contained dioxin, the deadliest chemical made by man—and 2-4-D. Agent Blue contained cacodylic acid (arsenic); and Agent White was a mixture of a picloram and 2-4-D, and was contaminated with dioxin.

Over seventeen million gallons of the various herbicides were applied in South Vietnam. Reports began to come from Vietnam concerning an increase of miscarriages, birth defects, people becoming ill, and of farm animals dying. These reports at first were dismissed as enemy propaganda. Scientists began to study the herbicide program, and finally convinced the government to discontinue it. The damage had been done to South Vietnam and its people, as well as to the American personnel and their allies. The areas that were sprayed the most were in the III Corps military region and the I Corps area. The area that my unit operated in was the III Corps area, in War Zone C and parts of War Zone D. Some of the names of places that we were in are: Phouc Vinh, Quan Loi, Anh Loc, Loc Ninh, Phu Loi, the Iron Triangle, and Lai Khe.

The health problems that I have did not begin to appear until around 1975. At that time, I developed two skin growths. One was on the upper back portion of my right arm, and the second was on the right side of my head near the temple. These growths were removed, and the diagnosis was that the growth on the arm was nonmalignant but the one on the side of my head was basal-cell carcinoma.

In 1979, I first heard that the herbicides were suspected of causing serious health problems in Vietnam veterans, and that the chemicals were suspected of causing birth defects.

It is suspected that dioxin becomes deposited in the fatty tissues of the body and may remain dormant for many years. Once the dioxin is released, it may attack different parts of the body.

The Vietnam veterans have had to resort to the largest class-action lawsuit in the history of the nation. This class-action lawsuit is necessary because, by law, we cannot bring suit against the military for health problems that may have been caused when one served in the armed forces. The legal system is again being used against the veterans. To try to remedy this situation, the Vietnam veterans have brought suit against the manufacturers of the herbicides.

When the Vietnam veterans began to ask for help, we were told that one major problem was that records of the individual units could not be obtained. These are the records that have the grid location and areas that a unit operated in—and would help the veterans to prove that they were in the sprayed areas. After much time and research, I was able to obtain these records for my time in South Vietnam. These records are titled "Operational Reports—Lessons Learned" and "Staff Journals—After the Action Reports." They can only be obtained after twelve years have passed since one was in Vietnam. They are important for proving that the veteran was in the areas that were sprayed with the herbicides, i.e., Agents Orange, Blue, and White.

To obtain these records, a request must be sent to the Department of the Army, Office of the Adjutant General, Research and Rulemaking Branch, Records and Management Division, Alexandria, Virginia 22331, along with the veteran's name, service number, and the complete unit he was assigned to in Vietnam and the dates served in Vietnam. Doing so will enable a Vietnam veteran to obtain the unit records that have been denied him in the past.

Even with the unit's records, the proper sector maps are needed to plot the herbicide missions. The maps can be purchased from Winter Soldiers Archives, c/o Clark Smith, 2000 Center Street, Box 1251, Berkeley, California 94704. The title of the Book is *The Vietnam Map Book* and costs the Vietnam veteran $25. The book also contains the herbicide tapes.

When I began to research the Agent Orange issue, I attempted to locate the herbicide tapes from the Department of the Army. I finally got them from the Department of Commerce, National Technical Information Service, in Springfield, Virginia, at a cost of $29. With this printout, I tabulated the gallons for each province in South Vietnam for the three herbicides—Orange,

Blue, and White. (See Appendix 2.)

Even with all of this information, my claim and those of the other Vietnam veterans continue to be denied.

United States Senator Arlen Specter (R-Pa.) held hearings in June 1981, on the problems of the Vietnam veterans and Agent Orange. At this hearing, I testified and met another Vietnam veteran. He showed the senator and the people his little girl. She was eighteen months old, and was born with no left arm. His other children have no health problems as serious as hers. He believes that his child's birth defect is the result of his exposure to the herbicides while in the military in Vietnam.

At another hearing in Washington, D.C., a veteran stated that he has "five screwed-up kids." One has three kidneys, another a defective heart, one a brain dysfunction, one an immunological problem, and the last has skin problems. He told the panel on Agent Orange that the VA treated him like dirt when he asked for help.

These are the main reasons that the Vietnam veterans are demanding help for themselves and their children. We need serious research, and not more political rhetoric.

When I was drafted I weighed 185 pounds, and upon my return from Vietnam I weighed 143 pounds. The first symptom that I developed was numbness in the hands and feet; later I developed the skin growths; and at present I have nerve damage. I have had almost every type of test there is for Agent Orange. In 1981, I was a patient at the Philadelphia Veterans Administration hospital; a nerve biopsy was conducted on my right leg. The sural nerve was removed, and the results were that I have peripheral neuropathy and was informed that there is no way to determine how this will progress. So there is still no answer to my health problems and those of other Vietnam veterans.

The time is now, not ten or twenty years from now, to help the Vietnam veterans and their families. We are not asking for pity, but only to be treated fairly.

"DEMENTED VETS" AND OTHER MYTHS
THE MORAL OBLIGATION OF VETERANS

George Swiers

On that February afternoon in 1970 there were, unarguably, scores of curious individuals wandering around the San Francisco airport. But none could have been more outwardly curious or as purposefully driven as the young Marine. He had just turned twenty-one, though he looked and certainly felt much older. And he had just returned from the once-upon-a-time Republic of South Vietnam, a speck on the planet where reaching that age was something of a miracle.

Perched upon his bar stool like a silent sentinel, watching the sea of airport passengers, he was struck by the business as usual, etched upon face after face after face. The absurdity of it all was overwhelming. He was, after all, the survivor of an honest-to-god magical mystery tour. A timeless, lysergic nightmare . . .

• where ideals and illusions could disintegrate as rapidly and violently as the human being beside you;

• where rules seemed as without boundary as the confusion and misery you existed in;

• where humiliation was so constant, so everywhere, that you stopped thinking of yourself as human.

And so, with a bravado inspired by two hours' worth of drugs and alcohol, and his uniform disheveled beyond embarrassment, he set out to speak with his Fellow Americans. To share with them his hideous secrets, to tell them what went on daily *in their names.*

Needless to say, it was impossible to find an audience, impossible even to find someone willing to hold his stare. This, he thought, is how lunatics come to speak exclusively among themselves.

The incident occurred when he happened upon the smiling middle-aged couples seated before the television. Their sin was to prefer the wisdom being offered by a program called *My Mother The Car.* The young Marine, whose very survival was owed in part to inordinate discipline, suddenly and completely lost control.

The security officers who escorted him away weren't really that rough with him; they were even tolerant of his incoherent rambling; and one of them actually said, "Listen, buddy, have a drink. You'll feel better."

This week, exactly thirteen years have passed since I was last in California. I return to a place where Vietnam is *all* that is spoken of. And there is some measure of comfort in that. But if I have learned anything in these thirteen years, it is this: *I'm not supposed to feel better.*

My friend Patrick Finnegan, a fellow activist and former grunt, often marvels at the government's willingness to permit *any* Vietnam veteran reaccess to America. For we brought with us the awful, suffocating truth of the war: that lies, though they be cleverly camouflaged, neatly packed and endorsed by presidents, are *still* lies. And that no lie clicked out in a military press release could bury deep enough the death, dishonor, and defecation that was Vietnam.

The government was quick to discredit the living proof that evil had been done; to silence those returning who hadn't already been numbed into silence. In 1971, when veterans threw their medals at the White House in protest of a war that disgusted and degraded them, the Nixon administration implied that they weren't really veterans but actors. At Miami in 1972, when we marched on the Republican Convention, broken men, reminders of a broken faith, the same administration pointed to our freshly scrubbed, non-veteran peers as a shining hope that would not "stain America."

The message sent from national leadership and embraced by the public was clear: Vietnam veterans were malcontents, liars, wackos, losers. The die was cast for a decade's indifference toward the social and economic reintegration of veterans. Hollywood, ever bizarre in its efforts to mirror life, discovered a marketable villain. *Kojack, Ironside,* and the friendly folks at *Hawaii Five-O* confronted crazed, heroin-addicted veterans with the regularity and enthusiasm Saturday morning heroes once dispensed with godless red savages. No grade-B melodrama was complete without its standard vet—a psychotic, ax-wielding rapist every bit as insulting as another one-time creature of Hollywood's imagination, the shiftless, lazy, and wide-eyed black. The demented-vet portrayal has become so casual, so commonplace, that one pictures the children of Vietnam veterans shivering beneath their blankets and wondering if Daddy will come in with a good-night kiss or a Black & Decker chain saw.

America needs its myths about the war, just as it once needed the lies. We are all of us convinced, though not all will yet admit to it, that Vietnam was a shameful abomination. *Someone* should be punished for it, indeed, deserves to be stark-raving mad because of it. The myth of 2.5 million walking time bombs tells us that someone, somewhere, in some way, is paying the price for our national sin. Absolution is lent to all others. We can live with Vietnam, without ever having to look at it.

Writing for the *Atlantic Monthly,* novelist Ward Just noted, "The Vietnam War must be scaled down to life rather than up to myth."

A detailed public autopsy on the war, and what it did to America, one in which truth is not permitted to become a casualty, should be the permanent issue of Vietnam veterans. For only through a full reckoning, a demand for examination and accountability, can the war's demons be purged.

In his January 1973, prime-time speech announcing an end to America's longest war, Richard Nixon used the phrase "peace with honor" five times. With that, the dishonorable task of sweeping the war under the rug was formally begun. Though four successive presidents have exploited the war, none of them had the moral courage to present a candid fireside chat entitled: "Vietnam Reconsidered: Lessons From a War." The legacies of Vietnam hold hostage millions of Americans who have neither seen nor heard of that faraway land: millions whose lives are ravaged by an economy still reeling from a trillion-dollar war, millions whose faith in America has so eroded that we are as gypsies—without sense of national purpose. One day, in another faraway place, other teenage Americans may fight and die for a reason as criminal as our mere reluctance to discuss Vietnam. For if we do not speak of it, others will surely rewrite the script. Each of the body bags, all of the mass graves will be reopened and their contents abracadabra-ed into a noble cause.

Vietnam veterans have their memorial now, of course. It didn't turn out to be the one-ton condolence card many of us envisioned. To the contrary, the memorial, beautiful and moving in its simplicity, provided the necessary catharsis for more than a few Vietnam veterans. November '82 also brought with it our parade. And who, this side of Pasadena at New Year's or Macy's at Thanksgiving, ever saw such a grandiose procession? There, leading it all, was none other than Gen. William Westmoreland (presumably unedited by CBS). Lovable, white-headed, reverent Westy—basking at last in the light at the end of the tunnel. Still, there were Vietnam veterans who completed the long, nightmarish path of readjustment through that process, that simple gesture of recognition.

What of readjustment for the remainder? What of those who dismiss parades and monuments as panaceas for deer hunters? What of the faceless many that Siegfried Sassoon called "The Unreturning Army"? By now it is an old and too-often told story: an inadequate GI Bill; a catalog of social problems that was staggering; employment opportunities limited or nonexistent; complicated health problems entrusted to an archaic system. In a scenario that would have pleased Kafka immensely, funds desperately needed to rebuild lives were, instead, financing an orgy of death ten thousand miles away. It is from this rubble, wrought by treachery and betrayal, that Vietnam veterans must now declare their independence. To reject forevermore the label of pitiful, helpless victim. To refuse to allow our pain to be weighed against the pain of others, or have our suffering so exaggerated as to become an indictment of the innocent.

Unemployment and underemployment are not restricted to the Vietnam veteran community. Neither do we hold the copyright on exposure to dioxin. The body count of suicide, divorce, incarceration, and substance abuse is not, all things considered, terribly discriminating. To suggest that Vietnam veterans are alone denied decent educational opportunities is ludicrous. And millions upon too-many-millions of Americans suffer from insufficient and inept health care.

A veteran who endures, and survives, the trauma of war has a moral obligation to articulate that experience to others. Not to do so is to totally abdicate one's responsibilities to the living, the once-living, and to generations yet unborn.

I remember an Edgar Lee Masters poem, "Silence," I obediently memorized as a high school junior. "Silence" in part concerned a conversation between a young boy and a very old, one-legged Civil War veteran. Asked by the boy how the leg was lost, the old soldier relives in his mind the horror of Gettysburg, but unwilling and unable to share with the boy that which his conscience demands, he answers instead, "A bear bit it off."

During 1969—a year when, for the most ambiguous of reasons, I walked the jungled mountains of someone else's country carrying a high-velocity weapon intended to terminate the lives of those who would defend it, watching those whom I loved being brutalized by the real-life spaghetti western we starred in and realizing, all of it, much too late—I often thought of the old soldier. I thought then, and know now, that his inability to share with the boy his profound grief, his unwillingness to recall the hows and whys of a leg ruined, then discarded like an insignificant chunk of meat, doomed the child to one day surrender a portion of his own anatomy and, perhaps, humanity, in the trenches of France.

There must come, through national discussion, a reckoning for Vietnam. And, very clearly, it is the war's veterans, those with insight born of deep personal tragedy, who must cry out the loudest. For it is mainly they, abandoned first on one front and then another, who have the capacity to return hope to the process.

Whether it is fair to burden the veterans with such awesome baggage is moot. We may well be asking them to step onto an emotional merry-go-round that becomes for them, and for the nation, eternal. And the result might best be described by dipping into Vietnam's macabre lexicon, where real estate, ideals, and human beings were routinely destroyed in order to save them.

But any risk is acceptable. How ironic it would be if our unwillingness to discuss Vietnam became the war's final, unpardonable sin.

This time, the hearts and minds that are there to win or lose belong to Americans.

THE TREATMENT OF VIETNAM VETERANS

FROM RAP GROUPS TO COUNSELING CENTERS

Shad Meshad

The Vietnam veteran fought an unconventional, unpopular war, in a foreign country eight thousand miles from home. Upon coming home, he was welcomed with indifference, fear, or hostility by the American public and many of his friends and family. These "warrior-teenagers" (their average age was eighteen, as opposed to twenty-seven for the typical World War II soldier) had no one to understand their experiences, especially the brutality they had seen: the Phoenix assassinations, recon patrols, villages leveled, positions overrun, and friends crippled and killed.

If he turned to anyone for professional help, the Vietnam veteran received "conventional" treatment. In the late sixties, few mental health professionals understood the special problems of the Vietnam veteran: his alienation, survivor guilt, his "street" culture, or his retreat into drugs. The flashbacks, lack of affect, and uncontrollable rages suffered by many Vietnam veterans (especially those who served in heavy combat) were too often classed as schizophrenia and dealt with by heavy sedation at Veterans Administration hospitals. Mental health professionals, schooled in the problems of veterans returning from "patriotic" wars like World War II and Korea, tended to dismiss the Vietnam veteran as a "junkie" or a "hippie." The media reinforced and sensationalized the image of the troubled Vietnam vet as a crazed, drugged, time bomb. As a result, the Vietnam veteran had no one to turn to and retreated even further into alienation, isolation, and drugs. The government had "ripped him off" by sending him to Vietnam; society had called him a "baby-killer" on his return; and then the VA (which he called the "green machine" like the army) was finishing "the job."

The first recognition of the special problems of Vietnam veterans came through the work of Robert J. Lifton and of Chaim Shatan, in the early seventies. Lifton, who based his book *Home from the War* on "rap groups" (informal group-therapy sessions he led), focused on the pain, the flashbacks, and the homecoming trauma. Shatan, in his *Grief and the Vietnam Veteran,* explored the mourning process. But it was not until 1973—when Vietnam veterans began to develop their own ways of treating themselves and their fellow veterans—that the special problems of Vietnam veterans were recognized and treatment began.

A personal aside here: I went off to the war in 1970, a true son of the South, a believer in "mom's apple pie" and "defend your country." But I was a "psych" officer, and right away I came up against the absurdity and senseless brutality of the war. What did it mean to announce to a unit that had been fighting its way through the jungle for thirty days in monsoon rains that "next week the psych officer will be on board, if anyone needs to talk to him"? How could a kid who'd been pounding through the jungle without sleep for weeks, and who'd just lost his three best friends, march right up and "talk to the psych officer"? Most vets, even now, twelve to fifteen years later, can't talk about Vietnam. Sometimes my work there—and my work here—is just "holding on to someone." But the point is: It's a Vietnam veteran—whether he's a trained therapist with graduate degrees like me or just a guy who's been there—who understands that.

Most people doing anything about Vietnam veterans are Vietnam veterans themselves. We understand that the anger, frustration, and confusion Vietnam veterans feel is not a "sickness" but a normal reaction to an abnormal situation. It has taken a decade for that to be recognized. And it was through the initiative of Vietnam veterans themselves that what we now call "post-traumatic stress disorder" was defined, pushed, and shaped into treatment programs. In the early seventies, I was working at the Brentwood

VA hospital in Los Angeles. I began to discover that veterans' self-help groups like "Flower of the Dragon," "Swords to Plowshares," and "Twice-Born Men," were seeing more Vietnam veterans than the VA itself. A small group of dedicated organizers—men like Ron Kovic, Jack Smith, Jack McCloskey, and Harold Bryant (themselves Vietnam veterans)—were trying to understand and treat Vietnam veterans outside any conventional medical institution. Their success was based on the fact that troubled Vietnam vets were only comfortable around other Vietnam veterans. At the VA, few staff members were Vietnam veterans, and few understood the Vietnam experience. They dismissed the real guilt, anger, and grief as mental illness.

By the mid-seventies, a network of "rap groups," similar to the ones pioneered by Robert J. Lifton, but now run by Vietnam veterans, had sprung up around the country—in Los Angeles, San Francisco, New York, and Saint Louis. When vets came together in groups led by other vets, they opened up, and the "rap groups" became forums to vent and analyze the anger, alienation, and powerlessness that sprang from their Vietnam experience. Research task forces were formed, as well as a committee on "post-traumatic stress disorder." They emerged from a 1973 conference run by the National Council of Churches, and a study at Purdue University under the direction of Charles Figley. (Figley's 1978 book, *Delayed Stress Reactions Among Vietnam Veterans*, was to become the Bible of the movement to diagnose and treat troubled Vietnam veterans.)

By the late seventies, what I call the "circle of treatment" had become the established way to begin the healing of Vietnam veterans. The process began with drawing the vet into a treatment facility (whether it be a VA hospital, a mental hygiene clinic, or a vets' self-help program), diagnosing him, treating him, helping him back into the world, and following up on his readjustment.

But a final step had to be taken: to draw the Veterans Administration—with its massive financial and treatment resources—into the process of treating those veterans who still felt alienated from the government. It was out of this experience that the idea of the Vet Centers—storefront treatment centers funded by the VA but separate and apart from the hospital system itself—was born.

In 1977, Max Cleland, himself a wounded Vietnam veteran,

became head of the Veterans Administration. Veterans who had been developing their own treatment programs for Vietnam veterans, including me and Rev. Bill Mahedy (who had been working with me in Los Angeles), presented Cleland, other VA officials, and Sen. Alan Cranston, head of the Senate Veterans' Affairs Committee, with the idea of a nationwide network of storefront counseling centers. A task force was formed, and Congress passed on June 15, 1979, a Psychological Readjustment Act, setting up the National Vet Center Program. Eighty-one centers were set up around the country, staffed by veterans (many of them trained psychologists or psychiatrists) and by Vietnam veteran counselors trained on the job to run "rap groups."

It has been a long struggle to bring home the nearly three million American boys and girls who served in Vietnam. Our work is not finished. The war is not over. But we have learned that the troubled Vietnam veteran can be treated and that he has "talent" as a survivor from which all Americans can learn and benefit.

RACISM IN THE ARMY AND BACK AT THE VA

Frank Walker

Almost 50 percent of the ground casualty victims in Vietnam were minority troops. Blacks suffered almost 20 percent of the deaths in Vietnam; Chicanos 20 percent; Asians and Puerto Ricans 7 percent. They were also awarded a disproportionate number of less-than-honorable discharges: 300,000 of the 800,000 bad discharges during the Vietnam era went to black GIs. Hate groups like the KKK were allowed to breed like rats, unhampered by military regulations or harassment. And to top it off, unemployment among black Vietnam veterans is now at 18 percent.

I am a Marine. One of my main problems when I came home was nightmares. They were of death—the death of young Americans. I did not know how to explain it to my family. I come from a family that has served in the military a lot. My father was a Marine. My uncle was a Marine. My grandfather was in the army. When they returned from their wars, they were heroes in my eyes. So when I returned home, talking about my problem, they did not understand. Well, hell, I didn't either. So I did like a lot of Vietnam veterans and headed toward the VA. That didn't help me. I have found since I have been working with the vet centers that 90 percent of the blacks or minorities discharged with a medical are classified as schizophrenic paranoids. That is the way they classified me. There must be a hell of a lot of s.p.'s in this world, then.

VOICES OF THE VETERANS

Twelve speakers from the floor

LELAND LABINSKI:
I think a lot of us vets came to the wrong conference; we should have been at a conference entitled "America Reconsidered." I have a friend who has sat at home for the last ten years building models. He went to Vietnam five months after being drafted. He was sent on a five-man patrol: it was ambushed; his best friends were killed beside him, and the top of his skull was blown off. Due to our fine medical staff in Vietnam, he had a frontal lobotomy. The VA considers a man who sits at home and builds model airplanes as lazy—especially since he is a Mexican. The Department of Defense and the rest of the government have a Vietnam lesson for him: Maybe you should have stayed in Vietnam and not survived. Most of us vets see his situation a little differently—he was out there on patrol for us. One of the reasons we survived was that we watched each other's backs. He suffered brain trauma and post-traumatic stress and from alcoholism, and recently from a new disease—Reaganitis.

He came home. He went through the hospital. They handed him a check and sent him home. And ten years later, there was an agency-wide review and his compensation was cut from a thousand dollars a month to four hundred. For a year and a half, we have been fighting the VA to reestablish that minimum. The VA throws up bureaucratic impediments. A VA psychologist tells him that there is no such thing as post-traumatic stress. We all know about delayed-stress syndrome but it does not exist for that man. We go to a Vietnam vet center and find it understaffed; it can only provide a group. This man needs a little bit more than a group, and veterans need a little bit more than a group. What veterans need is understanding of how to turn our anger into energy and to understand who our friends are and who our enemies are. This man cannot provide for his parents, who hope to retire on social security and do not know whether it will be there. He is being taken care of by his brothers and sisters, who now face prospects of unemployment. We have to form political action committees. We have to get Congress to dance to our bidding, not to the bidding of Chrysler Corporation.

NICHOLAS ROSE:
I served in Vietnam with the 101st Airborne and I was wounded. I have been back since March 1968, and I am still trying to catch up on about ten years, between my nineteenth birthday and my twenty-ninth (I am now thirty-five). Many of us suffer that. We thought that the VA would continue helping us in our readjustment. It is too late to punish anyone. I have been carrying a guilt trip around with me.

AN AIR FORCE VET (THREE TOURS ON PARA-RESCUE):
For over ten years, I buried Vietnam in my closet. I threw everything away; I did not want to talk to my family, to my friends, to anyone. I woke up at night screaming; I woke up at night tearing my room apart; I woke up at night living all the missions we flew and all the bodies we brought out and all the people we could not get to in time. I had the reality about a year ago of waking up one night and finding myself in the hallway with a hole punched in the wall again and my thirteen-year-old son asking "Daddy what is wrong? You scared me." That scared the crap out of me. I began to go to the veterans' outreach center. I have received more help from my brothers sitting in a group than I have received from anybody. I do not want Vietnam left out of my memory; it is something that has to stay there. We cannot forget it, and the American people should not forget it.

AN ARMY VET:

I look at my life as a pre-Vietnam, a Vietnam, and a post-Vietnam one. When I was serving over there, with the 173rd Airborne Brigade, in 1969, they told us that there was an NVA battalion in a village; and they put us on line and told us to charge across a rice paddy. (Anyone who has been there knows you do not charge across rice paddies. You walk very slowly and very ploddingly.) A mute testimony to the hold they had over us is that we got in line—like the fools we were—and moved out, fully expecting to be opened up on within the next thirty seconds. I still cannot believe I did that—when I fully believed I would be killed in the next minute. It was a dud. There were only a few villagers and some domesticated animals. Word came through that the lead platoon had run into something as we filed through the village. A woman was screaming and cursing at us as we filed through. I do not know for sure what she was saying. It was not complimentary. Why is she yelling at me? I come ten thousand miles, march in the rain, monsoons, tropical sun, rice paddies, rivers, hip-deep in slime, tripping over vines, falling over dikes, being bitten by uncounted species of bugs, carrying unknown sicknesses, always tired, getting diarrhea, being fucked with by the lifers, living on crap I wouldn't have given a dog I hated, getting shot at, ambushed, booby-trapped, hand-grenaded, my friends getting fucked up to save her sorry fucking ass—and she is going to stand there and spit and curse at me? A voice in the back of my head started speaking softly, very softly, because there was a lot of misguided patriotism in the way. Misguided patriotism makes it hard for sensible thoughts to linger for any amount of time. It was saying, "Hey, man, this woman don't care how noble you are for coming all this way to save her from her neighbors; all she knows is that you or someone just like you just set her house on fire. You may call it a hooch and laugh because it doesn't have a door, but it is her house and it has just been torched, for whatever noble reasons. That's why this woman is cursing you and all your ancestors. Because you, and not her evil neighbor, just Zippoed her home and destroyed all the things valuable in her life. As far as having no door goes, she is so far ahead of you, you will probably never know. She has a society that does not need a door, let alone a series of locks on the door, as opposed to the noble society you come from. That's right, asshole, you thought you were so civilized; you thought you were going to do so much for these poor, ignorant savages. Maybe in a thousand years, if your society lasts that long, it will have evolved to the point where it can live without the fear that causes people to put locks on doors. And then after another thousand years, it will get to the point where even the doors won't be necessary. Think about that for a while, shitbird." I did think about that, and two months later, during my seventh month of duty upcountry, I told them to shove it; they would have to win the war without me. I didn't care what they did; I was not going out there anymore. Burning people's houses down to save them from Communism does not make any sense.

PHIL CUSHMAN (EX-MARINE):
Vets have been stripped of their due process constitutional rights for the rest of their lives concerning any injuries they sustained defending their country. There is no recourse from VA decisions. Under Section 211a of Title 38 of U.S. Codes, every court in America is closed to veterans. Under Section 3404c of Title 38 USC, a veteran can pay an attorney no more than ten dollars for total services rendered. We carefully protect the rights of those who violate the rights of society, but the people who get injured defending those rights are stripped of them.

ROBERT VAN CARIN:
This country has made a mistake: it has confused the war with the warrior. America, through that war experience, became Vietnam veterans. It was an individual experience; everyone had his own war over there. We all had that commonality of being in combat.

HAYDEN FISHER:
For the first time, we are people who fought on the American side of a war that was lost. And because of that, because of the beating we were taking and the length of the war, we were forced to look at what we were doing over there, forced to think about what we were undergoing and carrying out against other people. We have been portrayed as crazies, lunatics, hijackers, rapists, muggers, and what have you, because they do not want us to talk to others about

those experiences. They saw what happened when we did—when many of us came back and joined the antiwar movement and when we had the Winter Soldier investigation[1] that revealed our role as pawns in that war. It was not just that we got shot up, but what we had done to other people. They saw what happened when we threw our medals back. They were afraid of that, and they wanted to bury it. Now, some forces want to talk about Vietnam. They want to get back into another Vietnam, and so they have to reverse what people have talked about and what people have learned.

JUDY MILLS TABER—representing the POW's and MIA's still unaccounted for:
There are 2,494 men who still remain unaccounted for in Southeast Asia.[2]

A VET:
No monument, no memorial, no national healing or apology, with self-righteous pleas for unity, can dissipate my anger. Nor do I want it to. You say that I am too emotional, subjective, personal, but so is death, humiliation, and Agent Orange. And for most, the war did not end when the credits came up on the screen. Yes, I will go to the wall to read the names of hundreds of friends and cry for my brothers and sisters of America who died in Vietnam; yes, I will go to the wall thinking fearfully and frightfully of the day in Germany, in 1967, when I refused orders for Vietnam; yes, I will go to the wall regurgitating all our dreams and drugs; yes, I will go to the wall looking for the day when death can ensure that there will be peace and no more war.

BOBBY SANCHEZ:
After several years as a vet counselor and of visiting the families of vets, I realize that America is suffering from a specific form of post-traumatic stress. Whether people were pro- or antiwar, they experi-

---

1. See Vietnam Veterans Against the War, *The Winter Soldier Investigation: An Inquiry into American War Crimes* (Boston, Beacon Press, 1972).

2. According to a newspaper story by Tyler Marshall, 2,452 Americans are officially listed as Missing In Action. That represents 4 percent of those killed in action, as compared to an MIA rate of 20 percent in World War II and Korea. Los Angeles *Times,* Section I (March 29, 1983), p. 1.

enced the guilt of our involvement there. Those who were prowar, in light of the evidence we now have, stop and reflect on their behavior then, and feel they have been manipulated, and abused, and mismanaged. Those who were antiwar feel some guilt over whether their participation in demonstrations was responsible for deaths in Vietnam, for the downfall of Vietnam. All these feelings are beginning to surface in these individuals. The vets are willing to talk about Vietnam; are you? Are you ready to admit the mistakes that were made, and, upon admitting them, are you ready to take remedial action to rectify those mistakes? If not, there may be another war, and will soldiers then be willing to put their asses on the line and risk the kind of treatment we have received?

RICK BERG:
We are talking to ourselves again. Veterans are put on display to be looked at. We stand up here and tell stories. They hurt. They are not going to keep people from going to war. If the war had been reported, we wouldn't have these lines of people waiting to talk. The lessons I learned in 'Nam I could have learned in this room. We know we were had. We know which children will be had again. We have inherited something from the antiwar movement; something from our enemies, who were in some sense our friends. They fought for the exploited, and we came home and found out that we were the exploited. It is a strange thing to recognize that you are killing your friend. They won the war; we lost the war. Good. America needed to be kicked in the nuts.

A VET:
The media lacked the ability to take its own eyes, the eyes of the investigator, the eyes of the reporter, and look at itself. I am ashamed. Vietnam set me free, and today I am even freer. I am free of my illusions about this country and my illusions about the press. We have a lot to contribute to this country. We have the truth of frustration. We can no longer go to the press and ask them to speak for us. We stand naked before this country, and no one can clothe us but ourselves. We take responsibility for what we have done; this country must also take responsibility.

CONCLUSION

Peter Marin

Vets are in an ambiguous situation—they were the agents and the victims of a particular kind of violence. That is the source of a pain that almost no one else can understand. It is necessary for the vets to speak about that pain, and for that pain, because no one else has experienced it. And without their speaking, no one else will understand it. I do not want the vets to forget their pain, but there are certain kinds of suffering that, although it closes you off from a world that seems to be causing that suffering, ought to be able, also, to join you to other persons who have suffered pain from the same source.

The vets feel that without a particular kind of dialogue or acceptance they cannot become whole. That may or may not be true. But the people from whom they expect this dialogue have their limits. Most vets will not be able to move on from the place where they are stuck unless they understand that the ones from whom they want dialogue are no better, no more whole, than veterans are at this moment. They are no more capable of the dialogue or the response than vets were at a particular point. You are not going to get this by demanding it; you will have to get it some other way; and I do not know what that way is. You are going to have to get it by teaching the others how to do it.

•THE VIETNAMESE•

Editor's Note

Saddest of all the stories are those of the Vietnamese themselves. America, they said, lost a war. We lost our country.

Their low-pitched voices hardly carry beyond the microphones, but their tales are tragic. Why did America come to Vietnam if it was not going to abide by its commitments to its small ally? What was its purpose in Vietnam? Was it really to bring freedom and democracy to Southeast Asia?

These were not only the voices of supporters of the final government of President Thieu. These were the voices of opponents of the Thieu government, some of whom had stayed behind because they believed in reunification and conciliation. But when the last Hueys flew off from the U.S. Embassy in Saigon, it was as though Vietnam had been erased from the American map. It was left to sink back into the ruins of the defoliated land, the hatred and passions of the terrible war, the futile machinations of an inefficient and sometimes indifferent Communist regime.

Saddest of all was the message of the boat people. No one, they said, had ever left Vietnam before. Not in the proud history of Vietnam. Not in the two thousand years of struggle against China, no matter how savage the defeat. Not in the great famine of 1945 when so many died in the North, a famine intensified by the war against the French. The northerners did not even leave the North and come South where there was food. Two million starved.

Now, and only now, were people leaving Vietnam—anyone who could get out by boat or slip away in any manner. And, as Ngo Vinh Long points out, even this was not understood, because from the beginning Americans had not bothered to understand or study Vietnam and its culture. They did not know the people—not those they thought they were helping, not those whom they were fighting. They did not know the deep roots of Ho Chi Minh's Communist movement. They did not realize that, for practical purposes, the Communists had already by the late 1930's won the country, both North and South, won it by superior political ability, organizing strength, and dedication to the cause of Vietnamese independence and nationalism.

Ngo Vinh Long recalled that, in 1983, both Richard Nixon and Henry Kissinger said that the United States should have won the war in Vietnam. This, he believed, showed that even ten years after the Paris truce, neither Kissinger nor Nixon had yet begun to understand the dynamics of the Vietnamese situation which had, from the beginning, precluded an American victory or a victory for an American-supported or directed Saigon regime.

The whole of Vietnam, in the opinion of the American specialist in Indochina, Joseph Buttinger, had become Communist by 1945.

Echoing through the discussion were the voices of the Vietnamese refugees themselves asking in a thousand ways: Why? Why? Why?

———————————————

THE WAR THAT DESTROYED MY HOMELAND

Michael Huynh

Frankly, I have a dilemma in reconsidering the war in Vietnam. As a resident of the United States, I was able to see the war from a U.S. perspective, and that perspective is what causes my dilemma. As a resident of this country in the early seventies, I was an observer of the final stages of the war as seen by the American people. As has so often been reported, the evening news presented a view of the war that both horrified and humiliated the American people.

The view which centered on the activities of the Army of the Republic of Vietnam (ARVN), the American forces, and the South Vietnamese people emphasized the tragedy of war—death and injury. Like clockwork, each evening the American people saw the bodies of soldiers, both American and ARVN; civilians were given the count as to what the grand total of dead was for that day. Additional comments and editorial views most often described the lack of morale, fighting spirit, and popular support for the Vietnam war in both Vietnam and the U.S. Very little attention was directed at the state of affairs in, or excesses of, North Vietnam in the war.

For me, this was a view that did not reflect my experience, understanding, or belief of Vietnam and the war. As an observer, I realized that my country was being physically portrayed, but not my home. It was a view which did not accurately or adequately represent my land, my home, my culture, my history, and my people. In stating this, I am not saying that these things did not happen. I am simply saying that this view did not reflect an appreciation of the reality of Vietnam as the Vietnamese people saw it. It was as if Americans were looking at the war through another, more carefully filtered, pair of glasses. The Vietnamese, on the one hand, saw the war in terms of its historic antecedents, how it affected the fabric of the society, how it uprooted and displaced the people, and the role the U.S. played in its outcome. All of Vietnam witnessed the war firsthand. Most of the people of the U.S. witnessed it in their living rooms; they realized their relatives or friends were in it, but did not understand why. The land and the people were foreign. It was as if Vietnam got the U.S. into the war.

Two examples. For the American people, as well as for the press, involvement in the war was seen from the outset as a questionable activity, and later as an outright mistake. The mounting criticisms within the United States regarding the war, the reported problems in successfully carrying out campaigns, and the ever-mounting death toll became so great that it became impossible for the U.S. to continue. During the same period, the Vietnamese people saw the U.S. response as a lack of commitment to fight for freedom in Vietnam. In a war in which two superpowers are waging an ideological conflict within the borders of a small country, the commitment of each superpower must remain resolute for the people who are to carry on the conflict to remain committed. Over time, because of political upheavals in this country, the Vietnamese first detected concern, and then saw a genuine lack of support for the war among the American people. Whether real or imagined, this lack of resolute support for the war affected our ability to continue fighting it.

Likewise, as the U.S. entered the war, it brought a perspective which emphasized technical superiority without understanding the conditions under which a war should be fought. From your vantage, there were a host of technical innovations that could be introduced in this war. From the Vietnamese point of view, the war should have been fought in a more traditional manner. The relative merits of these different methods of carrying forward the fight involved uncertainties and possible excesses. It seemed to the Vietnamese people as if the war was being fought on a day-to-day basis, with the major variable being the use of different strategies. It was as if, in treating a sick person, the doctor kept experimenting with drugs—ultimately disabling the patient permanently, rather than diagnosing the illness in the first place. The longer we fought the war, the more the U.S. introduced new technical devices, without understanding the nature and causes of the war.

Regardless of the relative merits of the U.S. role, the ultimate impact was that more than a million people were forced out of Vietnam at the end of the war. These people fled from fear of being persecuted for the rest of their lives. The consequences were that the people had to leave their country. *Never had this happened before.* Even during the famine of 1945, when more than two million people died from lack of food, we did not leave our country. The results of this war displaced a whole population. We are here now because of the involvement of the U.S. Rightly or wrongly, we chose to support and be friends of the United States. Promises and commitments were made. We are here now as refugees who believe in freedom. However, the most recently arrived refugees, having had to spend some years incarcerated in reeducation camps, find themselves arriving in an atmosphere in this country which at best ignores them or at worst describes them as being too dependent upon welfare and other forms of support.

There is insufficient thought about how these people, who have been displaced from their land by force, placed in prison and kept in resettlement camps which forced them to become dependent, might be affected. We need to understand that the great number of Southeast Asian refugees seeking asylum in the U.S. now are a result of the U.S. involvement in Vietnam, Cambodia, and Laos. Without bearing witness to these homeless people, we deny the role the U.S. played in much the same way the U.S. failed to understand the Vietnam war. Most important, Americans deny to these people the chance to live their lives out in a free country, a society that was promised to them by the U.S. at the outset and during the war. It is no wonder that the Vietnamese now residing in this country believe America came to Vietnam to remake our country in its image without trying to understand who and what we were, are, and hoped to be. Consequently, it is not inappropriate for us to believe that the U.S. should help us resettle in the U.S., while keeping our hearts in Vietnam in the hopes of one day returning.

PROS AND CONS OF THE U.S. INTERVENTION
A VIETNAMESE VIEWPOINT

Bui Diem

In perspective, for the Americans the war in Vietnam was perhaps only a bad, unhappy chapter in their history. The same cannot be said, unfortunately, for the Vietnamese. The war for them was a tragedy of indescribable proportions, involving hundreds of thousands of people who lost their country, families, and homes. Eight years after the fall of Saigon, thousands of people continue trying to get out at the risk of their lives, in search of freedom and social justice.

As a Vietnamese, I do not pretend to talk in terms of American interests and pass judgment on whether it was right for the Americans to intervene in Vietnam. I do, nevertheless, have some observations to make regarding how the Vietnamese perceived the U.S. intervention—and the effects of the intervention on the conduct and outcome of the war.

In general terms, it can be said that in the early fifties and sixties, not many Vietnamese understood either U.S. policies or U.S. politics. The few things they knew about the U.S. were the Marshall Plan in Europe, the strong anti-Communist, moralistic stand of John Foster Dulles, or the idealistic Inaugural address of John F. Kennedy. For them, the U.S. was the natural leader of the "Free World," and the U.S. intervention in Vietnam was only the continuation of the U.S. intervention in Korea. The "right" or "wrong" question did not come up in their minds. If there were concerns about the effects that the presence of foreign troops might cause, especially in a war with an enemy who claimed to fight against foreigners for the independence of the country, the concerns were quickly put aside by several arguments: there is a ferocious war to be waged; there is no substitute for victory; the U.S. is not a colonialist power; and, above all, the most powerful nation on earth cannot be defeated.

In addition to this, the Vietnamese knew very little, or had misconceptions, about the U.S. political process, the check-and-balance system, the influence of the news media, and the importance of public opinion. There was a "blind trust" in the U.S. which, in many instances, lasted until the final days of the war.

This was obviously unjustified, and the Vietnamese paid an extremely high cost for their blunder. But, in retrospect, if we turn back the clock to the early sixties, who, at that time, even among the Americans, could have doubted the determination of the mighty U.S.? The Vietnamese did not have time to ponder the pros and cons of the U.S. intervention. In a struggle for life, who could resist help from a rich and powerful country? They were nevertheless deeply disappointed by the way the help was terminated. In this regard, it is worthwhile quoting a typical Vietnamese reaction to the negative decision of the U.S. Congress in 1974 concerning military and economic aid to South Vietnam.

A containment policy or help to South Vietnam, you can call it what you want, but the U.S. somehow forced its way into South Vietnam by sending hundreds of thousand of troops into the country. Whether it was good or bad, a big nation and world power like the U.S should bear the consequences of its decision and accept its moral obligation to help the South Vietnamese out of a situation that the presence of U.S troops helped to create. The Americans should not simply call it quits and go home, saying that U.S. intervention was a wrong decision.

Responsible Vietnamese strongly believed that if a non-Communist South Vietnam was to survive and emerge as a viable nation, the prime responsibility was on the Vietnamese—and that, consequently, whether the U.S. involvement was right or wrong, it was up to them to make the best of it. They failed to develop a strategy required by the international circumstances, the rapidly changing mood of the U.S. public, diminishing U.S. aid and support, and the new situation created by the Paris Agreement in 1973. All this was their mistake, but the U.S. intervention through the presence of half a million men in Vietnam affected, in many decisive ways, the development of the situation. The Americans acted in the mid-sixties as if the war in Vietnam were strictly an American affair. Partly, perhaps, because they were convinced they could finish the war in a short time, and partly because they are impatient by nature, they tried to do everything by themselves. They did not realize that, in the process, they spoiled the Vietnamese and made them too dependent on American aid. In effect, the Vietnamese acquired, during the period of heavy U.S. involvement, the bad habit of relying on American firepower, and had the false expectation that their allies would stay until victory.

The Americans neglected to train and equip the Vietnamese for a job which should have been theirs: the defense of their country. Not to win the war was so unthinkable a proposition that training was not even considered, or at least not so seriously considered as it should have been.

In the eyes of the Vietnamese, the Americans made the war too expensive. It was a kind of "affluent war" never seen before or even thought of by the Vietnamese. They opened their eyes in bewilderment when they looked at the helicopters bringing hot food to the fighting men. They saw the thousands of gadgets piled up in huge PXs for the use of the GIs, the hundreds of planes flying back and forth across the Pacific for the transport of U.S troops and supplies. They witnessed the more-than-generous use of bombs and amunition; and the hours and hours of bombing and strafing by planes and artillery barrages, triggered in many instances by mere sniper fire. They shook their heads in despair when they saw that the critics of the war put all these billions on the shoulders of the Vietnamese. During the difficult days of 1974, when their request for additional military aid was rejected by the U.S. Congress, they said that if the Americans could only have saved part of the cost of just a few weeks of the "affluent war" for some sort of long-range aid to South Vietnam, the outcome of the war could have been different.

The Vietnamese were more critical of the Americans in terms

of overall military strategy against the Communists. They thought that, in dealing with an enemy who waged an unlimited and total war, the Americans were basically wrong in their concept of "limited war" and "gradual pressures." In fact, the resourcefulness of the Communists was underestimated. The "limited war" concept simply gave them shelter, time for healing their wounds and preparing for other offensives.

These observations represent only a kind of token reaction from the Vietnamese, reflecting their view on some aspects of the war. There is one general observation that can be made: the Vietnamese fully realize the share of responsibilities they have to bear in the loss of their country; they did not blame the Americans for helping them, but they disagreed with the way the Americans intervened and especially with the way the Americans withdrew. The disagreement was almost total, whether it was in military, political, or diplomatic terms. The Vietnamese were of the opinion (and still stick to this opinion, especially now with the eyewitness reports coming from the boat people) that the defeat of South Vietnam was avoidable, and that the Communists won by default.

Critics of the war used to say that South Vietnam had no chance at all: the regime was corrupt, the political and religious factions were fragmented, and there was no cohesion. All these assertions are nonsense for those who understand the history of Vietnam and the nature of the war. When it was started in the mid-forties, the war was against the French and for the independence of the country. Later on, in 1954, the Geneva Agreement created a new dimension to the conflict, and it became a war for political control of Vietnam between Communists and non-Communists, a war between two different ways of life or, in legal terms, between the Democratic Republic of Vietnam (North Vietnam) and the Republic of Vietnam (South Vietnam)—two sovereign states duly recognized by the nations of the world. South Vietnam was a pluralistic society, with all the shortcomings and weaknesses of such a society common to all the underdeveloped nations arriving at independence after the Second World War. It was not a paradise on earth, but it was not hell, either. Obviously, the various governments in power in South Vietnam from 1954 to 1975 did not succeed in making life much better for the Vietnamese people, but certainly they did not make life worse, as the Communist regime is doing right now. Eight years after the war, can anyone point out any evidence of progress in South Vietnam?

It serves no purpose to defend the defunct regime of South Vietnam (and it is not the intention of this essay to do so). But for the memory of the hundreds of thousands of Vietnamese fighting men who died for the cause of a "free Vietnam," for the thousands of "boat people" who continue to risk their lives going abroad, and beyond that, for the memory of the more than fifty thousand Americans who accepted the supreme sacrifice in Vietnam, it is necessary to have a fresh review of the war in Vietnam and to try drawing some useful lessons from this tragedy which cost so much to the two countries.

FREEDOM AND THE VIETNAMESE

Doang Van Toai

From 1945, when I was born in a poor village in South Vietnam, until May 1978, all my life in Vietnam, I have never enjoyed peace. My family house was burned three times in the war against the French, and, in 1968, during the Tet offensive, my family house was again burned by American bombs. In 1975, when the Communists took over, my house was not burned, but they confiscated not only my house but the house of my brothers and my sisters and my parents.

I grew up in the countryside. My family and I suffered from the bombs of the French. My compatriots and I grew up with a hatred for foreign intervention. I hated also the Saigon rulers, men like General Thieu and Marshal Ky, former soldiers of the French colonial army. These were the men who helped the French destroy the Vietnamese resistance. They rose to power over the years by helping to commit these crimes against their people, and then became leaders themselves. America naively came to Vietnam and supported these men.

Like others of the opposition movement in Vietnam and in the United States, I was hypnotized by the political programs advocated by the National Liberation Front, which included the famous and correct policy of national reconciliation without reprisals, and a policy of non-alignment with and independence from the

Americans, the Russians, and the Chinese. That is why I refused to flee the country in April 1975. I decided to stay in Vietnam, under the illusion that I would help to rebuild the country. I was ready to sacrifice myself, my life, to accept the hard conditions, to cooperate with the new regime, if it would honor and keep the promise of no reprisals and carry out the reconciliation policy.

I think that many antiwar activists in this country shared my hopes of that period in 1975, when the Americans withdrew their troops from Vietnam. Many of us in that period, throughout the world, talked about how the Vietnamese people would no longer suffer repression or hunger, but would enjoy freedom and democracy. But, in fact, what happened to these hopes?

Under the domination of the Japanese, there were almost two million Vietnamese dying of hunger, but no one fled Vietnam. Under the Saigon governments during the war, hundreds of thousands of prisoners were arrested and jailed, but no one fled the country. Yet those who are pro-Hanoi or are hypnotized by the propaganda of Hanoi claim that the boat people are economic refugees. In the history of Vietnam, no one ever fled for economic refuge. We came to the U.S. not with the hope of sharing American or Western prosperity, not to share the riches of these countries, but to share the freedom of these countries. There were among the boat people not only the Thieu supporters, not only the killers of Saigon, but also the Vietcong, the former opposition leaders, and even the former justice minister of the Vietcong. You can imagine the situation of justice in a country if the justice minister of that country had to flee.

We all debate who is responsible for the situation in Vietnam now. Some claim it is America because American jets bombed there, because America came to Vietnam, but I ask all of you to separate the government from the people. I ask all of you to think about the fate and lives of fifteen million Vietnamese people, rather than the small group of leaders in the Hanoi Politburo. The Vietnamese in America, including myself, have many relatives in Vietnam. We do not oppose economic aid to Vietnam. But can we be guaranteed that that aid will reach our relatives? Or will the Hanoi government take it to support its troops in Cambodia and Laos? If the Hanoi leaders really love their own people, they should withdraw all troops from Laos and Cambodia; they should concentrate their efforts on their own country, to build Vietnam, to help the Vietnamese people.

When I lived in Vietnam under the Communist regime, they put me in jail because I refused to obey their orders. The Communist jailers crammed over 100 prisoners into one cell. Every night I watched many old men die; my friend died under my foot. At home, my mother was not admitted to a hospital because she had a son in jail. And my whole family was considered a reactionary family by the government.

At the Fifth Congress, in 1982, Le Duan, the secretary-general of the Vietnamese Communist party, insisted that "the Soviet-Vietnam relationship is a cornerstone of Vietnamese foreign policy," and asserted to all the party members that "we should teach the whole country, all party members, all the people, that not only in this decade, but in the following decades, the Soviet-Vietnam relationship would be unbreakable." Vietnam today is totally dependent upon the Soviet Union. Pictures of Soviet leaders were hung in public places, in schools, in offices, including pictures of Stalin.

To all of you who were antiwar and supported the Vietcong during the war years, the principles of independence, liberty, peace, and democracy must be defended not only in the non-Communist countries but also in the Communist ones. There is still a confused feeling among progressive people that they should necessarily support the Socialist regimes of the world. My compatriots and I learned, through suffering in our lives and witnessing the fate of our countrymen—and it is a lesson that must eventually move the conscience of the world, especially of the former antiwar activists—that progressives should always defend the victims, not the leaders or government officials.

THE WAR AND THE VIETNAMESE

Ngo Vinh Long

During the last ten days or so, many former American policymakers, reporters, and other old Vietnam hands have taken to the air waves to draw the lessons of the war for the American people. By and large, most of these people have claimed that the war could have been won or that South Vietnam could have been maintained if the United States had been more decisive in its efforts at different stages of the war and if enough American arms had been made available to the Saigon regime.

On January 27, for example, Howard K. Smith and his son, Charles Smith, appeared for almost an hour on ABC's *The Last Word,* saying that the United States should have invaded North Vietnam and gone into the other Indochinese countries very early on to destroy the North Vietnamese bases and infiltration routes to the South. Charles Smith said that to try to maintain South Vietnam without invading North Vietnam or striking at troops in the other countries of Southeast Asia was like trying to defend France during the Second World War without going directly into Germany and the surrounding countries. Howard K. Smith stressed that the United States should have gone all out—short of nuclear weapons, of course. On the same evening, Henry Kissinger and Richard Nixon appeared on ABC's *Nightline* and blamed Congress for having made it impossible for the United States to enforce the Paris Peace Agreement and for having made the conquest of South Vietnam inevitable by cutting aid to the Saigon regime. They both added that the loss of South Vietnam weakened the conduct of American foreign policy. Howard K. Smith spelled this out a little more clearly when he said that the real tragedy of the Vietnam War was that it had made the United States afraid of intervening in other countries.

These remarkable statements, ten years after the United States was forced to withdraw all its troops from Vietnam, do not suggest that these intelligent men have not learned anything from the Vietnam experience. Rather, they seem to indicate that there are significant Americans willing to risk continued recrimination at home in order to get certain segments of the American public to overcome the so-called Vietnam syndrome—so that the American imperial ideology can be rebuilt. But this is something that I will not go into here.

What I want to do, rather, is to show very briefly how total American disregard for Vietnamese history and culture, as well as for the welfare and aspirations of the Vietnamese people, made it impossible for the United States to maintain a "free and independent South Vietnam." (The word "disregard" is used advisedly here because, from the vantage of his ivy tower at Harvard University, this writer had discussed very extensively, with quite a number of influential intellectuals and key policymakers, Vietnamese history, society, culture, nationalism, and other such irrelevant things, and found that these people were not all that ignorant. The point was, one of these influential intellectuals explained to this writer, "Every society, like every human being, has a breaking point.") To be sure, the United States could have destroyed Vietnam many times over with its military machine—and totally wrecked Vietnamese society and culture with its economic and cultural penetration. But as this writer pointed out to Henry Kissinger in a long letter in the spring of 1967 (later published in the June 2, 1967, issue of the *Harvard Crimson*), anything short of this would result in an eventual victory for the Vietnamese revolutionaries.

There were many reasons for this inevitable outcome. First, there was the historical factor. By 1930, the Indochinese Communist Party (ICP) had emerged as the undisputed leader in the struggle against French colonial rule and exploitation. Massive

French pacification efforts and wholesale arrest of thousands of Communist cadres and sympathizers, as well as the terrible impact of the world depression, could dampen the revolutionary struggles for only three years, from 1932 to 1935. But beginning in 1936, when many of the cadres were released, thanks to the influence of the Popular Front in France, revolutionary struggles surged not only in the countryside but also in most towns and cities. At times, tens of thousands of peasants were brought into cities like Hanoi, Hue, and Saigon for massive demonstrations. Most interesting, by this time the population fully understood the importance of protecting their leaders and of listening to their analyses and instructions. As a result, we can now learn from existing French police reports and archival sources that there were very few political activities in the latter half of the 1930s that ever occurred without prior directives from the Indochinese Communist Party.[1]

In fact, it can be said that the Communist party had already captured Vietnamese nationalism and gained deep-rooted support among the Vietnamese people by the latter part of the 1930s. The Second World War and the Japanese occupation of Vietnam further strengthened the political position and prestige of the ICP. By the time of the August Revolution of 1945, Ho Chi Minh and his ICP followers had captured the whole nation, not because of any political vacuum created by the Japanese, but because of the tremendous political and organizational efforts of the ICP in rallying the Vietnamese people against colonialism and imperialism for about a decade and a half. Joseph Buttinger, a noted Vietnam historian and an early mentor of Ngo Dinh Diem of South Vietnam, was correct when he concluded some time ago that the policy pursued by the United States in Vietnam was doomed to fail because:

It was bad enough not to take into consideration that the Vietnamese people had struggled for over two thousand years against being absorbed by China, and had for almost one hundred years fought against colonial rule in order to regain independence. Much worse still was not to know, or knowingly to disregard, the fact that as a

---

1. For detail, see Ngo Vinh Long, "Peasant Revolutionary Struggles in Vietnam in the 1930s" (Ph.D. diss., Harvard University, 1978), 745 pp.

result of French colonial policies in Indochina, the whole of Viet-
nam had become Communist by the end of World War II.
I say the whole of Vietnam, not only the North—something
which, in spite of thirty years of French and American propaganda,
remains an undeniable historical fact.[2]

The deep-rooted popular support for the Vietnamese revolutionaries was again thoroughly tested during the 1946–54 period,
when France, Great Britain, and the United States thought that
they could destroy the Ho Chi Minh government with overwhelming military might. But the Vietnamese revolutionaries were only
to emerge from this so-called First Indochina War victorious, not
only at the famous battle of Dien Bien Phu, but also in almost
every village and town in the whole country. The anti-Communist
columnists Joseph and Stewart Alsop were forced to write, after a
trip through southern Vietnam, that, "In the area I visited, the
Communists have scored a whole series of political, organizational,
military—and one has to say it—moral triumphs. . . . What impressed me most, alas, was the moral fervor they had inspired
among the non-Communist cadres and the strong support they
had obtained from the peasantry."[3]

Because of the obvious reason that the Vietnamese revolutionaries already had overwhelming support among the population,
when the United States and Ngo Dinh Diem decided to install an
"independent South Vietnam," contrary to the stipulations of the
Geneva Agreement, there was not much they could do except to
carry out wholesale repression and "pacification" of the rural areas.
Massive forced relocations of the rural population under programs
such as the "qui-khu/qui-ap, agrovilles, and "strategic hamlets"
were carried out in the effort to control the population and to root
out the "Vietcong," or literally, "Vietnamese Communists." Resentment ran high among the population. Demonstrations, peti-
tions, and protests multiplied. Troops who came to demolish the
people's houses and to destroy their gardens met with fierce resis-

---

2. See Joseph Buttinger, *Vietnam: The Unforgettable Tragedy* (New York,
Horizon Press, 1977), p. 17.
3. "The Dike and the Tide," New York *Herald Tribune,* August 29, 1954,
Section II, p. 1.

tance. Women, children, and old folks disputed every inch of land with the Saigon soldiers and policemen. Repressive measures backfired, and resulted in the downfall of the Diem regime. After that, the United States realized that there was nothing it could do to prevent a Communist victory except introduce American troops into the southern part of Vietnam, bomb the northern part, and in effect, start the "Second Indochina War."

The second factor making an "independent South Vietnam" all but impossible to achieve was the American conduct in that war. An area with fewer than eighteen million people, South Vietnam had a total of more than ten million refugees by 1972.[4] Most of these people had been made refugees many times over through the American policy of "emptying the countryside." In order to "secure villages" and to root out "Vietcong infrastructures," bulldozers, bombers, and chemical defoliants were used. The villagers were forced into the "New Life" hamlets, the camps for refugees fleeing from Communism, and the towns and cities. To begin with, the tactics used in "pacification" ran counter to traditional Vietnamese customs and beliefs—the cultural and religious significance of the house, the land, the tomb. Then there were the horrible living conditions in the refugee camps, and the humiliation the refugees had to face there as well as in the "New Life" hamlets and the urban centers. The conditions of the refugees were so bad that Saigon newspapers felt compelled to run long articles on the misery. Even *Song,* a Saigon daily specifically created to justify the pacification program, had to say, on December 10, 1967, in a long article entitled "Looking at the Face of the Two Quang Provinces in War, Hunger, Misery, and Corruption":

This is a free area—free for depravity, corruption, irresponsibility, cowardice, obsequiousness, and loss of human dignity. What the devil is dignity when people sit there waiting to be thrown a few hundred piasters and allotted a few dozen kilos of rice a month? . . .

---

4. *Relief and Rehabilitation of War Victims in Indochina, Part IV: South Vietnam and Regional Problems,* hearing before the Subcommittee to Investigate Problems Connected with Refugees and Escapees of the Committee on the Judiciary, United States Senate, 93rd Congress (U.S. Government Printing Office, 1973), p. 8.

I believe that even if a certain Communist had in his pocket a few dozen "open-arms" passes, after witnessing the humiliation of life in a refugee camp, he would be so shocked that he would run away without a single look back.

From February 1 to February 2, 1972, *Tin Sang,* a Saigon daily published by a group of Catholic deputies in the Lower House, ran a long report entitled "Hunger is Rampant in the Central Region," which documented the causes of the hunger and described the heart-rending condition of the population. The article described the hunger facing a "resettlement area," an area people were herded into after their villages had been destroyed:

At present in the settlement area of Gia Dang, where the population of the villages of Trieu Phong and Hai Mang districts is now living, starvation is widespread and is threatening the lives of the entire population living in this resettlement area. In the coastal areas of Thua Thien province it is the same: people have to eat banana roots and leaves after days of having no rice and greens. Let us witness these scenes: mothers have no more milk for their babies to suck at; fathers stare helplessly at their children lying about in hunger. Will the fathers die before the children or will the children die before them? Death appears before them. . . . In early January, 1972, dozens of people left the resettlement area to beg for food. Since January 15, every morning about a hundred persons from villages such as Co Luy, Da Nghi, Phuong Lan and Ba Du go up to the district town of Hai Long or the town of Quang Tin to beg. . . . Getting up on an empty stomach each morning, they walk across the hills and dunes to beg for food. Unable to lift their feet anymore, they lie down here to die. Each day brings new corpses.

The situation in the urban areas was a little brighter, but not by much. According to the February 25, 1974, issue of *Hoa Binh,* a Saigon daily, Deputy Premier Phan Quang Dan who was in charge of refugee resettlement, among other things, disclosed that from three to four million persons were unemployed in the urban areas. The premier gave the number of orphans as 800,000 or more.

Too much, and not too little, aid from the United States to the Thieu regime, especially after the signing of the Paris Agreement, brought about the fall of Saigon. Propaganda to the contrary, in the two years after the signing of the Paris Agreement, Congress actually voted more economic and military aid to Saigon than ever before. Immediately before and after the signing of the Paris Agreement, the Nixon administration sent nearly $1 billion worth of military aid to Saigon. The United States supplied the Thieu regime with so many arms that, as Maj. Gen. Peter Olenchuk testified before the Senate Armed Services Committee on May 8, 1973, "We shortchanged ourselves within our overall inventories. We also shortchanged the reserve units in terms of prime assets. In certain instances, we also diverted equipment that would have gone to Europe."[5]

In fiscal year 1974, Congress gave Saigon $1 billion more in military aid. Saigon expended as much ammunition as it could—$700 million worth. This left a stockpile of at least $300 million, a violation of the Paris Agreement, which had stipulated that equipment only be replaced on a one-to-one basis.

For fiscal year 1975, Congress again authorized $1 billion in military aid, but appropriated $700 million—about what was actually spent in 1974.

The military aid granted Thieu encouraged him to sabotage the Paris Agreement by attacking areas controlled by the Provisional Revolutionary Government (PRG). A study by the U.S. Defense Attaché office in Saigon revealed that "the countryside ratio of the number of rounds fired by South Vietnamese forces (since the signing of the Paris Agreement) to that fired by the Communist forces was about 16 to 1. In military Regions II and III, where South Vietnamese commanders have consistently been the most aggressive, and where some U.S. officials said that random 'harassment and interdiction' fire against Communist-controlled areas was still common, the ratio was on the order of 50 to 1."[6]

---

5. *Fiscal Year 1974 Authorization for Military Procurement, Research and Development, Construction Authorization for Safeguard ABM, and Active Duty and Selected Reserve Strengths,* hearings before the Committee on Armed Services, United States Senate, 93rd Congress, Part 3. Authorizations (U.S. Government Printing Office, 1973), p. 1383.

6. *Vietnam: May 1974,* Staff Report Prepared for the Use of the Committee on Foreign Relations, United States Senate, August 5, 1974, p. 22.

Father Nguyen Quang Lam, an ultraconservative Catholic priest, wrote in the February 1975 issue of *Dai Dan Toc:*

Yesterday I wrote that whether there is an additional $300 million or $3,000 million in aid, South Vietnam will still not be able to avoid collapse. . . . In the afternoon a reader called me up and said that I should have put it more strongly. I must say that the more the aid, the quicker the collapse of South Vietnam. All I had to do was to take a look at our society.

Ever since the United States began to pour its troops and its dollars into South Vietnam, our society has been turned completely up-side-down. A prostitute is regarded with highest esteem because she can get lots of money from the American soldiers. Prostitutes are even ranked higher than priests and monks. . . . Come to think of it, the reader has a point there. The American dollars have really changed our way of thinking. People compete with each other to become prostitutes, that is to say, to get rich in the quickest and most exploitative manner.

Father Lam continued: "No wonder whenever our soldiers see the enemy they run for their lives, even though they might have a basement full of ammunition which they could presumably fire till kingdom comes."

It is clear that the American government's disregard for Vietnamese history and culture and its massive military, economic, and cultural penetration of Vietnam brought untold destruction to Vietnamese society and the consequent "loss of South Vietnam." President Jimmy Carter was quoted by the Los Angeles *Times* on March 25, 1977, as saying: "The destruction was mutual. We went to Vietnam without any desire to capture territory or impose American will on other people. I don't feel that we ought to apologize or castigate ourselves or to assume the status of culpability."[7] During my seven-month research trip to Vietnam in 1979 and 1980, many Vietnamese kept on reminding me of this remarkable statement. A professor at Hue University likened it to a rapist saying that his victims hurt him as much as he hurt them. Victims,

---

7. *Don Irwin,* "U.S. Owes No Debt to Hanoi, Carter Says," Los Angeles *Times* (March 5, 1977), p. 1.

he said, usually don't talk much about their suffering because they have to go on living. This writer hopes that, as Americans begin to assess the economic, political, psychological, and cultural impacts of the war on America, they will also begin to understand how much more that war hurt the Vietnamese. This is not to make Americans feel guilty so that they will castigate themselves or apologize to the Vietnamese. There is no need to do that. The damages have already been done. The hope here is that America will not inflict the same wounds elsewhere.

VOICES OF THE VIETNAMESE

Five speakers from the floor

A RESPONSE TO THE PANELS ON THE PRESS:

As photographers, do you always have to shoot and display pictures that are sensationalist—pictures of a Vietnamese colonel shooting a Communist captive in the head? Isn't war more than combat scenes, the gory details, the bloody, gruesome murders? Do you ever realize the anguish, the mental torture of a Vietnamese soldier who has to shoot his own brother? How many of you have ever considered the wife who has to wait nights on end for her husband to return and in the end see only his coffin? How many of you remember the statistics of the Vietnam soldiers who have died? What is the good of all these descriptive accounts of the war? What is the purpose? Were we in this war because of sensationalism, or because of the high ideals of some Americans who believed in bringing democracy and freedom to Vietnam? Somehow that has been lost sight of.

On behalf of the Vietnamese people here, I would like to thank the American vets, those who have died and those who believed that they fought in a just cause. Many of you here have contributed to the cause of peace, to the antiwar movement, which was all grandiose and idealistic. But face it, what have all those grandiose ideals brought to us today? What have we seen?

All the things in Vietnam you journalists reported before

1975, are you doing the same today? Or are you just sentimental-
ists who dwell on your achievement, such as the footage of showing a Vietnamese sergeant knifing his fellow countryman?[1] Is that
what you consider achievement? Is that what you consider accom-
plishment? Why don't you do the same kind of reporting today?
Those of you who still have an interest in Vietnam, why aren't you
doing the same thing for the Vietnamese people today? What are
you doing today? Are you really and truly looking at all the questions involved?

WHO ARE THE UNDERDOGS?

For too long the people of the United States have tried to
champion the cause of the underdog, without knowing who the
underdog was. The underdogs in Vietnam were not necessarily
those bombed by China or the United States. I am a product of
Vietnam, and the sad thing about it is the untenable position in
which I am today because I speak for the South Vietnamese—
actually, for all the Vietnamese people; they are the underdogs, not
Ho Chi Minh, not the politburo of Hanoi or any of that leadership.
And I am in a very bad position because I am not an apologist for
my former government in South Vietnam nor, for that matter, of
the United States' misgoverned, sometimes obfuscated policy
toward Vietnam. Nor am I bitter about U.S. involvement in Vietnam; I am only bitter about the misunderstanding, the lack of
education Americans have shown in coming into Vietnam.

The Vietnam War was not at any point a civil war. The
Vietnamese people wanted to drive out the French, or for that
matter, any form of domination of their soil. And they were united
in their desire to get rid of the colonialists. In that sense, they
rallied under the banner of the Vietminh, or as you would say, the
Communists. Actually, the Vietminh were just the offshoot of
many nationalists. If you want to find the roots of the war, you
have to look further than just the U.S. involvement; you have to
find the causes of the war. It is a fallacy and error to consider
Vietnam a civil war. It was never a civil war. It was a war waged by
Ho Chi Minh because he wanted to believe that the path that led
him to Communism was the path that could save Vietnam from

---

1. The subject of a CBS news report narrated by Don Webster.

French domination. In that sense, he waged a one-man war, bringing along with him many other Hanoi leaders who also believed that Communism was the way to salvation, to reunification. It is belaboring the point to condemn your government, to condemn the policy in which you shared. You should, instead, consider the point of view of other people, mainly the South Vietnamese and the Vietnamese.

UNITED BUDDHIST CHURCH OF VIETNAM:
The position of the United Buddhist Church was miserably misunderstood in Vietnam during the war. Its heartfelt cry for a Vietnam free of all foreign domination was misinterpreted by almost every government in South Vietnam during the war, and labeled Communist, pro-Communist, or neutralist. After the Communists took over South Vietnam in 1975, many of our leaders were imprisoned or murdered by them. They consider these people, who had been denounced by many as Communist or pro-Communist during the war, to be CIA agents. How awful it is to be neutral. How awful it is to be telling the people the truth of what happened in Vietnam.

Since the French took control of Vietnam in 1883, the Vietnamese people have constantly struggled to regain their independence and sovereignty. The objectives of their struggle have been, quite simply, national independence, social justice, peace, and freedom. The resistance movement started shortly after the French occupied Vietnam and has lasted until the present. It has been led by kings, mandarins, scholars, revolutionaries, religious leaders, and common people. This movement has been repeatedly betrayed, led astray by friends and foes alike.

First betrayal: Two of our leaders went to Japan in 1905 and 1906 to found The Association for the Modernization of Vietnam. They smuggled hundreds of young Vietnamese into Japan to be trained for clandestine organization and political propaganda. They were, however, expelled from Japan when that country received an economic development loan from France.

Second betrayal: During the Second World War, the Chinese, as well as the Americans, who needed intelligence about the Japanese in Vietnam, made Ho Chi Minh head of the Vietnam Independence League, even though, at that time, Ho Chi Minh was known as a Communist leader. The Vietnamese nationalist leaders who helped the Allies by fighting against the Japanese were abandoned by the Allies.

Third betrayal: Despite the sacrifices made by the Vietnamese on behalf of the Allies in their fight against Germany in Europe and against Japan in Asia, they were rewarded by the Potsdam Conference's confirmation of the French claim to Indochina.

Fourth betrayal. Ho Chi Minh was given financial aid and weapons by the United States OSS. He entered Vietnam in October 1944, and when the Japanese surrendered in August 1945, Emperor Bao Dai abdicated in favor of the government set up in Hanoi under Ho Chi Minh, in order to avoid bloodshed and suffering for the Vietnamese people. The French reconquest of Vietnam started in September 1945, and drove Communists and non-Communists alike into armed struggle. Ho Chi Minh, to obtain public support, deceived the public as to his true identity, by dissolving the Communist party which he had founded in May 1930. Realizing that his leadership might be challenged, due to pressure from the Chinese, Ho Chi Minh reached an agreement with the French in March 1946, which stipulated that in return for permission to station troops in Vietnam, France would recognize the Vietminh government and consider Vietnam a free state in the French Union. When the nationalists denounced the March agreement as a surrender to the French, Ho Chi Minh cooperated with the French in suppressing the nationalists and all the nationalist movements.

[Time limitation prevented a reading of betrayals five through eight.]

Ninth betrayal: Since 1883, the Vietnamese nationalists fighting for independence, peace, and democracy have been misunderstood, abandoned, and betrayed, while the Communists have been staunchly supported by friends and foes alike. Many well-meaning people in the United States and Europe want to forget Vietnam, partly because of the United States' military involvement, and partly because of guilt, shame, and frustration. They do not wish to influence the current situation in Vietnam. The Communists have a legacy, whether in Russia, Eastern Europe, Asia, or Africa, of exploiting national liberation as a cover, and have succeeded in manipulating public opinion in their favor. Dien Bien Phu and Tet were not military victories, but political triumphs for the Hanoi government. The skillful propaganda used to justify the Cambodian invasion and the imprisonment of hundreds of thousands of Vietnamese is readily accepted by many people.

Can we make use of the Vietnamese experience in our dealings with various movements of national independence in various parts of the world? Can a free national-independence movement get a sympathetic ear among well-meaning people and organizations, or will it be buried under misunderstanding, frustration, and guilt?

A VIETNAMESE REFUGEE:

Millions of refugees have fled South Vietnam. Those who have left by boat, especially, have risked their lives and left behind everything, their families and their nation, to get to the free world. If you think that they have come over here for any other reason than the lack of human rights in Vietnam now, let me point out that at the end of World War II, when there was a shortage of food supplies in North Vietnam, millions died without trying to flee North Vietnam, even to the South, where the food supply was plentiful. They did not leave because the family tie was so strong. But now, under the Communist regime, they have risked everything to get out. They have even abandoned family ties, because of the repressive government that respects no human beings. They did not leave to get a better life in another country. The lack of human rights in Vietnam is the cause of the refugee movement to the free world. It is not true to say that any government that emerged in Vietnam after the war would have been the same.

A VIETNAMESE REFUGEE:

What has happened after the war has justified the American troop involvement in Vietnam, because the troops did help our people defend our freedom—not successfully, but they did try. The American presence has been justified by the atrocities that have driven hundreds of thousands to the sea. The new government is not creating economic zones [return to the villages] but new economic zones, in remote jungles. Instead of using the resources to feed the people, they are using them to invade Laos and Cambodia. Normalization of relations should not occur with a tyrannical regime.

•VIETNAM•

Editor's Note

Of the fate of Vietnam since the war, sharply divergent images have emerged. To the specialist Douglas Pike, a strong supporter of the Vietnam War, what has emerged has demonstrated the fecklessness, the lack of ability, the rigid doctrinaire nature of Hanoi's leadership, unable to cope with the economic, political, and diplomatic problems which have arisen.

In his view the disarray in Hanoi is so profound that it may even lead to the disintegration of the government and possibly its system.

Everywhere, insoluble problems abound—Cambodia, the conflict with China, an economy which is slowly sinking into the Mekong, rising intolerances of the Soviet Union, a generational struggle between old cadres of the politburo and Young Turks.

The cruelty of the Vietnamese in herding opponents into "reeducation" camps, the desperation of the "boat people" risking their all for a chance to leave the country he interprets—as do others—as justification for the American intervention in Vietnam. Here, he believes, is proof in abundance of the inherent evil of the Communist regime in Hanoi.

But to others, many of Vietnam's problems seem stamped "Made in America"—the product of postwar American hostility, measures designed to harass and cripple Hanoi if possible, and to bring down the regime. In this category they place the economic embargoes, the refusal of the United States to provide aid of any kind, the diplomatic isolation, the continuing hostility over the MIA issue.

Along with these, to be certain, has been the sharp breach in relations with China, the open war and border conflicts between Beijing and Hanoi centering over the Cambodian question.

Not all of the issues are presented in these papers. There is no discussion, for example, of the remarkable provisions which Nixon and Kissinger placed in the Paris protocols for the provision of hundreds of millions of dollars of American aid—a carefully crafted bridge which both Americans and Vietnamese hoped would lead to the emergence of the U.S. as the principal supporting power for the postwar Vietnamese regime. These wise provisos, to be certain, sank into the mire of Watergate with its weakening effect on Nixon's ability to persuade a sullen Congress that it was in American interests to help a former foe and win a friend in Southeast Asia (as we had done with Japan in East Asia).

Nor does even William Shawcross explore the effects of American policy in Cambodia, the rise of Pol Pot, and the whole catastrophe which ultimately opened up in that sad land.

THE CONSEQUENCES OF THE WAR FOR INDOCHINA

William Shawcross

The consequences of the war for Indochina were appalling. The destruction of the infrastructure and the society were atrocious, and any government that would have taken over in 1975 would have faced unbelievable problems. To give you just one banal or anodyne statistic, but an important one: in 1976, Vietnam was planting less rice than it had in 1940. So much of the cultivated area had been lost during the war; so many of the farmers had fled as refugees to the cities.

I do not have any answers or any prescriptions for what has happened, or any final analysis; and I do not have any prescriptions for what ought to happen. I would just like to raise some questions. Vietnam today is one of the poorest countries in the world. It has an income of $160 a head per annum. It has been cut off since the war from most of the economic aid that went in during the war—to the North from China, and to the South from America. The poverty of Vietnam and Cambodia is awful and unbelievable. But which of us would have predicted that poor Vietnam, this impoverished country, would have the third-largest army in the world and be spending about forty-seven percent of its GNP on defense? (Even Caspar Weinberger had no dreams of that.) Who would have expected, back in 1975, that today Vietnam would have two hundred thousand troops occupying Cambodia and another forty thousand in Laos? Who would have expected China and Vietnam, once described as "lips and teeth" because they were so close, to be at war today?

Perhaps we could have foreseen that the United States would have turned its back bitterly on Vietnam, a tragedy in my view. But who could have foreseen the agonizing irony of the Chinese leader Deng Xiaoping cavorting around Texas in a stagecoach, wearing a ten-gallon hat, denouncing Vietnam, and then going home and invading Vietnam with at least the tacit support of the United States? That same China, whose advance, we were told, the United States was in Vietnam to prevent.

Did we who were in Vietnam, and opposed the U.S. effort there, expect the instant eclipse of the Provisional Revolutionary Government and the imposition of rule by the North? I didn't. Did we anticipate reconciliation, as happened in Hungary after the revolution? That is what I hoped for. Did we foresee a whole chain of reeducation camps in which tens of thousands of people would be incarcerated without trial for indefinite periods? Did we expect the liberators to be condemned a few years later by Amnesty International as violators of human rights? Did we expect hundreds of thousands of boat people to take to the sea and to leave the ancestral lands that they valued so highly?

By 1974, there were signs of a terror in Cambodia. They were reported by journalists in Phnom Penh, but we did not wish to imagine that it could really happen. Martin Wollcott, an English journalist who was there, described afterward, with grief and anguish, how journalists would sit in the Hotel Phnom in the last days of the war singing a little ditty to the tune of "She Was Poor but She Was Honest." It went like this: "Will there be a dreadful bloodbath when the Khmer Rouge come to town? Oh, aye, there will be a dreadful bloodbath when the Khmer Rouge come to town."

And there was. The evidence was there, but we did not wish to consider the implications of it. It was too confusing. Too frightful. And why, when the bloodbath began—and it began very quickly—did it take us so long to realize what was going on and still longer to do anything, after 1975, to mobilize against it?

Who would have thought that the Khmer Rouge, after they had been overthrown by their former ally, Vietnam, in 1979, would still have their claim to the Cambodian seat in the United Nations supported by a majority of the world's countries? (And when does a liberation become an occupation?) Who would have thought that today, in 1983, the majority of the world, not just the United States and China, not just Vietnam's ancient and old enemies, but also many, many of her former supporters throughout the world would be arrayed against her and against her continuing occupation of Cambodia? Who would have thought that this very week (February 6), Vietnam would be shelling a camp on the Thai-Cambodia border in which there are military troops of the anti-Communist group resisting Vietnam, and in which there are also thirty thousand refugees, pawns of both sides. The troops are there because the Thai authorities want the troops to be hidden among the civilians; and the refugees are once again the victims.

Who would have thought about these things? I did not think about them back in 1975. Did any of us consider that these things were likely to come to pass? They did come to pass. They are not the only things that have happened to Indochina since 1975. They are not the only questions we might raise and reconsider. I wonder whether somehow, back at that stage, we clung too tenaciously to the consolation and the hope of progress—striving, in the words of Percy Bysshe Shelley, "till hope creates from its own wreck the thing it contemplates." That hope, I think, has been dashed, and now we must reconsider how that hope can be rebuilt.

VIETNAM TODAY
THE OFFICIAL VIEW

Madame Nguyen Ngoc Dung

Ten years have elapsed since the Paris Agreement was signed and U.S. troops were withdrawn from South Vietnam. Yet the Vietnamese people are still unable to have a real peace; a war of attrition in all things is being waged against it. After 1975, the Vietnamese people should have enjoyed real peace so as to begin healing the wounds of war, developing the economy, and rebuilding the country. But an independent and reunified Vietnam has become a major obstacle to the Beijing authorities' ambition of expanding into Southeast Asia. Because of this they have pursued their historic policy against Vietnam; they have attempted to turn Kampuchea into a military base, encircling Vietnam with a pincer movement. They used the Pol Pot clique to provoke armed conflict in the Vietnam-Kampuchea border in 1975 and to extend that conflict into a border war in 1977. And in 1979, China unleashed a border war involving six hundred Chinese troops against Vietnam. It is regrettable that Beijing's reactionary policy has been pursued with Washington's complicity and backing. Consequently, relations between the United States and Vietnam, which once reached near-normalization, have deteriorated seriously.

Beijing's threat to "teach Vietnam a lesson" and its policies of blockade and sanction were closely combined with Washington's efforts to apply political, economic, and military pressure. If in the past the United States attacked Vietnam under the pretext of containing Chinese Communism, then nowadays China's pretext for doing so is to prevent Soviet hegemony. This is an obsolete rationale cloaking a colonialistic motive. China has set in motion a colossal propaganda machine to paint the picture of a Vietnam torn by starvation, political isolation, and imminent economic collapse.

In reality, postwar Vietnam has to confront many difficulties. In the first few days, Vietnam faced the danger of losing her newly won independence and sovereignty. In the North, large Chinese military contingents were massing just 150 kilometers from Hanoi, while in the southwest, Pol Pot's troops were deployed along seven border provinces. And the scene of the heaviest fighting was Tai Nin province, only seventy kilometers away from Ho Chi Minh City. Under such a situation, Vietnam had to take action to wipe out the Pol Pot clique aggressors, to defend Vietnam's security and sovereignty, and at the same time, respond to the urgent call from her Kampuchean neighbors, who were being massacred at the bloody hands of the genocidal Pol Pot clique and its thirty thousand Chinese advisors.

The whole world witnessed these acts, but still a number of countries, including the U.S.A., China, and the allies, have refused to end the Pol Pot resistance. On the contrary, they have openly provided arms and assistance to the remnants of that genocidal clique, which, using sanctuaries inside a neighboring country has undertaken frequent intrusions into, and armed attacks against, Kampuchea. In the face of the aggressive and warlike policy of the most populous power of the world, in collusion with the world's richest power, unity of the free countries of Indochina is the only way these countries, small and weak as they are, and just out of the war, can cope successfully with the challenges and survive. That path lies in the combat solidarity, the spirit of sharing, will, and hope among the three countries [Vietnam, Kampuchea, and Laos], and in the combined strength of their determination to preserve their independence, sovereignty, and territoriality achieved through seven decades of fighting side by side against foreign aggressors. That explains why the Sino–U.S. dream of the collapse of Vietnam cannot come true. Instead, what they now see is a stable and confident Vietnam in a position of unprecedented solidarity with the revolutionaries of the other free Indochinese countries.

With respect to other Asian countries, Vietnam has persevered in building new relationships with them. Despite Chinese machinations, Vietnam, together with Kampuchea and Laos, advances with persistence and determination along the line of cooperation and friendship and has taken the initiative in advocating a dialogue which has improved and strengthened mutual understanding and mutual respect among the Asian and Indochinese countries.

With regard to China, the Vietnamese people always treasured the long-standing friendship with the Chinese people and have spared no effort to restore this friendship. We stand for a peaceful solution of contentious issues and have more than once proposed the resumption of the bilateral negotiations suspended since 1980. Also, we have proposed the signing of a pact of mutual nonaggression and peaceful coexistence. It is regrettable that so far there has been no concerted response from China.

Regarding our national reconstruction, I wish to state that the achievements our people have made over the last eight years still fall far short of our expectations and of the requirements for improving the people's standard of living after the long and arduous years of war. As a matter of fact, if our country did not have to face up to a war launched by China, our people would have been able to build up their country much more. On the other hand, our shortcomings in social and economic management were also causes of the slowdown of the advance of the Vietnamese people on the road to recovery. These shortcomings have been overcome. The Vietnamese people have enjoyed the wholehearted and ever-increasing assistance of friends throughout the world: a paper mill built with Swedish assistance; a cement factory built by the Soviet Union; a cement factory built by Denmark; a thermo-electricity plant built by the Soviet Union. These are significant projects for the Vietnamese economy. With the support and assistance given by its friends, Vietnam was strong enough to face up to the worsening situation with China, to defend fruitfully its national independence and sovereignty, and to oppose the policy of expansion and annexation pursued by Chinese hegemonism.

In March last year, the Fifth Congress reviewed the revolutionary period since peace was established and made an assessment of its achievements and shortcomings. The Congress affirmed the great achievements, such as the reunification of the country, the stabilization of the people's lives, the overcoming of the extremely grave trials, the firm preservation of sovereignty, the maintenance of the living conditions without any famine after the war, the making of progress in the rebuilding of the country, the healing of the wounds of war, the taking care of orphans, widows, and the disabled, the elimination of illiteracy in the southern part of Vietnam, the advancing of culture and education, and the development of science and technology. The party Congress made special efforts to organize severe self-criticism from the grass-roots levels to the Central Committee level. The main shortcomings were recognized by the Congress, and many guidelines and policies have been changed.

The way of thinking and doing things by the leadership during wartime had not been adapted to the rules and requirements of building the country in peacetime. Many aspects of the economic planning and central management have not been carried out properly. Since 1975 Vietnam has undergone three phases: from war to peace, then from peace to war, and now peace with wars of destruction brewing on all sides. It is by no means easy to carry on the organization and structure of the state's machinery and the social and family structures, given such great and sudden changes. The Congress worked out many resolute measures to expel from the party ineffective cadres, to substitute for those who are inefficient, to illuminate the membership, and to enhance the leadership's knowledge of science, technology, and economic development.

The readjustments realized in policies for economic development and management are producing positive results. In 1982 Vietnam attained a record-high food output of sixteen million tons—fulfilling, for the first time, the food plan. Also marked in 1982 was a significant change for the better in Vietnam's economic life.

With respect to relations between Vietnam and the United States, our people always bear in mind, with profound gratitude, the valuable contribution of the millions of Americans who formed the antiwar movement. Normalization of relations would mean that the two countries could meet the interests and aspirations of the peoples of both countries. This normalization must be based on equality and proceed without any preconditions. Much to our regret, the United States has set one precondition after another. They are presently using the MIA issue to incite the American population against Vietnam. Recently, William Clark, the national security advisor, said, in effect, that by failing to act rapidly in searching for MIAs, Vietnam has created perceptions of incredible cruelty and suffered political isolation as a result. How ridiculous is that statement, when millions of Vietnamese continue to bear sufferings and pains as a consequence of the U.S. war. Why are so many of the war wounds brought to Vietnam left unhealed? What kind of cruelty is more incredible than the U.S. denial of export licenses for food to staunch hunger, for medical supplies for the sick, for the supply of milk for children? An economic blockade and sanctions—are they not cruel? The U.S. administrations have to bear responsibility for their missing citizens, because it is they who forced these people to leave their families and to come and fly over another country and to get killed or become an MIA in the process. By contrast, Vietnam's attitude toward these people is that when they were flying bombing missions, they were enemies, but when they were captured, they were considered pitiful victims of the U.S. administration's policy of war, and given humanitarian and lenient treatment. All the captured Americans were released to the American side by Vietnam. The Vietnamese government has done its best in searching for the MIAs and has returned over seventy-nine sets of remains and material evidence to the U.S. side. These efforts were made while the Vietnamese people were coping with many difficulties in their lives, especially those caused by the hostile policy of China. If Vietnam had full peace, it would have better conditions to seek information about missing persons. But the United States administration, instead, has entered into collusion with the Chinese expansionist hegemonists against Vietnam, thus posing a threat to the peace, sovereignty, and security of Vietnam. This constitutes the main obstacle to the seeking of information about U.S. missing persons.

Right now, on the soil of the country which prides itself as the champion of freedom, Vietnamese are still subject to discrimination. Permission has not been granted to me to go to Los Angeles to exchange views. This reflects part of the obstacles hindering the normalization of relations between the two countries. Nevertheless, it is my conviction that these obstacles will be overcome.

Question from the floor: What is the state of the counter-revolution in Vietnam today?

Madame Dung: There are a few people who try to make trouble, but they are captured by the army or the Vietnamese militia. It is nothing, and the people and the country move ahead.

Question: Why have you jailed Buddhists and murdered one in jail?

Madame Dung: We have freedom of religion in Vietnam. All believers can exercise their rights to participate in their religion. The people are not put in jail because of their religion but because they are criminals. They try to hide their crimes by taking a religious cover. Many, many foreign observers who are traveling in Vietnam can attest that religion is free in Vietnam. And, I repeat, only the criminals who are working against the security of Vietnam are put in jail. I do not have the dossiers with me, but I know certainly that those in prison have acted against the security of the government and the people.

Question: Why are Vietnamese in Kampuchea?

Madame Dung: We have a duty to help a neighboring friend and brother in need. They were massacred by Pol Pot, and I think that not only Vietnam, but all colonized people all over the world facing such a situation, could not stand aside, but had to go and help the Kampuchean people. The second reason is that Pol Pot was supported by China, an aggressor against Vietnam. It was for the defense of our independence and sovereignty. We, the three small countries of Indochina who face the aggression of the big powers, must unite together.

Question: Why have 500,000 Vietnamese laborers been sent to Siberia to work?

Madame Dung: It is an entire fabrication and a campaign of slander. A very long time ago we made an agreement with the Soviet Union for assistance in training Vietnamese workers, and for the last ten or fifteen years, it has trained sixteen thousand Vietnamese workers. It is to help Vietnam to rebuild the country and develop the country. We want the technology and the know-how to rebuild. It is logical that we should receive help and cooperation from the Soviet Union, another socialist country, as well as from nonaligned countries, to train our young people.[1]

[**Another question:** about the arrest of two Buddhists, the government consolidation of the Vietnamese Buddhist churches under its control, and the takeover of An Quong pagoda.]

Madame Dung: It is not easy for foreigners to understand the complicated situation in Vietnam. During many decades, under colonialist regimes and during the war, there were maneuvers and attempts to use religion as a cover to hide reactionary activities against the government. I cannot explain to you or give you all the activities of the reactionaries in this case, but I have spoken some years ago about these problems. However, I am sure of the freedom of religion in my country, and that only the criminals are arrested and punished.

[**Question in the form of accusations:** arrest of Buddhists, enslavement of workers, occupation of Cambodia, and stealing of South Vietnam's gold.]

Madame Dung: It is not serious to continue this way of debate. I am willing to inform, to explain, but I refuse to carry on this form of polemic, to respond to remarks that are not meant to gain information or promote real discussion. It is slander. I have already talked about this issue, and to continue this same discussion is not serious. It is useless to continue.

---

1. According to a State Department report on forced labor in the Soviet Union, made public in February 1983, eleven thousand Vietnamese are serving in Russia under individual contracts that, in effect, make them "indentured servants." They are reportedly paid less than Soviet citizens doing comparable work and "a substantial portion" of their pay is withheld, to be credited to Hanoi's debt to Moscow. Robert C. Toth, "4 Million Forced Soviet Laborers Reported," Los Angeles *Times,* Sec. I (February 15, 1983), p. 7.

VIETNAM TODAY

AN AMERICAN VIEW: I

Douglas Pike

The Vietnamese Communist system, with its unique leadership, which performed so well in the service of its golden cause—unification of North and South Vietnam under the Communist banner—and against such a formidable foe over such a long time, has been totally unequal to the lesser peacetime challenges of binding up the wounds of war, launching a nation-building and economic development program, and establishing reasonably good relations with neighbors and the world.

Since that moment in April 30, 1975, when Soviet-built tanks smashed through the wrought iron gates of Independence Palace in Saigon to end the protracted conflict that was the Vietnam War, a shroud of failure has settled on the survivors, victor and vanquished alike, measurable in any term one chooses to employ—economic, sociopolitical, diplomatic, military; above all, psychological. The failure is traceable to the dozen men of the Hanoi politburo, with their unchallenged monopoly of power, who have been incapable of dealing with the peacetime, postwar world.

Out of the events that have visited the region since the end of the war, three of overriding historical significance stand out.

The first was the emergence of holocaust, bloodbath, psychological trauma, or social pathology, depending on whether one chooses to use pejorative or clinical terminology. In any event, it has been human suffering on an unprecedented scale, far worse than war.

Cambodia, or Kampuchea as it became known, almost immediately descended into a surrealistic hell of anarchy, starvation, disease, and mass migration, savaged by an extraordinary death rate. Essentially, the condition of suffering engendered by anarchy continues today, although now, mercifully, at a lower level.

The Kampuchean brutalization in the name of social perfection is particularly difficult to relate, because ordinary description is unbelievable or incomprehensible. Events there seem to belong only in a science fiction novel or in some black-humor social satire. The hideousness of the suffering has been made even more grotesque by being offered up rationally: terror and holocaust in the name of the highest of mankind's virtues. Kampuchea has become a grim example of what happens to men who are caught up in an ideological dream which blinds them to the fact that human beings are the reason for all social change—and who become willing, even eager, to sacrifice all humanity for the sake of some political abstraction.

In Vietnam, the northern party cadres descended on the South with a looter's vengeance. Their orders were to "break the machine," that is, reorganize southern society by installing new social and political institutions which would emasculate existing social relations—concentrating on the villages where live two-thirds of all Vietnamese—that have endured for a millennium. Middle-class southerners, ethnic Chinese, even independent-minded proletarians, such as fishermen, were driven out, often literally as boat people—sometimes with malice, but mostly because there simply was no place for them in the new order.

Suffering at the holocaust level did not occur in Vietnam, we believed earlier, but now new studies are underway which indicate that executions and vengeance killings in the first few years were far more numerous than anyone outside Vietnam had believed, and amounted to a bloodbath.

The social reconstruction campaign by the North against the South was punitive, which is perhaps understandable if not excusable, considering the passions unleashed on both sides in the most emotional of all wars, a civil war. But the mean-spiritedness of the campaign is being reinforced daily, by new directives from the politburo, which mindlessly continues to "wave the bloody shirt"—to use the term coined by southerners in the U.S. after the American Civil War. That the leaders should not permit this emotion to abate is somewhat puzzling, since the leadership itself is the chief victim of its effects. Apparently these old men are so isolated, so encrusted with hatred, that they are incapable of putting the past behind them.

The second major development has been the disastrous decline of Vietnam's economy, which never was what could be called model. In North and South alike, the economic scene is in far worse shape today than during the darkest days of war. Poverty is widespread, inflation is rampant, food is in short supply, and food consumption is averaging fifteen hundred calories a day per person—just above the subsistence level. Efforts to rectify the condition are constant but ineffectual. The basic affliction is stagnation, the sheer inability of the leadership to get the economic sector in gear. There is less food available in the North than at any time during the war. Buses and trucks red-lined (out of service for any reason) averaged about 5 percent in the North during the war; now the nationwide average is about 25 percent. Industrial plants in the North always operated at least at 70 percent capacity; in the South at about 90 percent; but today the nationwide average is 50 percent (due chiefly to lack of raw materials and spare parts). By every major economic indicator, Vietnam is worse off than ever before. It survives only because of the Socialist world dole.

It should be stressed that this is entirely a postwar phenomenon. There are other wartime heritages plaguing the society, but the declines cited here have occurred since 1975. Rice production, for instance, reached a postwar high in 1975–76 and has been declining since. That cannot be blamed on American neo-colonialism or Chinese hegemonism, only on the leadership's poor judgment, wrongheaded policies, and outright blunders. Those who contribute to the fiction that America and others are responsible for Vietnam's present economic plight do Vietnam a disservice.

Recently Hanoi launched a new program to lift the economy by its bootstraps, called the Resolution Six program. It is an effort to decontrol and decentralize authority and decision-making in agricultural production and in the food distribution sector. It employs capitalist methods but labels them experimental Marxism.

Initial results from Resolution Six are promising. Rice production for 1982 will probably equal or exceed all earlier postwar harvests.

The third major postwar development is regional: the changed geopolitical scene that has yielded two new strategic balances of power, one within Indochina, the other throughout Southeast Asia. Overnight, in May 1975, Hanoi and the Indochina that it would come to control were elevated to new martial prominence. Vietnam is the third-largest Communist nation (eighteenth largest country in the world), with the third-largest armed force on earth (one million men), greater in size than even the American army. Hanoi's ability to project force in the region is limited only by its undersized air force and navy, a shortcoming the USSR is now correcting. The geopolitical configuration that has emerged is this: a polarized region—Communist Indochina vs. the ASEAN states—upon which is superimposed a triangular big-power rivalry involving the USSR, China, and the United States.

The American withdrawal from the Southeast mainland—certainly a psychological withdrawal—created a political vacuum the USSR found irresistible. Lured by what has always been its weakness—seductive opportunism—Moscow rushed into a void it perceived to be full of strategic potential. Its plunge was facilitated by Vietnam's falling on a time of troubles—and badly needing Soviet aid. Soviet opportunism was matched by Vietnamese dependency. Hanoi was, and is, dependent on Moscow for some fifteen percent of the rice it consumes and for all military hardware required in Kampuchea and against China.

There is reason to believe Moscow is now reexamining the bargain struck with Vietnam. The question is whether the relationship—a military alliance in all but name—is as advantageous as once believed. The Moscow-Hanoi relation, probably never so close or durable as many outsiders believed, may be on the threshold of marked change.

The ASEAN states' initial reaction to the victory by Indochinese Communism was enormous dismay and anxiety. This forced the five nations to assume more authority over their own security along the only feasible road, a joint effort. That, in turn, gave an enormous boost to the force of regionalism, beneficial not only to the ASEAN countries but to all in the Pacific basin.

China's postwar behavior has been perhaps the most extreme. The Hanoi victory was not an outcome it had seriously anticipated or even recognized until quite late. In the months following the end of the war, China assumed a new posture toward the U.S., set about creating an Asia-wide mutual support (read anti-USSR) united front, and began a chain of events that led to war with Vietnam.

The breach in Sino-Vietnamese relations had subliminal roots, but was more directly a product of three Hanoi actions: ever more intimate relations with the USSR, intrusiveness into Kampuchea, and mistreatment of overseas Chinese in Vietnam. Beginning in 1977, the association steadily deteriorated, culminating in a brief open war in early 1979, now settled into a more or less permanent cold war. None of this needed to happen. The Chinese could have been handled by a more careful and empathetic Hanoi leadership.

The inversion of Sino-Vietnamese relations was part of a broader pattern within the Indochina geopolitical scene—that is, the breakup of the fraternal brotherhood that linked the militants of China, Vietnam, Cambodia, and Laos. The Hanoi–Pol Pot split was made likely from the start by ancient, deep-seated ethnic antipathies. The trigger was Pol Pot's perverse determination to "reverse history" by institutionalizing hatred for Vietnam, thus moving Indochina away from Hanoi's goal of federation. The politburo had several options. The one chosen, a Moscow-style quick military fix, was designed to solve the problem in six months but failed when Pol Pot managed to turn the struggle into a protracted conflict. Hanoi now would dearly love to extricate itself from Kampuchea. Eventually, the leadership—or a new leadership—may agree to a negotiated settlement.

Within Indochina, the Vietnamese-Kampuchean relationship—and increasingly, it appears, the Vietnamese-Lao relationship—is being caught up in the fires of nationalism. The aftermath of the Vietnam War in Indochina is an unrelieved record of failed leadership. Victory presented the Hanoi politburo with an opportunity to create the brave new world Ho Chi Minh had so long promised. These leaders, old, dogmatically anachronistic, of an implacable mind-set, bugs in amber isolated from younger minds even within the party, made a series of initial judgments, and issued policy instructions on the basis of these. When the policies demonstrably failed, the politburo piled on further wrong policies, compounding the error. They laid blame on a nearly endless list of culprits, internal and external, never once on themselves. All the while, their political system is being lashed by that great curse of Chinese politics, factionalism, and the great debilitating political game of *bung di,* or faction-bashing.

In the final resolve, however, historians may conclude that while the wrong people tried to run postwar Vietnam, there was a more fundamental reason for the failure—what the French love to castigate as *le système.* The party-state *apparat* created in wartime was a fighting machine, totally hierarchical, tightly knit, disciplined—exactly what was needed. But in peacetime those virtues became vices. The party-state institutions are over-organized, excessively centralized, full of cross-purpose—all of which smother initiative, prevent flexibility, and mitigate against innovation.

The pessimistic conclusion one is forced to reach is that this condition—the wrong system being run by the wrong people—will not be changed voluntarily by those in command and cannot be changed by others. Therefore, time and human mortality are Vietnam's best hopes.

VIETNAM TODAY
AN AMERICAN VIEW: II

John McAulif

The aftermath of the second Indochina War has been as tragic as
the war itself. The suffering has been different and certainly less
than that of the war period, but it has been just as unnecessary.

The perception of the public and the media has been that the
fault lies in Hanoi. In fact, it lies at least as much in Washington.
U.S. postwar policy toward Indochina has been a moral travesty.
Moreover, in the long term it is a disaster—based on the same
profound misunderstanding of Vietnamese history which took us
into Vietnam and made it so hard for us to get out. Perversely,
American policymakers have helped bring about what they ostensi-
bly oppose: an increase of Soviet and Chinese influence and power
in Southeast Asia.

It did not have to be that way. Whether from a sense of moral
responsibility for the destruction created by U.S. military power, or
humanitarian concern for the victims of wartime devastation, or
from a natural human desire for reconciliation with former enemies, we could have followed a different path. The American people were prepared to. A poll in the *New York Times* of July 1977
showed that two-thirds of Americans supported sending food and
medicines to Vietnam, and a majority favored economic assistance
which would have helped the country rebuild.

The failure lay in the political leadership of our country—

perhaps no surprise, since their defeat in war had not driven them from positions of power. Besides having an understandably vindictive feeling toward the uppity people who had successfully defeated the world's greatest power, they needed to ensure that postwar Vietnam was as terrible a place as possible. Vietnam's very real problems are increasingly used as a retroactive justification for the U.S. war effort, as a basis for attacking opponents of the war.

To understand the aftermath, we must begin with the Paris Agreement on "ending the war and restoring the peace in Vietnam." The revisionist mythology which is being constructed tries to persuade us that it must have been the other side which violated the peace agreement, because they were the ones who ultimately won, on April 30. Obviously, both sides violated the agreement, or the war wouldn't have ended in a military debacle, but the vital question is whose violations came first and were most subversive to the agreement's purposes. There is not time here to make the case, but the record demonstrates (and Frank Snepp has confirmed much of it) that it was the Thieu regime which was determined that the agreement would not be implemented politically or militarily, and the Communist side which initially favored and honored it. Echoing the post-Geneva experience of 1954, one side thought it could win and the other felt it would lose through implementation.

Had the agreement been implemented, it is likely several things would have come about:

1. a more gradual transfer of power
2. a more complex balance of forces within the South, and between northern and southern parts of the country
3. an opportunity for an orderly and safe departure of people who could not fit into the new Vietnam
4. greater economic stability because of uninterrupted links with the West and assistance in rebuilding from the war's destruction.

The precipitate collapse of South Vietnam surprised the Vietnamese revolutionaries. In their own planning, they expected the war would go on another year—and they were not politically prepared to administer the South. To their credit, the bloodbath that the U.S. government so often predicted (and which had happened in China after its revolution, in Indonesia to the Communists, and in France to Vichy collaborators) did not occur. To their blame, tens of thousands of persons were detained without trial in reeducation camps. The numbers held and the conditions of the camps are subject to heated controversy; suffice to say that many were detained who could not truly be accused of war crimes, and that conditions were, at a minimum, harsh.

The political structures of a Communist state were imposed, including prohibition of organized opposition. It is easy to condemn Vietnam today from the viewpoint of Western democratic values. It is harder to remember that the regimes the U.S. backed were not noted for their commitment to real democracy or civil liberties, although their dependent relationship on the U.S. did create some openings for dissent. Only the most extreme and suspect of refugee accounts describe postwar conditions of imprisonment and torture which approximate those that were routine and widespread in the Republic of South Vietnam.

From the viewpoint of Vietnam's revolutionary nationalists, northerners and southerners (including those who had temporarily regrouped to the North in 1954), April 30, 1975, was the culmination of more than thirty years of struggle to achieve the independence of their whole country from Japanese invaders, French colonizers, and American neo-colonialists. But the country they won had been profoundly dislocated economically and socially by the war. The South's economy depended on large U.S. subsidies and food aid which created an artificially elevated life-style; the North relied on food aid from China and had lost much of its economic infrastructure. In the South alone, according to a 1977 UN report, nearly ten thousand hamlets had been damaged; over 1.5 million oxen and buffaloes were killed; there were 800,000–900,000 orphans; and millions of people had been forced off the land.

Harsh internal policies toward defeated enemies and an ideologically rigid desire quickly to socialize the South led to many injustices and mistakes. Undeniably this has contributed to Vietnam's postwar suffering. However, it is hard to imagine how any regime or any system of government could have had an easy or successful time without massive postwar assistance similar to the Marshall Plan in Europe or the reconstruction of Japan.

The exodus of refugees from Vietnam began in the final days of panicked collapse of the Thieu regime. Frank Snepp's *Decent Interval* makes clear that it was the Ford-Kissinger administration's unwillingness to accept the reality of defeat which contributed greatly to the chaos at the end—and to the abandonment in Vietnam of tens of thousands of persons whose position was compromised by their former relationship to the U.S.

The refugee flow continued, reaching its peak when tensions between Vietnam and China affected the status of the *hoa* (ethnic Chinese) in both North and South. Interviews with refugees suggested a variety of motives: political, economic, but fundamentally a deep alienation from what Vietnam had become. It was not a new phenomenon in history, but for the individuals involved, it was a terrible experience. It didn't have to be. Had the U.S. and other Western countries been prepared to negotiate a massive, orderly departure program between 1975 and 1978, immense suffering and loss of life could have been avoided. A limited Office of Displaced Persons was finally set up in 1979, but the criteria for being accepted to it by the U.S. were far stricter than for those who came out by the dangerous boat route.

The anger of the refugees should not surprise us. Because of U.S. efforts in the 1950s to create an anti-Communist government in South Vietnam, what had begun as a nationalist anti-colonial revolution did take on the aspects of a civil war. The refugees represent one side of the bitter and deep divisions produced; the other side involves the often harsh treatment of the persons whom the victorious Vietnamese revolutionaries regard as puppets of the U.S.

I am not arguing that the Vietnamese revolutionaries did the morally right thing, or even that it was a necessary step to protect their victory. There are people in Vietnam's government itself, as well as others in Saigon and Hanoi, who are critical of the treatment and distrust of people who were on the other side, as well as of those who had not—in their terms—played a sufficiently patriotic role.

But again the central question is, Did Western and U.S. behavior affect their situation in a positive or negative fashion?

Tiziano Terzani wrote one of the first articles in the Western press exposing and condemning the reeducation camps. He argued at the time that if the U.S. normalized relations and provided reconstruction aid, it would have a positive effect in terms of human rights issues. Such a policy would have diminished among revolutionaries the fear that the former middle and upper classes would be agents of an implacably hostile U.S.

The Ford and Kissinger policies toward Vietnam were indeed unambiguously hostile. They even refused to allow Vietnam in the United Nations, a reprise of past policy toward China. The Vietnamese, in turn, were bending over backward to open up relations with the West. Much to the dismay of the Soviet Union and to the surprise of the West, they refused to join COMECON and instead took the Saigon seat in the World Bank and the Asian Development Bank. The investment code they developed for joint enterprises with foreign capital was analogous to the process underway in China. Vietnam resisted Soviet requests to gain access to Cam Rahn Bay port facilities.

The Carter administration was more ambiguous. Although Carter was one of the longest supporters of the war in the Democratic party, a number of key advisors were people who had been identified with moderate antiwar attitudes. At the beginning, his administration moved to close the book on the war. The Woodcock Commission went to Vietnam, concluded that there were no U.S. prisoners still alive, and felt that progress was being made in obtaining cooperation on searches for the bodies of MIAs.

The Vietnamese made a big mistake at this point. They connected the questions of normalizing relations, MIA body searches, and reconstruction aid. Carter's response was morally obtuse, to say the least. Responding to a press conference query as to whether the U.S. had a moral obligation to help rebuild Vietnam if MIA information was provided, the president said, "The destruction was mutual. . . . . We went to Vietnam without any desire to impose American will. . . . I don't feel that we ought to apologize or to castigate ourselves. . . . I don't feel that we owe a debt."

He did leave open the door for possible "normal aid processes" after diplomatic relations were established. Later he ended U.S. opposition to Vietnam's membership in the UN. However, if Carter had taken the lead in acknowledging partial U.S. moral responsibility for the war's destruction, he could have rallied substantial public support, as shown by the July 1977 poll.

Into the vacuum of leadership stepped the most conservative forces in Congresss. A series of lopsided votes in the House in the spring of 1977 sought to prohibit any direct or indirect U.S. assistance to Vietnam.

At this point, one of the most bizarre espionage cases in U.S. history erupted. In February 1978, David Truong and Ronald Humphrey were indicted for passing low-classification political documents to Vietnamese in Paris. Listed as an unindicted co-conspirator was Vietnam's ambassador to the UN, Dinh Ba Thi. Although Thi's name was later dropped, and the only testimony at the trial about him by the paid U.S. government informer completely cleared Thi, the U.S. had already expelled him, and all negotiations between the two countries had ceased. (Truong and Humphrey have just completed the first year of their fifteen-year sentences at Ray Brook and Danbury federal prisons respectively.)

In the early summer of 1978, Vietnam sent increasingly clear signals that it was dropping the aid linkage; and Washington did its best to ignore them. In the fall at the UN, the U.S. and Vietnam worked out all the details for an exchange of ambassadors, but the signals changed in Washington.

The official justifications for the U.S. backing-off have to do with Vietnamese policy toward Cambodia, refugees, and economic relations with the Soviet Union. Some observers share the Vietnamese view that it was Washington's higher-priority interest in relations and strategic alignments with China which intervened.

In May of 1978, National Security Advisor Zbigniew Brzezinski had visited China. He is reported to have played a significant personal role in opposing normal U.S. relations with Vietnam. This has been attributed to his desire not to allow anything to interfere with normalizing relations with China and establishing anti-Soviet cooperation.

Representatives of U.S. humanitarian aid organizations were shocked by the bitter personal antagonism expressed toward Vietnam by staff members of the National Security Council during private meetings in 1978 and 1979. While some Carter appointees to the State Department had opposed the war, their priorities, once in office, were Southern Africa, Central America, and human rights—preventing the next Vietnams. Although they may have favored a different policy toward Vietnam, this was not the issue on which they would go to the mat. Most of the State Department professionals responsible for U.S. policy toward Indochina had formed their perspective on Vietnam during wartime assignments there and were not particularly sympathetic to the problems.

Ultimately, a fundamental change must be made in U.S. policy toward Indochina. If we are not to slip deeper into a third Indochina war, real peace must finally be declared. We must recognize the reality of the governments which have replaced those we supported and/or created. In the interim, there are several specific changes which should be undertaken by the U.S. Government. Their primary purpose is humanitarian, but each can contribute to an improvement in atmosphere which may facilitate the larger political change:

1. Humanitarian aid provided by non-governmental religious and secular agencies should receive a blanket exemption from licensing requirements
2. A liberal policy should be instituted of granting visas to visitors from Indochina to the U.S. and travel permission for members of Vietnam's mission to the United Nations.

By denying what was done, and our part in it, and its living legacy, we have denied ourselves the opportunity to mourn and regret and learn. By denying the reality of our past, and its consequences in the present, we cheat ourselves of choosing our future.

VIETNAM AND AMERICA

Robert Muller

What we are talking about here is not history, but contemporary concern: the fate of Indochina today. What responsibility do we, the American people, have for the very dismal state of affairs in Vietnam and throughout Indochina? And what is our obligation, morally if not legally, to help relieve some of the despair that is so rampant throughout that part of the world? As we look to address those concerns, it is helpful to look closer to home and see how we have dealt here with our legacy of involvement in the Vietnam War. As a Vietnam veteran, who has been an activist for thirteen years now, I can simply say to you that America has failed to deal with her own. Not only have we failed here to provide the healing and the assistance to those who have been directly affected by the war, but we also have failed to muster the courage for addressing the important issues that the war raised. The silence surrounding our overt, obvious involvement in Vietnam has been both deafening and the most offensive aspect of our involvement. That silence is taking a terrible toll in this country—not only of our sense of morality and conscience as a people, but perhaps by allowing the greatest tragedy of all to happen, which is not learning anything from our recent history and therefore setting the stage to have it all happen again.

In my capacity with the Vietnam Veterans of America, I have

had the opportunity to travel in the past year to thirty-five college campuses across the country to lecture on the Vietnam experience. And what I have encountered has been stunning and appalling. I realize just how stunning that war was to my generation and the country as a whole, and I remember that the average age of a combat soldier was nineteen, and then I go to a college campus today, and the eighteen- and the nineteen-year-olds ask questions such as, "Mr. Muller, what side did you fight on, the North or the South?" When I started to lecture, I thought the audiences knew something, and I talked about the My Lai massacre and the celebrated trial of Lieutenant Calley—only to be asked on successive campuses, "What is My Lai?" and "Who is Lieutenant Calley?" If we do not have the capacity to deal with our own legacy here, you should have some hint by now as to how we have handled a far-off land and an alien people.

We do not have normal relations with Vietnam now. We do not even have the threshold steps of diplomatic recognition of Vietnam. And when you ask why and consider the impact of it, you should consider the following: In November, when we dedicated the national monument to the Vietnam War, in Washington, D.C., I was invited to meet with President Reagan. He used the opportunity of hosting a group of Vietnam veterans to denounce Vietnam, citing the hundreds of thousands of people, as he put it, who were being murdered and tortured—and citing the plight of the people who risked their lives by fleeing the country— as the justification finally for our war of a decade ago. He said, what you see in Indochina today is proof that our war was a just war. There may be, in other words, some political considerations involved in frustrating any recovery in Indochina and continuing to portray the leadership there as the bad guys.

The American war effort battered Vietnam. In the Second World War, we dropped 2.5 million tons of bombs in Europe and the Pacific; in Vietnam, by air alone we dropped over seven million tons. When you add to that the naval artillery and other explosives we dumped on that country, it totals more than fourteen million tons of explosives dropped on Vietnam—the most heavily bombed country in the history of the world. The result of that kind of violence was that one out of thirty people in all of Indochina was killed. One out of twelve was wounded. And one out of five was made a refugee. Add to that what happened after the war—natural disasters, flood, famine, typhoons—and you can start to appreciate just what kind of rubble and disaster confront the efforts to begin rebuilding Indochina.

Just over a year ago, I had the opportunity to lead the first delegation of Vietnam veterans to return to Vietnam since the war. We had no idea what the North was going to look like. I remember flying into Hanoi with great nervousness over the reception we would get. The first shock was the airport at Hanoi itself. We expected a terminal and control tower and so on, and what we landed in at Hanoi International Airport was nothing more than a field, without the buildings and the hangars. The ride into Hanoi was on roads that were bumpy and pitted, and there were no other vehicles. To get to the city that loomed so big in my mind and in those of the other veterans, the capital of the country with which we had fought our war, and to see something that was as basic, as Spartan, and as hard-pressed as Hanoi, was nothing less than stunning. We expected smokestacks and factories and production capabilities in the city, and what we found was nothing more than a town. The people were scurrying about on bicycles and a couple of motor scooters, and the only cars we saw were the ones we rode in.

To say that Vietnam is economically hard-pressed today does not begin to convey just how desperate the situation is. We met an American woman, the only national that we knew of, who has been living on the outskirts of Hanoi for four years. And when she heard that some Americans had come, she came to visit us at the hotel. And what she said confirmed our worst fears. She works in a medical facility, and she said fully fifty percent of the children are suffering from diseases of malnutrition; infectious diseases are rampant; if people do manage to eat two meals a day, they are considered fortunate. There is no protein nor protein substitutes; there is no milk for the children. In terms of the conditions where we were, which were considered the most luxurious, it was not a place where anyone would want to stay. Even the dining room—their best effort—had perhaps half a dozen rats running around the floor while we were having our dinner.

We were particularly nervous about the reaction of the Vietnamese people to us, since we arrived on the ninth anniversary of the 1972 Christmas bombings—the celebration of which was announced on posters around the town. (It should be remembered that in those ten days, we, the United States, dropped on Hanoi and Haiphong more bombs than Germany dropped on Great Britain during the entire Second World War.) And yet, never once in all of our travels and all of our encounters with the Vietnamese people did we have one negative look, one negative comment and we were warmly welcomed and warmly embraced.

The leadership was much the same. There is a certain level of communication, perhaps, that goes on between soldiers; and suffice it to say that as we discussed, late into the evening, those subjects of common concern—the Agent Orange spraying, the status of the MIAs, and the accounting for their remains—we ended up raising our shirts, and they raised theirs, and we compared scars of bullet wounds and shrapnel wounds.

It is an understatement to say that going back to Vietnam changed my life. It was the same for us all. We have carried with us, for more than a decade, the time-frozen images of our earlier encounter with Vietnam: of villages exploding, of people dying, and of untold suffering and misery. To be able to return and replace those images with those of a country—albeit suffering and poor but still at peace—went a long way toward helping us relieve ourselves of some of the baggage we have carried. To look no longer upon the Vietnamese as the objects of war, as gooks or dinks, as we had been trained and conditioned to regard them, but now to look upon them as people who were fathers and mothers and family people, added an element of compassion that many of us have continued, since we have come home, to try to adjust to and resolve.

When we came back to the States, we were roundly criticized in some quarters for having the audacity to go and talk to the Communist leaders of a country with whom we do not have formal relations. And I came to understand that we are the ones who are suffering perhaps even more for the failure to end the war in Vietnam. To encounter the amount of hatred and bitterness from so many Americans toward the Vietnamese after having seen them look upon us as friends and allies and having witnessed them place the war in perspective, a part of their history, said an awful lot. And I think not only to benefit the people of Indochina and Vietnam, but also to benefit us as a people—for our hearts and minds, for our morality and our conscience and our soul—we have to end the war against Vietnam. We have to stop portraying them as the bad guys; stop isolating them politically and economically, and take the step we have taken with even greater enemies in the past: start the process of diplomatic recognition, work toward normalization, and ultimately help rebuild that country—and in doing that recapture part of what the American people historically have been.

SOUTH VIETNAMESE PEOPLE

Don Luce

People have said a lot
About the countryside
In difficult and lofty phrases
With feelings dark as night,
As cryptic or bitter
As the words of a lover betrayed.

But I would like now to say some simple things,
Simple as a field of rice or sweet potatoes,
Or a silent early morning.
Please let me breathe again the air of yesterday,
Let children frolic in the sun
With kites over bamboo bridges.

Just a narrow little space will be enough
Four rows of bamboo trees around it;
And leave a little space for an entrance,
A place for a girl and boy to tell the story of the moon,
For old women with babies to gather and chatter.

Please give me back these things I've mentioned—
A story as simple
As a bird's unbroken song,
As a mother, as a baby
As the life of long ago the poets used to tell. . . .
   —"Please Give Me Back"
   by Hoang Minh Nhan[1]

Our lives became like those of animals desperately trying to escape their hunters. . . . Human beings, whose parents brought them into the world and carefully raised them with overflowing love despite so many difficulties, these human beings would die from a single blast as explosions burst, lying still without moving again at all. And who then thinks of the blood, flesh, sweat, and strength of their parents, and who will have charity and pity for them?. . . . In reality, whatever happens, it is only the innocent who suffer. And as for others, do they know all the unimaginable things happening in this war? Do they? Or is it rather that this war is something which benefits us and thus need not be stopped?
   A thirty-year-old woman refugee from the Plain of Jars[2]

In its effort to win the war, the U.S. government forgot the Vietnamese, especially the poorest Vietnamese. And most Americans have never heard their voices.

The devotion of Vietnamese to their family is practically unlimited, and the sentiment toward the father is one of near-reverence. In every home there is a family altar where sticks of incense are lit on family anniversaries and holidays, and where offerings are made and prayers are said in memory of those who have passed away. Nearby, their ancestors are buried and their graves tended with great respect. To leave the graves untended,

---

1. Jacqui Chagnon and Don Luce, eds., *Of Quiet Courage: Poems from Viet Nam* (Washington D.C., Indochina Mobile Education Project, 1974), pp. 142–43.
   2. Fred Branfman, ed., *Voices From the Plain of Jars: Life Under an Air War* (New York, Harper Colophon, 1972), pp. 42–43.

many believe, condemns their souls forever. In the words of Vietnam's greatest poet, Nguyen Du:

Your abandoned souls are roaming in strange lands
No incense is burning for you
You wander, helpless, in the night[3]

In a traditional Vietnamese village, life follows the rhythm of the seasons. When the rains come, the men plow the fields; the women plant the rice; and the children carry water, tend the buffalo, and catch fish for the evening meal. At harvest time, the village gathers to thresh the rice and sing centuries-old songs to speed their work (or to court a favored one). At home, in the evening, the grandparents tell stories of when they were young— or repeat legends of ancient heroes (often about the generals who drove out the Chinese generations ago).

Imagine the damage to the culture when these people were driven from their homes. Imagine the depth of their anger. Imagine how a new society can repair the damage done to the family structure after the dislocation of this war.

The effects of the war were much more devastating on the southern half of the country. In the South, the bombing and defoliation occurred in the countryside, forcing people into the cities. In the North, the bombing was on the cities and infrastructures like roads, bridges, and factories. This encouraged northern families to send the children into the countryside to live with grandparents or relatives. Thus, while the North must repair or rebuild its roads, factories, etc., the South is faced not only with the physical problems of rebuilding but also with the problems of readjustment for most of its citizens.

The U.S. and Saigon military forcefully moved about half the population into strategic hamlets, New Life hamlets, refugee camps, and overcrowded slums—and called it pacification. "Country Fairs" brought rock-and-roll music, hot dogs, and Kool-Aid to remote villages—while the Marines searched the people's homes for VC and deserters (and souvenirs). Leaflets fluttered down on

---

3. "Calling the Wandering Souls," in Chagnon and Luce, *op. cit.,* p. 16.

villagers telling the inhabitants that "the wicked Vietcong" were in their village. Therefore, "gunfire is going to be conducted on your village. . . . Take cover, as we do not wish to kill innocent people." Five million acres of land[4] was defoliated, killing the rice, coconuts, papaya, bananas, and forests. Those fortunate enough to escape the devastation in the countryside were fed bulgur wheat, cooking oil, and powdered milk.

The height of the refugee movement was around 1965. An eight-year-old farm boy moved that year was eighteen by the end of the war. For a decade, he existed by shining shoes, pushing drugs, washing cars, stealing from cars. In the process, many of these young men became addicted to the drugs they were pushing. Even if you could have convinced this young man to return to the farm after 1975, you would still have to teach him how to farm. The best way to learn to farm is by farming. A whole generation of Vietnamese have missed this practical education.

For many young women, the only way that they could survive was by working in the bars and brothels. According to authorities in Vietnam today, two-thirds of these women had venereal disease, and many were addicted to hard drugs. Making these women part of the work force involves teaching new skills and motivation as well as physical rehabilitation.

It is true that the U.S. taught many Vietnamese new skills. Unfortunately, many of these skills are needed in limited numbers now (language interpreters, drivers, typists, people working in the service industries). Other skills, especially those of factory workers, are dependent upon spare parts for factories that were left behind (which Vietnam can't get because of the trade embargo). Another problem is that most of the doctors, dentists, and engineers left after 1975.

As we think of U.S. responsibility toward Vietnam, we must think of the condition of the farmland. In 1977, I took the three-day drive from Da Nang to Saigon. On the left, was the narrow band of rice paddies that stretch along the coast and, on the right, mountains rose dramatically to the sky. Throughout the trip, I could see the continued effects of the defoliation. The sidehills

---

4. Don Luce and John Sommer, *Vietnam: The Unheard Voices* (Ithaca, N.Y., Cornell University Press, 1969), p. 170.

were nearly bare from the continued use of defoliation on these hills. Two obvious problems of this devastation are the destruction of most of the forest wealth of lumber, charcoal, and even export products like rubber and cinnamon. Secondly, each year, when the monsoon rains hit those hillsides, there is little to hold the water. And floods result.

I visited a wounds ward in Qui Nhon; nearly all the patients were there because they had stepped on an old mine, their plow had hit a shell, or the child had picked up a "butterfly" mine.

The Pentagon and the U.S. government in general have refused help for these victims. The Pentagon has refused to share information on the best ways to defuse the mines, bombs, and shells. Our government will not provide mine sweepers or devices to detonate electronically the mines. Nor will the Pentagon provide the maps that would show where U.S. troops planted land mines. After a detailed explanation of how the mines were affecting the farm people, one Pentagon colonel said, "The goddam Vietnamese should have thought about those things before they started the war."

It is, of course, the poorest Vietnamese who suffer most from these continuing effects of the war. A policy designed to make these people suffer more, in hopes they will eventually overthrow the government of the Socialist Republic of Vietnam, is both cruel to Vietnam's poor and an unrealistic evaluation of the country.

If the United States is serious about achieving stability and peace in Indochina, it will have to revamp its strategy. At a minimum, the U.S. should normalize diplomatic relations with Vietnam, take it off the "enemies list" so that customary trade can begin, and provide reconstruction aid and repatriation assistance for Indochinese refugees who may want to return home. It would also be desirable to try to involve the United Nations in settling the Cambodian conflict, perhaps by first establishing a seat for Cambodia in the world body, and then by working toward an eventual UN peacekeeping force. Finally, the United States might try to help establish a demilitarized zone between Cambodia and Thailand, as well as a reduction of the Chinese Army force on the Vietnamese border—both of which might be in exchange for a promise of the withdrawal of Vietnamese troops.

Such a policy would be more generous and more humanitarian than the present strategy articulated by Assistant Secretary of State John Holdridge: "We will seek, if we can, to find ways to increase the political, economic, and, yes, military pressures on Vietnam."

U.S. (and Chinese) policy has succeeded in further impoverishing the already devastated Vietnamese economy. But these policies have not succeeded in achieving U.S. goals of isolating Vietnam from the Soviet Union, reducing the strength of their military, strengthening ASEAN solidarity, or lessening the possibility of a widening war in Southeast Asia. It is time for a new policy. Helping to improve the situation for the average person in Indochina would promote friendship between our countries, ease Vietnamese dependency on the Soviet Union, and begin the process of lowering tensions in Southeast Asia.

VIETNAM TODAY

QUESTIONS AND ANSWERS

Douglas Pike, John McAulif, William Shawcross, Robert Muller, and Doang Van Toai

Question: Why does the U.S. support the Pol Pot regime?
Douglas Pike: The U.S. does not actually support the Pol Pot regime. Once a year, at the UN, it gets trapped on the credentials question. That is the only place it takes a stand. I do not believe that what happens at the UN is very important. U.S. policy toward Southeast Asia today is essentially one of letting ASEAN and China take the lead. Actually, I do not think Washington has a foreign policy toward Southeast Asia—not out of bitterness, but more out of benign neglect. I was told recently that ever since Ronald Reagan became president, the issues of Vietnam, Cambodia, and Southeast Asia had not been discussed at a Cabinet meeting. They do not sit around thinking up beastly acts to perform on those countries.
John McAulif: According to Elizabeth Becker, a former reporter from the Washington *Post,* speaking at a conference on Cambodia at Princeton in November, the U.S. played the midwife role in convincing the Thais to allow the Chinese to supply the Khmer Rouge through Thai territory.

Question: Who is responsible for the Pol Pot murders?
William Shawcross: The regime itself. The policies of the White House, between 1970 and 1975, created the conditions, the only conditions, under which the Khmer Rouge could have come

to power. But we must remember that that regime was, at heart, a Marxist-Leninist party; it was not a Fascist party.

Question: How can you call for normalization of relations with a regime, Hanoi, that mistreats its people?

McAulif: I do not think America should normalize or not normalize relations with governments on the basis of our moral approval of them. There are lots of governments in the world, not the least of which is South Africa, with which I think the U.S. should have relations. There are many dimensions to that. People I have talked to in South Vietnam, who are very critical of developments in the South since 1975, feel that from their viewpoint, normal relations—ending the trade embargo and beginning an aid program—would lead to an improvement. China and Singapore, which deeply disapprove of Vietnam, for instance, have normal trade relations with it. According to the *Far Eastern Economic Review,* in fact, Chinese trade with Vietnam jumped enormously last year. The current policy has not led us anywhere, and will not lead us anywhere, unless you think that it somehow is going to bring about a fall of the government in Vietnam. And that is unlikely to happen.

Question: Given the nature of Communism in Vietnam, will normalization really help the situation there?

Robert Muller: You cannot seriously argue against the proposition that you have to have people talking to each other before anything can happen between them. Normalization should not be considered an evaluation or a judgment on the morality of the government. We have many potential adversaries in the world with whom we have relations and to whom we talk—and through the process of dialogue, we at least work toward the minimizing of differences. Before the VVA contingent left Vietnam, in December 1981, we noted areas of concern to both sides, namely the status of the MIAs and the consequences of the use of herbicides. We had met with several U.S. government agencies before we left and they had told us the same thing: that there had been no discussions with the Vietnamese government for months; that they had not even been able to get together to arrange a meeting to put the issues on the table. As a result of our trip, our government began to meet four times a year with the Vietnamese government on a formal basis to discuss the MIA situation, and procedure to bring about resolution of this issue is on line.

McAulif: Carter, in his memoirs, said that one of his major errors was not to have immediately normalized relations with Vietnam, Angola, or Cuba. The suffering that exists in Vietnam today is not on the same level as that of the war. Nor do I think that the Vietnamese are highly enamored of the Russian advisors or the Soviet Union in general. There is only gratitude and a historical link.

Shawcross: The Soviets are not popular. When I was in Vietnam, eighteen months ago, the only phrase I really needed on the streets was "I am not a Soviet." It was astonishing to me the dislike with which the Soviets are regarded in Vietnam today by ordinary people. On one occasion, I saw at Hanoi airport the Soviets treating Vietnamese officials with extraordinary contempt and disregard, which reminded me of the way some Americans treated them during the war. Recognition, if it had come early, in 1975 or 1976, or even 1977, would have been far better for America and Vietnam. It didn't. And the question now is entirely bound up with political problems, and the problem of Cambodia in particular. Now, recognition is not something the U.S. politically can just give on a plate, without any *quid pro quo.* It has to be tied to a political settlement in Cambodia, and that is what the Vietnamese have continually resisted. It seems to me that the Vietnamese are the principal actors in Indochina today, not the Americans.

Question: Wouldn't normalization allow Vietnam to play the same role in Southeast Asia that the U.S. played in Vietnam?

McAulif: The question of Vietnam's role in Kampuchea, in particular, is very complicated because there are several different truths pertaining to it. One is the historical truth of the Vietnam-Thai rivalry over who will be the dominant power in Cambodia. The second truth is that the Cambodians did not care, in 1978, whether it was the Vietnamese or the Thais who liberated them from Pol Pot. In fact, it was the Vietnamese who did it; and from that has stemmed a reality which, because it does not fit U.S. perceptions, does not get across. The reality is that people in Kampuchea today, as long as there is the least bit of danger that Pol Pot will return, despite all the historical problems between the Cambodians and the Vietnamese, still regard Vietnam's presence as the lesser of two evils. I think there is a path out of there, but it has to follow a serious recognition of what has transpired since 1978: that there is a government in Phnom Penh, that it has in fact created extensive administrative and education structures. Life in Kampuchea is different today than it would be had the Vietnamese not come in; it is not going to be easy to unsort. But it can be unsorted if there is a serious effort to do that.

Shawcross: But the Vietnamese, from 1975 to 1978, consistently denied that anything was going wrong in Cambodia. They said that all the refugee stories from Thailand were CIA propaganda. And after they invaded, which I agree was a liberation, they denied that they were there at all; they said the situation was irreversible and that no one else had any right to discuss it. There has been no attempt by Vietnam to recognize that other countries do actually have the right to protest or to be concerned when two hundred thousand foreign troops cross borders. It has not just been the U.S. and China who have led the campaign against Vietnam, it is small countries like Yugoslavia which have a historic and real fear of invasion by a larger neighbor.

Yes, the Heng Samrin regime is better for Cambodia than the Pol Pot regime, but do we as Westerners have any right to say to the Cambodians, "This is good enough for you; this is what you must put up with"? I think not. You quoted Elizabeth Becker just now; she has just returned from Phnom Penh, Saigon, and Hanoi. One of the things she commented on, with irony, was the awful fact that if you are a former Khmer Rouge, you may very well be in the current Cambodian government, working for the Vietnamese; if you are a former ARVN, you may well still be in a reeducation camp.

McAulif: You should complete that by saying that if you are a former Lon Nol or Sihanouk government person, you also have a better chance of working in the government in Phnom Penh than if you are a former ARVN. There are other possible paths that could be followed than those being followed now.

Shawcross: Of course there are, if the Vietnamese want to.

McAulif: I think they want to.

Shawcross: They have not shown much sign of wanting to compromise.

McAulif: I disagree on that. I think that their current negotiating position represents a very substantial compromise.

Question: Are the prison camps better than a bloodbath?

McAulif: That is a when-did-you-stop-beating-your-wife question. I am not sure that those were the alternatives. I suppose in some sense, for the people themselves, and in some moral sense, to be in a reeducation camp is in fact far superior to being killed. In fact, many people have been released from reeducation camps. It was not desirable or commendable that people were sent to reeducation camps, but it is more commendable than executions.

Shawcross: But don't you agree that the reeducation-camp system, in which tens of thousands of people have been incarcerated without trial since 1975, is a system that has to be condemned absolutely? There was a doctor in South Vietnam, arrested in 1978, who spent eighteen months in a camp simply because he had once been a medic in Thieu's army. This is an appalling system, don't you agree?

McAulif: Yes.

Doang Van Toai: In the prisons and camps, there were not only Thieu supporters but also many Vietcong and former revolutionaries who had been allied to the Communists for a long time. I met one man, Nguyen Van Than, about seventy-five years old, who had been involved in the first resistance fighting against the French.

•THE MILITARY•

Editor's Note

The dark shadow of Vietnam today lies as heavily over the American military as over any segment of U.S. society.

Ten years after Vietnam, there has been no major examination by the military of its own role, its strategy, its tactics, its equipment, its operational concepts in Vietnam. Ten years after Vietnam the military has not incorporated Vietnam into its texts, into its courses for higher command officers. Vietnam is not taught at Quantico. It is not taught at West Point. It is not taught at Annapolis. It is not taught at the Command schools.

The conspiracy of silence prevails.

This extraordinary situation prevails although the higher commanding officers in Vietnam have all vanished from the scene and the brilliant young colonels and majors who saw the war from the bottom up are now rapidly taking their places. But the word still is out: Don't mention Vietnam.

It has been said that, classically, the military prepare to fight the next war in the manner they should have fought the previous war. That is, the mistakes are taken into account, the tactics and plans are changed. France built the Maginot Line after World War I to prevent the Germans from driving to the Marne as they did in 1914. Stalin thought he had gained ground for maneuver by dividing Poland with Hitler and occupying the Baltic States. Actually, he simply invalidated the defense systems he already had in place.

There seems no current prospect that the U.S. military will fight the next war on the basis of the lessons of Vietnam. It is erasing all memory of Vietnam as rapidly as possible from its Command structure. Its only response to Vietnam today seems to be a rather conventional yap that the war was lost by the politicians and the press.

This tragic and dangerous fact, as Cecil B. Currey notes, seems to make certain that should the U.S. again be involved in insurgency warfare in Asia, the Middle East, or Latin America, the errors of Vietnam will be repeated. Demands by general officers such as Maj. Gen. John R. Galvin that the military hold a scientific postmortem on Vietnam to discover its lessons have been ignored.

To the military, the Vietnam war was an aberration. It is not the war to which they have devoted and continue to devote their attention—a European war against the Soviet Union. That war they are preparing to fight on the basis of lessons of World War II. The consequences might be fearsome if such a struggle should occur. Those not restudying World War II are, presumably, inventing new and impossible tactics for winning a nuclear-fighting war.

An insight into contemporary U.S. military thought is provided by General Peers, who feels that Vietnam set back the U.S. Army by ten years in its research and development program. Funds for inventing new space weapons had to be diverted to equipment for fighting the unwanted jungle war. Even ten years after the end of Vietnam, the army hasn't caught up on its program for conventional (i.e., European-style) weapons planned before the forced diversion of funds to Vietnam (ordered by President Johnson in the mid-1960s).

In the words of James Fallows, "The military declared Vietnam was not a real war." It is a buried subject from which no one, at least no one in the military, is going to derive any benefit.

HOW DIFFERENT IS THE MILITARY TODAY BECAUSE OF THE VIETNAM WAR?

Cecil B. Currey

Did the military win or lose in Vietnam? The answer obviously depends upon the one giving the response. Three years after the collapse of South Vietnam, Gen. William Childs Westmoreland announced that "militarily we were successful . . . we didn't lose a single battle above company level."[1] Retired Marine officer, combat veteran, author of *The Betrayal,* William R. Corson writes of the military's "debacle in Vietnam."[2] Viet vet Joseph A. Rehyansky, writing in *The National Review,* proudly points out that the army "brought the enemy to its knees by the end of 1972."[3] Maj. Harlan Jencks, army reservist and expert on the Far East, describes Vietnam as "our most disastrous war."[4] Maj. Gen. John R. Galvin proclaims that when our army was withdrawn from Vietnam by the government, it was standing firmly on its own feet.

---

1. Associated Press wire service story, 30 April 1978.
2. Letter, Lt. Col. William R. Corson, U.S.M.C. (Ret.), to the author, 6 April 1981.
3. Major Joseph A. Rehyansky, "Divergent Views on the Problems of the Volunteer Armed Forces with One Point in Common," *National Review,* Vol. 33, No. 6 (April 3, 1981), pp. 367–68.
4. Manuscript copy of review of *Self-Destruction* supplied by Harlan Jencks to the author.

"No one," he writes, "brought the American army to its knees."[5] Prof. Paul Savage, longtime army reserve officer and coauthor of *Crisis in Command,* judges that our army was defeated in Vietnam "by an unkempt, undersized, ill-equipped . . . force of jungle fighters."[6]

Whether one believes that America won or lost the military struggle in Vietnam, even sanguine patriots and army leaders admit that this longest of the nation's wars was complex and that it was "an event we must reconsider with objectivity and care."[7] The army, however, has not yet become serious about such a restudy. There have been no official gatherings within the military—publicized or private—to ponder that late conflict and to gather from it lessons applicable to future combat actions. This dereliction has persisted despite warnings even from within the military that "With all its many wars within wars, like Chinese boxes, Vietnam may be prototypical of what the future holds for us." An exhaustive and accurate analysis of the army's performance there is essential if it is to better prepare itself for the next war. Yet, the army refuses to make "any kind of solid, objective study" of the Vietnam era.[8]

I maintained in a recent book that many of the army's problems were self-imposed; they did not grow out of civilian dictates. At least one military prolocutor, using words reminiscent of my own, warns that "the American military must stop blaming politicians for inhibiting tactical success in the war and must instead study carefully the . . . lessons that are there to be learned."[9]

Precedents exist for such an effort. After World War II, although many of those responsible for directing its battles were either still on active duty or else very much in people's memories, the army's Office of Military History brought together 210 scholars who wrote our official history of the Second World War. The

5. John R. Galvin, *Parameters: The Journal of the U.S. Army War College,* Vol. 11, No. 1 (March, 1981), p. 18.

6. Paul Savage, "Cincinnatus Recidivus: A Review Essay" (discussing *Self-Destruction*), *The Nation,* 232 (February 21, 1981), p. 214.

7. Galvin, *op cit.,* pp. 16–17.

8. *Ibid.,* 15, 15, 17.

9. *Ibid.,* 17.

resulting "Green Book" series was meticulous in detail and often analytic. After Korea, that same office produced another series of official studies analyzing that police action.

At present, the U.S. Army Center for Military History has only ten people working on twenty-three projected volumes covering the Vietnam conflict; although it has been nine years since our troops were pulled out of Indochina, none have yet been published. The primary reason for such a lackluster performance can only be military reluctance over having its Vietnam leadership subjected to careful scrutiny. General Galvin rightly criticizes this inaction. Writing in *Parameters: The Journal of the U.S. Army War College,* he notes that there is an urgency facing the army to learn how to respond to similar military confrontations. "We lack an answer to the question, *What was Vietnam, in its essence, as an American military experience?* Even if we wanted to, we could not turn away from the answer to that question." [10]

Our army does indeed want to turn away from that answer; to close its eyes to the black days of Vietnam; to move *tabula rasa*–like into the future. Those who must be counted upon to solve our army's problems were themselves deeply involved in command decisions during Vietnam. They need diagnosis, either from within or without. They have not yet been persuaded to entertain ideas suggesting institutional changes or structural reform. Troubled by spears cast by Vietnam War critics, their usual reaction has been hostile.

Col. David Hackworth, one of our most decorated officers in Vietnam, retired in frustration when his advice and criticisms were continually ignored. Lt. Col. Anthony *(Soldiers)* Herbert was forced into retirement after he accused two of his superiors of covering up war crimes. The "fact sheet" produced on him by the Pentagon contained base *ad hominem* arguments. Lt. Col. Edward L. *(Death of an Army)* King is dismissed as one who began to question the war only when he got orders transferring him to Vietnam from a cushy Fort McNair desk job. Lt. Col. William R. *(The Betrayal)* Corson only narrowly avoided a court-martial because of his book, and the decision not to prosecute was made reluctantly

---

10. *Ibid.,* p. 18.

after no breaches of security could be found in the manuscript. William L. Hauser, a West-Pointer with twenty-five years of service, retired only as a colonel despite a distinguished record. Author of *America's Army in Crisis,* which contained mild criticism of the military in Vietnam, Hauser may now appreciate the 1823 comment of Gouvion Saint-Cyr, the French field marshal who said, "I will remove from the promotion list the name of any officer I find on the title page of a book." Richard Gabriel and Paul Savage, coauthors of *Crisis in Command,* have been dismissed as part-time soldiers and ivory-tower academics, despite the force of their words. My own book, *Self-Destruction,* was denigrated as the effort of a part-time reservist and a "damn chaplain who never set foot in Vietnam."

Perhaps as a consequence, the army faces today the same predicament it faced in Vietnam. Gen. Maxwell Davenport Taylor described it well. "We didn't know the enemy, we didn't know our allies, and we didn't know ourselves." No wonder we faced failure then and have learned precious little since.[11]

One of the army's most tragic failures, which underlay and underscored so many other mistakes, has been described by an infantry officer who spent long years in Vietnam. "We were in a war that was a contest for people's minds. Their support was essential if we were to build institutions and organizations capable of regularizing functional behavioral patterns, of getting people active around local issues. In such a contest, there was an obvious correlation between our use of inordinate firepower in response to stimuli that had little to do with the outcome of the war, and the loss of legitimacy for our own government and for the ones we supported in Vietnam. When foreigners kill a lot of the wrong people—noncombatants—they hand the enemy free propaganda. The foe doesn't even have to make up its own. We ourselves created the necessary adverse feelings."[12]

The U.S. military unfortunately thought of Vietnam as a conflict to be won by firepower, by killing the enemy. It never under-

---

11. These words were recalled for me by Corson, *op. cit.*
12. Taped interview made in August 1977, Washington, D.C., during research for my *Self-Destruction: The Disintegration and Decay of the United States Army in the Vietnam Era* (New York, W. W. Norton, 1981).

stood that its actions only strengthened the opposition. It ignored persistent suggestions and criticism from dozens of its own mid-level officers, such as Colonels Hackworth and Hauser, Lieutenant Colonels Donald B. Vought, Carl F. Bernard, Jean Sauvageot, and many others.

Even in the midst of that war, the army looked upon its involvement in Vietnam as something of an aberration, unpleasant and temporary, to be borne stoically only for so long as it was necessary to be there. Combat in Southeast Asia did not call for any major reshaping of procedures, nor for any important rethinking of tactics, strategy, organization, equipment. Only minor tinkering was necessary to cope with the irregular warriors, the Vietcong and their North Vietnamese allies. The *real* enemy was the Soviet Union and its satellite cohorts.

"We do not," suggests the author of a recent article, "care to dwell on insurgencies that make up in moral ambiguity what they lack of the decisiveness attributed to conventional war. . . . This penchant is unfortunate, for [they] have much to tell us about how we fight and with what effect."[13] These words well describe the army's attitude, then and now. At its service schools during the Vietnam era, officer students learned not about infrastructures and cadres and people's wars, but about motorized divisions and electromagnetic pulses and echeloned attacks. Those same subjects are emphasized today.

One officer recalls that "As a career course student at [the infantry school at] Fort Benning in 1973, I was shocked to hear an instructor begin a class . . . with, 'Now that the Vietnam experience is behind us.' Nineteen seventy-three! He was stating an army policy that was never officially promulgated but was known by every serving officer: the U.S. Army consciously and actively is trying to erase the whole painful episode from its institutional memory. In its place there is only the semi-official myth that if it hadn't been for the cowardice and caprice of civilian populations, we could have won with more of the same—more firepower, more troops, more of the bullheaded brutality that was in fact so utterly self-defeating. That myth, and the army's refusal to remember the

---

13. Maj. Andrew J. Bacevich, Jr., "Disagreeable Work: Pacifying the Moros, 1903–1906," *Military Review*, Vol. 62, No. 6 (June, 1982) p. 50.

truth, means we are condemned to relive the past the next time we get involved in a 'people's war of national liberation.' "[14]

Another army officer has put it more succinctly: "Our army's penchant for forgetting nasty tropical wars is well known."[15]

I have a parallel experience. I attended the U.S. Army Command and General Staff College at Fort Leavenworth from 11 August to 19 December 1975. Probably the majority of my fellow officer students were 'Nam vets, full of their recent experiences there and interested in some directed effort to help them understand what it all meant. For the most part, however, the school did not emphasize the recent struggle in Indochina. In the total curriculum of 524 contact hours, perhaps sixty-eight hours dealt with the nature of irregular conflicts, and only a small portion of those focused on Vietnam. Still, some of my friends wrote insightful credit essays on Vietnam topics; and one staff member, Lt. Col. Donald B. Vought, Department of Tactics, sponsored a "Vietnam Studies Project." On the faculty at the time was Lt. Col. Jean Sauvageot, a man of intense intellectual curiosity and attainment. One of the army's most knowledgeable officers about Vietnam, he had served there many years; spoke the language well; had been a translator and advisor at the Paris peace talks. He left Fort Leavenworth early, at the request of the State Department, which required his specific talents. Later he worked for the Department of Health, Education, and Welfare resettling Vietnamese refugees. This man was a treasure trove of information and insight. Yet, at Fort Leavenworth he spoke at no mandatory, school-sponsored student assemblies, but was limited to voluntary out-of-class sessions. The school thought of him as "nice, but not necessary." He was "extra."

With so little appreciation of the need for officers to understand the nuances of revolutionary warfare, it is no wonder that the army, during the war years, made such haphazard personnel assignments. The experiences of an acquaintance of mine were typical of many. In only twenty-one months' time, he held successive assignments that included leading a Long Range Reconnaissance Platoon (LRRP), a heavy weapons platoon, command of a Special

14. Jencks, *op. cit.*
15. Bacevich, *op. cit.*

Forces "A" Team, service as a provincial Regional Forces/Popular Forces (RF/PF) advisor and as a senior district advisor. Those duties allowed him only an average of four-plus months on each job.

Those who brought us Vietnam, and who there produced the army's self-destruction, remain in control of our military apparatus and its doctrines. They are not eager to have their records subjected to public scrutiny or to admit that they made inept mistakes; not willing to admit that their own incompetence caused subsequent and consequent grave damage to the army—wounds so severe that a staff member at the Command and General Staff College once exclaimed to me that "the U.S. Army was in bad—in horrible—shape in seventy-three. My God, man, it was almost unusable because of the Vietnamese experience. . . . We didn't have a unit . . . that really was usable at all. . . ." [16] Even those who lead our military establishment today would admit, if pressed, that commanders are responsible for *everything* within their commands—both achievements and failures.

Armies in wartime function effectively and efficiently only so long as their "primary groups" do not suffer from rapid personnel changes; only so long as their members feel a "sense of the regiment, esprit, unit tradition and memories, of *legio nostra patria,* of immediate, known, trusted, and approachable commanders," [17] and only so long as they are well trained. All these factors were repudiated by those in charge of the Vietnam-era army.

16. Currey, *op. cit.,* p. 166
17. Savage, *op. cit.,* p. 213; and Savage, "Patterns of Excellence, Patterns of Decay," *Reviews in American History,* Vol. 9, No. 4 (December, 1981), p. 560.

CHANGES IN THE MILITARY SINCE VIETNAM

Lt. Gen. William R. Peers (USA-Ret.)

American involvement in the Vietnam War may have set back the army by as much as ten years. So many of the army's resources and funds were devoted to South Vietnam that little remained for research and development, procurement of new equipment, and other methods to improve the army's combat capabilities. It has only been within the past couple of years that new, modern equipment has begun to flow to active army units—and National Guard and reserve units, which had been stripped of equipment during the Vietnam War, are only now being resupplied. But this equipment is expensive, and it will be several years before all units are again at authorized levels.

The war created turmoil among army personnel. There were never enough qualified noncommissioned officers to serve as squad leaders, platoon sergeants, and so on. A large percentage of those positions were filled by privates first class and men of even lower rank. This, of course, increased the load on the already overburdened junior officers commanding lower-level units. Much of this has been or is being changed by the emphasis being placed upon the training, education, and development of those within the NCO corps.

But it has been the creation of the All Volunteer Force, combined with the effects of the current economic recession, that has improved the personnel situation even more than the impact of the Vietnam War. Today, there are more volunteers than there are positions to be filled. Standards have been raised, and nearly all of the new inductees are high school graduates. Likewise, there has been a sharp upturn in the percentage of reenlistments.

On the officer side of the establishment, the My Lai incident caused the army to conduct a systematic evaluation of the overall corps. Numerous deficiencies were found. But, more important, the army has and is taking action to correct these shortcomings. The word "management," which had been overused for many years, is being downgraded. The emphasis now is upon leadership, with particular stress placed on integrity.

It would be difficult to compare today's army to those of former years, but from what I see of it, it is a good army and it is rapidly improving.

RESIDUAL EFFECTS OF THE VIETNAM WAR ON THE MILITARY

James Fallows

There is usually one "good" effect that predictably comes from a war: military forces see how the theories, strategies, and equipment they have developed in peacetime actually work. That does not by any means justify warfare, but it is the only benefit that comes from it. That benefit has, by and large, not come from the Vietnam War, because the military, like the rest of the country, has declared Vietnam not a real war. Because military men can argue that it was not military factors, but rather political constraints, that kept them from prevailing, the war's lessons cannot be applied to tomorrow's contingencies. There are significant lessons to be learned about the way that different kinds of aircraft, missiles, human beings, and rifles performed in Vietnam; those have, by and large, been ignored both inside and outside the military.

In terms of the residual effect on the soul of the military from what it went through in Vietnam, there is a parallel between the residue in the culture as a whole and the residue in the military—namely, that it is a buried subject, something that people do not willingly turn their minds to, a thing that rests in the back of many people's minds, that bothers people, yet a subject they are occasionally tempted to explore. When I, as an outsider, talk with military men of all ranks about their view of those years, their first reaction is almost universally bitter, resentful, defensive. They say it was not the military's fault, that the media and government undermined their efforts. They were not allowed to win. And yet, once you get past that shell, it seems obvious that there is some effort at self-examination in the military about what it did wrong in those days and what it might do right if it were called on again to fight. It does register on individual soldiers that no member of the Joint Chiefs of Staff resigned in protest when told by Lyndon Johnson that he wanted them to fight a war, but he would not mobilize the reserves, nor would he try to make a case to the American public that this was a real war. People still brood about Gen. William Peers' report on My Lai, which asked about the military's values and how they were or were not defended. There are other indications of some professional ferment in the soul of the military: At a conference at West Point, not one among six or seven dozen officers responded to a question about what was the winning strategy in Vietnam; every military journal you pick up is replete with the phrases "professional ethics" and "leadership," and how the regimental system will correct some of the worst practices of Vietnam.

I still have some doubt as to how profound this self-examination is, because the real problem with the professional military in Vietnam was not the specific things it did, but the way that the careerist impulse, the desire to "punch one's ticket" and move into the next rank, got in the way of the historical truths of how human beings perform in combat. Even though this is a peacetime, not a wartime, military, it strikes me that careerism is at least as intense—a drive that shows up these days in procurement of weapons systems and military people being more loyal to a budget than to the U.S.

I also sense a generational split in the military forces. The people who were senior commanders in Vietnam are by and large out of the military these days. The people who were young officers in Vietnam, the lieutenants and captains of that era, are now majors, lieutenant colonels, and colonels, and I see them spending a lot of time trying to reflect on those days, because they were the people on the receiving end—they paid the price—when things went wrong at headquarters. But today's very junior officers regard this experience with indifference and vague resentment. It looks to them as if things might have worked out if the politicians had not been involved.

Finally, there is a residual effect in the relationship between the civilian world and the military. It would be astonishing if the military, which, in many cases, was unjustly blamed for a policy it did not create and was simply carrying out, and which felt itself unjustly victimized by the rest of the country, did not not carry some burden of resentment with it against the civilian society. I sense that resentment most acutely among those members of my generation in the military force—the middle-level officers who saw their own cohort split between those who went to war and those who did not go to war. It is still a subject of acrimonious conversation when people from those two worlds cross each other's paths. This suspicion of the civilian, outside world has had one beneficial effect: it has made professional military men far more skeptical than their political leaders about the application of military force in cavalier ways. I have found almost no brimming-over enthusiasm among professional military men for expeditionary forces in the Middle East or Central America. You do hear that enthusiasm from civilian defense analysts, but not from military men—because they are the ones who would be doing the job, and they have seen what happened before when they started out to do something whose end no one knew.

PART IV

THE LESSONS

Editor's Note

The lessons of Vietnam may be so pervasive as to defy definition. How does one define an age? But perhaps this is too pessimistic a suggestion. We are only now beginning to talk about Vietnam; to analyze ourselves, our society, our institutions; to try to understand our leaders and, perhaps most difficult of all, to understand the Vietnamese, their country, our friends, and our military enemies.

The "lessons from a war" remain to be learned. They are, in these presentations, roughly outlined. Vague silhouettes begin to be perceived. It was a war in which each man and woman saw it from his or her perspective, and it was a war which, like some streams, suddenly went underground, vanished from our active consciousness with its putative end, only now to begin to surface, more and more strongly in the consciousness of individuals and of institutions.

Some of the elements of our society have not yet begun to awaken from the drugged sleep into which its nightmares forced them—the American military, for example. With extraordinary controlled response, it hardly utters the word Vietnam. The Vietnam veterans only in the past couple of years have begun to talk to others than themselves about the bitter lessons. The political leaders of America seem to have taken vows of silence whether liberal or conservative. Firefights wage among the press and its critics, but even here no issue is fully joined.

Only perhaps the Vietnamese themselves neither forget nor remain silent, except be it the silence of the concentration camp. It was and is their country, their lives, their society which the war so grotesquely distorted in ways which can no more be corrected than can the dead be restored to life.

HOW DOES AMERICA AVOID FUTURE VIETNAMS?

Frances FitzGerald

This is an easy question to answer, for it was not at all easy for the United States to get into the war that costs the lives of tens of thousands of Americans, and millions, but literally countless, Indochinese. It wasn't easy a bit.

Vietnam was not a quagmire, in the sense that we stumbled into it and were sucked down and unable to get out despite our own efforts; though this is the textbook, and I think probably the cinematic, version of the war. In fact, the United States created the war. And if you count from the time of the Geneva agreements in 1954, that creation took over a decade. It took enormous amounts of time, expense, and the energies of a great many people. There is nothing easier than to avoid future Vietnams.

It's extremely easy not to intervene in the internal affairs of small third world countries, particularly ones of no economic or strategic importance to the United States. It's also quite easy not to get involved in weak, corrupt, and repressive governments, even if you do not have to go to the lengths of manufacturing those governments yourself. It is particularly easy when there are people around who remember the horrors of that war. And, of course, if any administration forgets the lessons of Vietnam, it has only to look to the lessons of the Soviet Union in Afghanistan, where there have been, according to the *New York Times,* some 12,000 to

15,000 Soviet casualties already, and countless casualties among the people of Afghanistan.

Of course, it's quite possible that our administration may forget these lessons and try to repeat history. Indeed, the current Reagan administration seems to be taking all the preliminary steps necessary right now in Central America. But if that's the case, there's very little that I or perhaps anyone else here can do about it. For to send CIA operators and U.S. military advisors into the social upheavals of Central America with the idea that they can stop them is, I would submit, evidence of some mental instability.

I can't tell the Reagan administration how to prevent another Vietnam, but I can try and draw some more detailed lessons from the Vietnam experience: some cautionary tales, some practical suggestions, and some pieces of wisdom that the individuals and the groups involved in the war have to offer us.

In the first place, for those who would play pro-consul in tropical climes, they could learn a great deal from the experience of Gen. Edward Lansdale and his successors with President Ngo Dinh Diem. The first lesson is this: You may create a leader; you may find him, put him in power, protect him to the best of your abilities, but his purposes will still not be yours. To paraphrase one North Vietnamese leader, you can create a puppet, but you can't make a good one. There are only bad puppets. There's a corollary to this proposition, and that is, you cannot bribe a man to end corruption.

A lesson that might be learned from the presidents and the pro-consuls in this war was also the following: Do not let your messengers know your intentions, or they will almost surely tell you what you want to hear. To tell them your wishes is to corrupt your reporting system. Secondly, if you really wish to maintain a civilian government, don't put all of your money into military aid, because the military in that country will grow and grow to the point where it will finally turn your civilian government out. Then you will be in the position of supporting a military dictatorship that will almost inevitably be oppressive, because it depends on you rather than on its own people. And it will almost inevitably be corrupt, because it will be dependent on you. It will hate that dependency, and therefore it will steal from you.

There's a lesson, I think, to be learned specifically from President Kennedy, and that is, beware of having too good a speech-writer—your phrases may be remembered.

There's a lesson to be learned from Secretary of State Dean Rusk, this particularly for future secretaries of state: Serving your president loyally, playing by the rules of the establishment and never making a fuss will not necessarily get you a reward—you may find yourself back in Athens, Georgia.

There's a lesson to be learned from Defense Secretary Robert McNamara, and that is, deception is dangerous, if only because it leads to self-deception. You cannot deceive the press, the public, and your own colleagues indefinitely without beginning to believe what you say. This in turn will disarm you, and David Halberstam will call you not just a liar but a fool.

There's another, perhaps more important, lesson to be learned from McNamara, and that is that in social revolutions, numbers are meaningless. You can count the dead; you can even count the troops on the other side, but that is counting the past. You cannot count what is becoming, and that is the only thing that matters.

There's a lesson that almost any leader in any country might learn from Ho Chi Minh, and that is, if you embark on a war of any duration, you must have the support of your people. This support is more important than weapons, for if people believe their cause is just, they are capable of extraordinary sacrifices. If they do not, all your weapons are useless.

There's a corollary to that, too, provided by North Vietnam's Gen. Vo Nguyen Giap—one which would be of some service to the guerrillas of Central America—and that is, there's a difference between a guerrilla war and a people's war. Guerrillas can separate themselves from the people, just as governments can, but in that case they will lose or they will remain guerrillas forever.

There's a lesson—quite a number of lessons, I think—that Lyndon Johnson would have for us, certainly for other politicians. One of them is, do not generalize from the experiences in East Texas. Some people are not interested in pork-barrel politics. And do not promise to eliminate poverty, ignorance, and disease when you yourself are invincibly ignorant as to the causes of the other two.

Johnson has another lesson for future presidents, and that is, do not let your line agencies write their own report cards. If the CIA is running an operation, believe the Pentagon, and vice versa. If you do not do that, you will run into what I call Robert Komer's general theory of relativity. Komer was the head of the "pacification" operation, and in 1967 he told us journalists when we asked what progress was being made: "Of course we're making progress. We're always making progress. It's just that sometimes the other side makes progress faster than we do."

Then, of course, there's a lesson from Sen. Wayne Morse, who was one of the two senators who opposed the Tonkin Gulf resolution—and this is a lesson for other congressmen—and that is, quite simply, don't take anything they tell you on faith, not "ma's apple pie" and not "reasons of national security." I think you'd have another smaller lesson, and that is, most of you congresspeople should not go to war zones if you oppose the administration's policy, because most of you are not as clever as the local officials and they will make you look like a fool.

The CIA in Vietnam certainly had some lessons for its successors—certainly lessons that were not observed by its successors in Iran—and one is, simply, to get good intelligence, you cannot be too closely involved with the client government, particularly if you are trying to save it from its internal enemies. For in that case, you will not be using it, it will be using you.

Gen. (William) Westmoreland has, I think, a linguistic lesson to teach us. He used language in a very extraordinary fashion many times during the war. But the lesson that most comes to my mind is this: If there is a verb "to attrit," it is almost certainly reflexive.

There is also a rather serious lesson that President Lyndon Johnson has for future presidents, and that is, if you choose generals and Cabinet members who will not resign for reasons of honor, then in the end you may have to.

There are many lessons to be learned from Henry Kissinger and Richard Nixon, but to select one of them, perhaps even at random: Do not say that the credibility of the United States depends on continuing American support for a war that you are just about to lose. Your allies may believe you.

There are a series of lessons that the American press corps learned in Vietnam, and the first one is that any official who talks about "credibility" is almost certainly lying.

There's also another lesson, a rather philosophical one, which they learned from Kissinger and Nixon, and that is, there is a difference between what people know, what they think, what they believe, what they tell you, and what they do. These are all separate categories, and you should not assume there is any communication between them.

A lesson that may be parochial to the press but nonetheless important is, do not write about land reform, even in the unlikely circumstance that you've grown up on a farm. It's too complicated. To talk of land reform is to talk of the economy as a whole.

Finally, journalists do not lose wars. They can't win them. And no more can they stop them. They represent public opinion more than they would like to imagine. Or in other words, a free country gets the free press it deserves.

The peace movement—what does it have to tell its successors? First, that it's not un-American or unpatriotic to oppose one's government, even when it's carrying on a war, even when it has fielded American troops. Secondly, that it's not necessary for a movement to have a single charismatic leader—a leader may be assassinated, or he may be discredited, and then the movement will break apart. A movement without a head may be mindless from time to time, but it will be more resilient. Popular protests are often more popular than electoral campaigns. Not everything in this country is done through the ballot box. On the other hand, movements which have only one issue may eventually fade away.

What do the veterans have to tell us? What do they have to tell future soldiers? First, that killing and risking one's life demands moral seriousness. Soldiers must ask the purpose, and if they do not do it sooner, they'll have to later, and it'll be far more painful then.

What the Vietnam veterans have taught the rest of us is this: We cannot simply write off our losses, declare failure, and get on with the matter, close the subject, because the young men we have sent to fight our wars for us will not forget. They will become our conscience. They will insist that there is responsibility.

What have the Vietnamese taught us? They have taught us a number of things. First, that there is nothing more precious than independence and freedom. Secondly, that life is not a series of problems with solutions. There are irreconcilable conflicts, without solutions and without any possibility of compromise.

Most important for this conference certainly, and for us in general, is that the past is not simply for historians. Strength and endurance come from having a connection with one's own history. The past and future are balanced in the present, and you have one only to the extent that you have the other.

You can have control over your future only to the extent that you are deeply and firmly attached to your own history.

IS CENTRAL AMERICA BECOMING AMERICA'S NEXT VIETNAM?

Robert E. White

Your nightmare images are of South Vietnam, and mine are of Central America, where I spent six years of my life. One nightmare image is the CIA-sponsored coup in Guatemala in 1954, where our country abandoned the traditional and correct method of influencing other governments through diplomatic persuasion and respect for sovereignty, and instead turned our diplomacy in Central America over to military and CIA stations. Another nightmare image is of serving more than two years under a United States ambassador in Nicaragua who conducted himself as nothing more than a toady of Somoza, thereby convincing the young people of Nicaragua that there was no hope in the United States and that revolution was the only proper path. Third comes from El Salvador, watching a bloodthirsty gang masquerade as a military establishment, routinely killing anyone who disagreed with them, under the guise of patriotism and killing Communists.

But I do have to say that some images are good. The tenacity of the democratic leaders in Honduras who still, today, in spite of the terrible things we are doing there, still have faith that they can make it, that they can find a way to avoid violence and bring about positive change through democratic methods. And I also recall the Panama Canal treaty, which was an act of great statesmanship, which turned a people who were potential enemies of the United

States into a country that believed, because they had the evidence of it, that the United States was capable of treating a small power in a fair and equitable fashion and of arriving at a commonsense agreement that served the interests of both parties. I also have the image of General Somoza, when I was serving as ambassador to Paraguay, arriving in Paraguay to deserved exile and meeting with his blood-brother General Stroesser and informing him that all his troubles began when White came to Nicaragua. And I also remember that I was the first ambassador fired by the Reagan administration, and that gives me some pleasure.

Vietnam has made some of our leaders more blind, and I see the demonstration of that blindness being played out in Central America where, among other developments, the foreign service is being purged. No nation can be great, no nation can discharge its responsibilities in the world today, unless it has a great career diplomatic service. The primary target of the Reagan administration has been those of us who have any particular or special knowledge of Central America or any area where a person's particular theology leads him to take a stand regardless of the facts. In Central America, the administration has, in effect, diminished the State Department, diminished the one group in our government that has no important program money. It doesn't have missiles, it doesn't have arms, it doesn't have great amounts of money with which to bribe people. Its basic objective is to report the facts and make foreign policy recommendations. And those are the people who have been ousted from our government. And I think that you would do well to recall the many, many foreign service officers who lost their careers in the past: first in China, then in Southeast Asia, and now in Central America.

If I had to sum up our foreign policy toward Latin America, it would be in the phrase "fear of change." We have been so absolutely frightened of any kind of change that we have uncritically supported dictatorships, winked at repression, tolerated corruption, and participated in the perversion of the democratic process. Now, there are two honorable exceptions to that unfortunate litany—and my standards here are minimal. In my view, the Alliance for Progress was an important initiative, and though it later went awry, at least Kennedy and the Alliance for Progress captured an important truth in those great words, "Those who make peaceful evolutions impossible, make violent revolutions inevitable." And the human-rights policy of Jimmy Carter gave a wonderful tool to the foreign policy man in the field, because for the first time we had a tool with which to distinguish between the dictator who was anti-Communist—because that was the only way he could get U.S. support—and an authentic democrat who might have also been anti-Communist but who shared some of the values that you and I hold and who had the support of his people.

The most important event in recent Central American history was the fall of Somoza in Nicaragua. United Nations Ambassador Jeanne Kirkpatrick draws one lesson from that event, and I draw another. She draws the lesson that as one dictatorship usually succeeds another, it is important that the United States shore up the dictatorship that is friendly and, at all costs, avoid the possibility or eventuality of a dictatorship that is unfriendly. I draw the lesson that once a dictator has lost whatever small support of the people he once had and is kept in power only by the support of the United States, when the inevitable day dawns and the dictator loses power, the more radical will be the outcome, and the more anti-American will be the succeeding government.

Now, the greatest success of the Reagan administration—and this I put down to the sort of "good guy–bad guy" intellectual sloppiness that I see as a result of the Vietnam War on many Americans—is to have convinced many Americans that there is no basic difference between the Carter administration and the Reagan administration; that the Reagan administration is merely a continuation of that sort of funny, generally retrograde policy of the Carter administration. Not so.

What was the Carter administration trying to do in Central America? One, at great political cost, it signed a Panama Canal treaty, ignoring the screams from many quarters that we were going to have Castro across the canal within six months. It made important efforts to shore up democracy in Costa Rica. It did absolutely everything possible to bring about an end to military rule in Honduras, and succeeded in bringing about elections there. It encouraged the Nicaraguan government, by passing a $75 million loan to the Sandinistas, in spite of the CIA's and the Pentagon's open lobbying against the Carter administration on this issue. In El Salvador, after the young officers overthrew the government of

General Romero and invited revolutionaries and Christian Democrats into the government, we did everything we could to speed up that change and to get behind land reform and other important reforms. And we isolated the killer regime of Guatemala in the hope that sooner or later the young military there would reject their pariah status. The objective was eventually to move Central America into a mode of positive change. The United States, in El Salvador, during the Carter administration, consistently supported negotiations with the revolutionaries. It was the revolutionaries who rejected negotiations with the government.

In the Reagan administration, policy has totally changed, Reagan policy is based on the support of the military establishments of Guatemala, El Salvador, and Honduras. In Guatemala we have, as Gabriel Garcia Marquez has said in his recent Nobel speech, a religious fanatic along the lines of General Martinez in El Salvador, simply killing people by the buckets. And what has been the Reagan administration's response? It says it opposes the killing, but the message sent is, "Do not tell us about what you do, but if you are successful, we will be willing to send you military assistance."

In El Salvador we are supporting, totally, the military, and we have defied the basic lesson we should have learned in Vietnam. We have put our policy in pawn to a hard-line military that cannot afford to compromise, because if it compromises, the minimum it will lose is power, and the most likely thing it will lose is the heads of its leaders. In Honduras, we have turned this relatively benign Honduran military into a mercenary arm of the United States as it seeks to overthrow the government of Nicaragua—one of the most profoundly immoral, blind, and stupid policies imaginable.

The Carter administration's objective in Central America was to provide a non-Communist model for change. Up until now, the only model for change in Latin America has been the Castro model—in my view, a disastrous example. What we were trying to say to these governments is that we understand your desire for change, but you do not have to look to Moscow or Havana for understanding and support—you can find it here in the United States. The Reagan policy has been to send arms and advisors to El Salvador. This was the first foreign policy initiative of the Reagan administration. In their ignorance, I suppose, the policymakers intended dramatizing the difference between the softhearted, softheaded, human rights–oriented Carter administration and the new, tough no-nonsense, *High Noon* Reagan administration. What they have dramatized is the total impotence of trying to bring about a military solution to the problems of Central America. And they are making the same basic error that was made in Vietnam: they see everything in an East-West context. For them, there is no such thing as authentic revolution. For them, all revolutions are imported from outside, and the bounden duty of the United States is to counter Communist aggression. How absolutely ridiculous! No twentieth-century revolution has been totally sealed off from outside support, but the Salvadoran revolution comes about as close as any you are likely to see.

For me, the unanswered question about Vietnam was always this: Why did *their* Vietnamese fight so much better than *our* Vietnamese? I do not know the answer. But I do know why their Salvadorans fight so much better than our Salvadorans, and that is because no amount of military advice, no amount of military assistance, can instill morale into a land led by a military leadership that routinely tortures and assassinates. These people are not held in respect by anyone; they are held in contempt by the entire world. Nor is there any way to send economic assistance that would do any good to El Salvador, when the rich of El Salvador are exporting six times the wealth that we are sending in, against the inevitable day when the whole thing falls apart. There is no way that a military establishment which has its bank accounts, its condominiums, and its families outside the country can be counted on.

I know why the revolutionaries fight so well. They did not choose to become revolutionaries; they were driven to it. They cannot give up. If they give up, they will be killed. So they are fighting not only for themselves, but for their families and their friends, because they will be killed, too. So the grit and the determination is theirs, and the military leaders know in their hearts that they are doing wrong.

There were people in these countries, and in leadership positions there, who were torn; and with proper policies, it would have been possible to find military officers who would have joined the vanguard for reform. Unfortunately, most of those people are now either out of the country, out of the military, in disgrace, or, in effect, hiding within the military.

However bad we are, however many mistakes we have made, I still think we have the capacity to improve, the capacity to change—providing the American people realizes the power it has and organizes itself in an intelligent way to bring about the desired objective of a humane, enlightened foreign policy. The bedrock of freedom in this country is still intact; its spoken values still have credence in Latin America. The people in Latin America do admire what the United States says it is, and they only turn away from us and to our enemies when they find out that what we say we stand for is not what we really stand for. The idea that Latin Americans are not capable of democracy is just racist nonsense.

THE LESSONS OF DENIAL

Arthur Miller

My theme is denial. The denial of Vietnam. The impact of Vietnam is and remains paradoxical. At the same time superficial and
passing and profound and lasting. The paradox arose out of denial,
a real process of denial that existed even in the face of the real
suffering the war entailed.

My confrontation with denial occurred early. Until somewhere in 1964, I had the war all wrong. I hated it, of course, and
the duplicity of Lyndon Johnson in getting us deeper into it. But
until the mid-1960s, and specifically at a teach-in at the University
of Michigan where I was one of the speakers, I never really doubted that we would win, whatever that meant. I also believed we
could almost indefinitely continue fighting a war in Vietnam without serious economic dislocations here at home. I thought we
would win because we had vastly superior technology. I am an
American; I believe in technology. I knew that politically we could
never win, but that in our case, as opposed to the French, we could
drown them in iron. At Michigan, I was earnestly and remorseless-
ly informed, by Jean Lacouture, among others, who had experienced Vietnam, that there was no way we could win a war there at
all. But, I figured, he was French. Also, there was a young corpo-
ral, a former Michigan student just back from Vietnam, who was
sure we could win. All we had to do, he said, was put a million

men on the ground and keep them there for at least ten and, better yet, twenty years. At Michigan, nevertheless, I started to worry less about robbing the Vietnamese of their independence and a little more about what Americans were going to do with the first war they could not win. I could not help recalling how the German army and the political Right, after the First World War, had successfully created the myth of the stab in the back: Germany had not lost, she had been betrayed by pacifists, liberals, Jews, and Bolsheviks. Would that happen here with some similar belligerent right-wing ascendancy?

This particular denial of reality was nibbled at by many Americans for a time, but has all but been abandoned. On the contrary, there exists a widespread resolve, which, God knows, may even be shared by some of the joint chiefs by this time, not to involve ourselves again in Vietnam types of warfare. We need only to recall Lyndon Johnson's smooth confidence in flying an army into the Dominican Republic—with hardly a bleat from Congress or the press—and compare it to Reagan's clumsy and transparent apologetics as he pokes around in El Salvador, repeating assurances of nonintervention that not even newspaper editors report with straight faces anymore.

If they left behind this legacy, this acknowledgment of reality, it was not altogether in vain that Americans died in Vietnam. Perhaps they will save us yet from even greater calamities.

In any case, it seems clear now that a major theme in American history was ended by Vietnam—the theme of our omnipotence. There were, of course, times when one did not imagine that it would end even this well. I am thinking of the streets of Chicago in 1968. Looking back now, the violence that occurred there appears as a rage of denial. Those police riots were fundamentally the violent reactions of authority trying to deny that its power in the world was limited. What else was Senator Ribicoff's confrontation from the convention platform with Mayor Daley, than the call to acknowledge the truth of Vietnam rather than to continue denying that a victory was no longer possible. Anyone witnessing the violence of Chicago had to fear for the consequences of an American defeat. Yet it would be absorbed, transmogrified, by a new leader, Richard Nixon, who was a past master of selective denial, who managed to withdraw while sounding as though he were charging ahead. To win, in short, by losing. Another form of denial.

To one who lived through World War II and had childhood recollections of the First World War, Vietnam seemed oddly remote, a war without apocalyptic feeling. It was striking that one never met defenders of our involvement who thought the war was going to change anything. The war was a kind of drudgery—a perhaps dubious battle, but one in which honor was somehow involved. One might occasionally hear that the Vietnamese had to be stopped on the other side of the Pacific before they got to Los Angeles, but few people seemed to take this echo of the previous war with any seriousness.

The atmosphere was a perfect miasma, fumes unwinding endlessly without purpose, climax, or mercy on military and civilian victims alike. It was like the cigarette habit: you smoke one more in order to smoke one more. In the meantime, the young men were dying, and at home the young generation was staring at its incomprehensible fate on the television screen. Not the least important element in this evil drain was that business remained good and Johnson was careful not to stick the public with higher taxes or even the usual restraints of consumption that go with real wars. The usual call for some kind of special effort was not even necessary. We could have big tanks and big Cadillacs at the same time. Month after month, only one thing became harder and harder to deny—it was not going to end soon.

Two civilian deaths, Howie's and Dan's, were desperate attempts to acknowledge that the moral legitimacy of the government's war upon Vietnam did not exist. Those two could no longer bear the mass denial around them. They wanted to count; they wanted to live. No one can think of their deaths merely as individual acts of desperation—in these two capable, sensitive young men, America's moral claims had failed and died. They refused the war at the cost of their lives.

Dan was the son of the local hardware store owner in my town in Connecticut. I had known Dan since his infancy; he was a fanciful, humorous kid in high school, and when his father died, he ran the store with his mother until he discovered that the area was covered with semiprecious rocks. Then he started a rock business. He was full of laughs and ingenuity, a handsome, intense boy with a lust for some distinction in life. At nineteen, he knew he would be taken by the war; and it changed him quickly. One night, I was sitting in my living room and heard a soft, uncertain knock on the sliding glass door, which startled me in the middle of a countryside like that. And there was Dan, and I let him in, and he stood there blinking, and he said, "Give me any idea, any fact, any color, and I will write you a great poem on the subject in five minutes, by the clock." He was drugged up to his ears. Within nine months, he was dead of an overdose. Drugs would probably have entered the United States in volume without the Vietnam War, but they would never have gotten to Dan enough to kill him.

Half a mile down the road, Howie lived—that is, when he was not hanging around my pond or my house. From the age of seven or eight, he loved to come and watch us eating, reading, digging in the garden. He was a lonely boy, the son of a family with lots of brothers and sisters. After he started high school, I hardly saw him. One day I ran into him in New York, and I gave him a ride, and he started asking me why I thought we were in the Vietnam War. I gave him all the answers that I thought would put the war in perspective, but he interrupted and asked simply why anyone should live anymore. I thought he was being a bit theatrical, but he seemed to have aged rather than grown up. The conversation gradually died between us, and whatever was happening to him was beyond my help. Nevertheless, he asked me, quite surprisingly, if I would help him get into the Neighborhood Playhouse, one of the best acting schools in New York. I was anxious to get him out of his blues, so I made a few phone calls and I got him in. But I thought that he had a doubtful future as an actor; he was short, pimply, wore glasses; his hair stood on end; he had a goofy, adolescent stare (like Dustin Hoffman who, incidentally, I also advised to get out of the theater). Two years later, having forgotten all about Howie, I spoke at the graduation ceremony of the Neighborhood Playhouse and casually asked the late John Morrison, the head of the acting school, if there were any promising students in the current class. Yes, he said, there is one, who we all think has a great career ahead of him, a really important talent. To my astonishment, it turned out to be Howie. I sought him out and shook his hand and congratulated him; but there was, I thought, something veiled about his joy. A year or so later, I heard of him again. He had sat down cross-legged on the grass behind his house, poured gasoline over himself, and lit the match. I do not believe he would have done that had there been no Vietnam War.

That immemorial yearning for a clear moral choice is still with us, but the war in Vietnam, if it left us with nothing else, opened us to a certain humility before the difficulty of making such choices anymore. Now, at least, a regime calling for our military help must demonstrate some respect for human rights; and even if this certification can be manipulated, as it is in El Salvador, there is nevertheless a wedge into which can be driven a standard of values, which was not the case before Vietnam. It needs to be said that Vietnam did not create, as would be expected, a total cynicism in our foreign policy, but allowed, at least for a while, a wholly novel attempt to inject morality into it: the standards of human rights. Like many a great empire before us, we have reserved liberty for ourselves while too often exporting oppression. But it must be said that ours is a unique attempt, feeble and uncertain as it may be, to make foreign policy consistent with democratic principles.

History, according to Henry Ford, was bunk. America was supposed to be the exception to all the rules of decay and enfeeblement that every civilization has experienced before it. The Vietnam War, from one perspective, joined us to the rest of the human race, in that the consequences of our errors were felt at home and not merely overseas. Vietnam demonstrated for anyone to see that ours, like any political system, rests upon, if not the consent of the governed, their collaboration. And when that is withdrawn, things indeed fall apart.

The mortality of the United States came onto the agenda during that war. I suggest that there may be a certain promise in that fact. I suggest that if President Reagan still can refer to the Vietnam War as a football game that was well played, the people know better than to feel anything but regret that we ever entered a war in that place and in that time and in those circumstances. I think it was the Vietnam tragedy that more than anything else, brought nearly seventy percent of us to support a nuclear freeze, despite the endless warnings and opposition of our recently elected administration. I think it is Vietnam in our memories that has forced Reagan to temper some of the easy truculence of his first statements on entering office. The people of the United States entered history in Vietnam for the first time since the Civil War; a vision of our dissolution appeared in the smoke of the battle. We denied the war in the midst of it and we denied the men who fought in it. The time to acknowledge it all has certainly come.

The War That Haunts Us Still

Harrison E. Salisbury

Ten years after the Paris Peace Accords brought the Vietnam War to a formal end, the embers of the "Fire in the Lake," as Frances FitzGerald calls it, still haunt America.

Nowhere was this more evident than on the pleasant campus of the University of Southern California last February, where eighty-five men and women—most of them journalists who had a hand in covering Vietnam, plus former military, CIA, and State Department officials and historians—met to reexamine Vietnam and study the "lessons from the war."

It was not an easy task. As they deliberated, the shouts of Vietnamese pickets, refugees from the lost land, echoed outside; and after each panel came poignant questions from Vietnamese interrogators and angry words from American servicemen who fought in Vietnam—questions about their nightmares, TV serials that depicted them as crazies, and about Agent Orange.

Behind all the questions was the basic refrain:

Why, why, why, why Vietnam?

It seemed clear that the conferees were engaged in a battle over what one speaker, Benjamin DeMott, an Amherst professor, called "the myth of Vietnam," that is, the image of the conflict that will pass into history and there remain to influence the minds of future American generations.

The legends of war are potent indeed. It was Adolf Hitler's "stab-in-the-back" thesis—that treacherous civilians had robbed Hindenburg and his Prussian military machine of victory in World War I—that led the Nazis to power in postwar Germany. Already neo-conservatives like Norman Podhoretz and others have advanced the theory that the cause of American victory in Vietnam was betrayed by the winking red eyes of the TV cameras and the "defeatist" dispatches of antiwar correspondents.

The concept of the "traitor press" and the cowardly correspondents found only the faintest echo at the gathering. Peter Braestrup, former Vietnam correspondent for the *New York Times* and the Washington *Post*, whose massive two-volume study, *Big Story,* heavily faults the press and TV for poor and misleading coverage of the Vietnam War, offered no support for the notion that the press "lost the war." In fact, as he noted, opinion surveys showed that TV coverage—contrary to the thesis of some myth-builders—had little effect on American attitudes toward the war.

Some participants were notably pessimistic about the role of the press. Seymour M. Hersh, whose exposés of the My Lai massacre and of the Watergate scandals have been widely credited with a strong impact on public and government conduct, viewed the future in tones of darkness. "No reporter can prevent another Vietnam from happening," he said. "Nothing has changed. If a government wants to lie, it can do anything."

But Barry Zorthian, for four years government spokesman in Saigon, suggested that everything has changed. There can never again be a "closed war," he believes. The television cameras can always be counted on to record the battlefield action, bringing the face of war into every American home in multicolored images. "The 'open war' is here to stay," he said.

One deep conviction emerged: almost all the participants repeatedly cited "the lies" the government told, and of how it lost credibility—first with the press, and then with the people. But Hersh insisted that nothing could prevent a government from lying, and he doubted that the armaments of the press were strong enough to penetrate that "bodyguard of lies" which Winston Churchill once said must be devised in wartime to protect the heroine, Truth.

Yet, George E. Reedy, one-time press aide to President Lyndon B. Johnson, blamed American ignorance—from LBJ's on down to that of ordinary citizens'—for the fatal errors. Americans, he insisted, hardly knew where Indochina was, knew nothing of the country, nothing of its people or its history.

Reedy felt it was fatuous scapegoating to blame any one element for Vietnam misjudgments, whether the White House, the State Department, the generals, or the journalists.

Reedy's remedy is the same as Zorthian's: education, education, education. But his years as a newspaperman and government official left him skeptical of America's resolve to discipline itself.

One conference participant listening to the efforts at a reappraisal of Vietnam recalled the words of the American officer who said during the war, "We had to destroy the village in order to save it." In the struggle over the "myth of Vietnam," the question remains open: Will America find a legend that erodes her democracy, or one that will heal and strengthen her? The debate of the next few years will give us the answer.

APPENDIXES

APPENDIX 1:
EXCERPTS FROM NSC-68 (APRIL 1950)[1]

I. BACKGROUNDS OF THE PRESENT WORLD CRISIS

Within the past thirty-five years the world has experienced two global wars of tremendous violence. It has witnessed two revolutions—the Russian and the Chinese—of extreme scope and intensity. It has also seen the collapse of five empires—the Ottoman, the Austro-Hungarian, German, Italian, and Japanese—and the drastic decline of two major imperial systems, the British and the French. During the span of one generation, the international distribution of power has been fundamentally altered. For several centuries it has proved impossible for any one nation to gain such preponderant strength that a coalition of other nations could not in time face it with greater strength. The international scene was marked by recurring periods of violence and war, but a system of sovereign and independent states was maintained, over which no state was able to achieve hegemony.

Two complex sets of factors have now basically altered this historical distribution of power. First, the defeat of Germany and Japan and the decline of the British and French Empires have interacted with the development of the United States and the Soviet Union in such a way that power has increasingly gravitated to these two centers. Second, the Soviet Union, unlike previous aspirants to hegemony, is animated by a new fanatic faith, antithetical to our own, and seeks to impose its absolute authority over the rest of the world. Conflict has, therefore, become endemic and is waged, on the part of the Soviet Union, by violent or nonviolent methods in accordance with the dictates of expediency. With the development of increasingly terrifying weapons of mass destruction, every individual faces the ever-present possibility of annihilation should the conflict enter the phase of total war.

---

1. *Naval War College Review*, May 1975, pp. 51–108; for a full study of its origins and import see Paul Y. Hammond, "NSC-68: Prologue to Rearmament," in W. R. Schilling, et al., *Strategy, Politics, and Defense Budgets* (New York: Columbia University Press, 1962).

On the one hand, the people of the world yearn for relief from the anxiety arising from the risk of atomic war. On the other hand, any substantial further extension of the area under the domination of the Kremlin would raise the possibility that no coalition adequate to confront the Kremlin with greater strength could be assembled. It is in this context that this Republic and its citizens in the ascendancy of their strength stand in their deepest peril.

The issues that face us are momentous, involving the fulfillment or destruction not only of this Republic but of civilization itself. They are issues which will not await our deliberations. With conscience and resolution this government and the people it represents must now make new and fateful decisions.

*   *   *

III. FUNDAMENTAL DESIGN OF THE KREMLIN

The fundamental design of those who control the Soviet Union and the international Communist movement is to retain and solidify their absolute power, first in the Soviet Union and second in the areas now under their control. In the minds of the Soviet leaders, however, achievement of this design requires the dynamic extension of their authority and the ultimate elimination of any effective opposition to their authority.

The design, therefore, calls for the complete subversion or forcible destruction of the machinery of government and structure of society in the countries of the non-Soviet world and their replacement by an apparatus and structure subservient to and controlled from the Kremlin. To that end Soviet efforts are now directed toward the domination of the Eurasian land mass. The United States, as the principal center of power in the non-Soviet world and the bulwark of opposition to Soviet expansion, is the principal enemy whose integrity and vitality must be subverted or destroyed by one means or another if the Kremlin is to achieve its fundamental design.

*   *   *

VII. PRESENT RISKS

A. General.
It is apparent from the preceding sections that the integrity and vitality of our system is in greater jeopardy than ever before in our history. Even if there were no Soviet Union, we would face the great problem of the free society, accentuated manyfold in this industrial age, of reconciling order, security, and the need for participation with the requirements of freedom.

We would face the fact that in a shrinking world the absence of order among nations is becoming less and less tolerable. The Kremlin design seeks to impose order among nations by means which would destroy our free and democratic system. The Kremlin's possession of atomic weapons puts new power behind its design, and increases the jeopardy to our system. It adds new strains to the uneasy equilibrium-without-order which exists in the world and raises new doubts in men's minds whether the world will long tolerate this tension without moving toward some kind of order, on somebody's terms.

The risks we face are of a new order of magnitude, commensurate with the total struggle in which we are engaged. For a free society there is never total victory, since freedom and democracy are never wholly attained, are always in the process of being attained. But defeat at the hands of the totalitarian is total defeat. These risks crowd in on us, in a shrinking world of polarized power, so as to give us no choice, ultimately, between meeting them effectively or being overcome by them.

* * *

CONCLUSIONS AND RECOMMENDATIONS

A continuation of present trends would result in a serious decline in the strength of the free world relative to the Soviet Union and its satellites. This unfavorable trend arises from the inadequacy of current programs and plans rather than from any error in our objectives and aims. These trends lead in the direction of isolation, not by deliberate decision but by lack of the necessary basis for a vigorous initiative in the conflict with the Soviet Union.

Our position as the center of power in the free world places a heavy responsibility upon the United States for leadership. We must organize and enlist the energies and resources of the free world in a positive program for peace which will frustrate the Kremlin design for world domination by creating a situation in the free world to which the Kremlin will be compelled to adjust. Without such a cooperative effort, led by the United States, we will have to make gradual withdrawals under pressure until we discover one day that we have sacrificed positions of vital interest.

It is imperative that this trend be reversed by a much more rapid and concerted buildup of the actual strength of both the United States and the other nations of the free world. The analysis shows that this will be costly and will involve significant domestic financial and economic adjustments.

The execution of such a buildup, however, requires that the United States have an affirmative program beyond the solely defensive one of countering the threat posed by the Soviet Union. This program must light the path to peace and order among nations in a system based on freedom and justice, as contemplated in the Charter of the United Nations. Further, it must envisage the political and economic measures with which and the military shield behind which the free world can work to frustrate the Kremlin design by the strategy of the cold war—for every consideration of devotion to our fundamental values and to our national security demands that we achieve our objectives by the strategy of the cold war, building up our military strength in order that it may not have to be used. The only sure victory lies in the frustration of the Kremlin design by the steady development of the moral and material strength of the free world and its projection into the Soviet world in such a way as to bring about an internal change in the Soviet system. Such a positive program—harmonious with our fundamental national purpose and our objectives—is necessary if we are to regain and retain the initiative and to win and hold the necessary popular support and cooperation in the United States and the rest of the free world.

＊　　＊　　＊

APPENDIX 2

GALLONS OF HERBICIDE APPLIED IN SOUTH VIETNAM
1965 TO 1971[1]

Military Region I Corps

	Agent Orange	Agent Blue	Agent White
Province #1 Quang Tri	515,615	25,790	111,410
Province #2 Thua Thien	753,385	78,367	186,751
Province #3 Quang Nam	352,945	19,450	63,200
Province #4 Quang Tin	173,275	44,770	50,470
Province #5 Quang Ngai	219,460	86,737	40,770
Province #91 Hue	No Information on the Computer Printout		
Province #92 Da Nang	No Information on the Computer Printout		

Military Region II Corps

	Agent Orange	Agent Blue	Agent White
Province #6 Kontum	910,415	74,700	131,340

---

1. Information Researched by George W. Ewalt, Vietnam Veterans of America, Chapter 67, Delaware County, February 1982.

Military Region II Corps *(cont'd)*

	Agent Orange	Agent Blue	Agent White
Province #7 Binh Dinh	497,952	97,242	64,711
Province #8 Pleiku	197,585	14,190	191,363
Province #9 Phu Bon	12,300	10,900	21,600
Province #10 Phu Yen	207,707	58,120	19,831
Province #11 Dar Lac	217,900	23,119	37,590
Province #12 Khanh Hoa	132,596	45,591	77,215
Province #13 Ninh Thuan	104,815	33,100	2,075
Province #14 Tuyen Duc	485	4,540	0
Province #94 Dalat	No Information on the Computer Printout		
Province #15 Quang Duc	277,575	12,500	135,400
Province #16 Lam Dong	32,400	49,735	2,890
Province #17 Binh Thuan	119,565	14,420	47,910
Province #93 Cam Ranh	3,915	0	1,320

Military Region III Corps

	Agent Orange	Agent Blue	Agent White
Province #18 Binh Tuy	294,360	33,500	86,640
Province #19 Long Khanh	983,582	16,745	612,356

Military Region III Corps *(cont'd)*

	Agent Orange	*Agent Blue*	*Agent White*
Province #21 Phouc Long	1,607,235	56,450	1,143,565
Province #22 Binh Long	139,740	0	209,735
Province #23 Binh Duong	395,835	40,510	373,873
Province #24 Tay Ninh	511,740	74,495	476,849
Province #25 Hau Hghia	483,215	10,345	51,273
Province #26 Bien Hoa	425,037	8,950	386,965
Province #27 Phouc Tuy	202,910	2,700	156,750
Province #28 Long An	109,090	0	28,300
Province #29 Gia Dinh	532,685	43,400	225,484

Military Region IV Corps

	Agent Orange	*Agent Blue*	*Agent White*
Province #95 Vung Tau	No Information on the Computer Printout		
Province #96 Saigon	No Information on the Computer Printout		
Province #30 Go Cong	6,000	0	3,095
Province #31 Kien Tuong	59,020	11,300	54,260
Province #32 Kien Phoung	13,760	990	4,895
Province #33 Dinh Tuong	8,720	965	7,316

Military Region IV Corps *(cont'd)*

	Agent Orange	Agent Blue	Agent White
Province #34 Kien Hoa	225,390	0	56,070
Province #35 Vinh Binh	174,595	5,000	17,360
Province #36 Vinh Long	5,490	1,180	12,735
Province #37 An Giang	No Information on the Computer Printout		
Province #38 Kien Giang	30,895	0	21,190
Province #39 Choung Thien	23,220	0	2,225
Province #40 Phong Dinh	30,775	12,700	15,722
Province #41 Ba Xuyen	27,820	1,280	3,546
Province #42 An Xuyen	474,240	0	106,760
Province #43 Bac Lieu	126,690	6,000	31,635

ABOUT THE CONTRIBUTORS

MICHAEL ARLEN, author of *The Living Room War* (1969), *Exiles* (1970), *An American Verdict* (1973), *Passage to Ararat* (1975), and *Camera Age* (1981), is a contributing editor to *The New Yorker,* commenting on television.

PETER ARNETT has been an Associated Press correspondent in Jakarta (1961–62), Vietnam (1962–70), and New York (1970–present). He received the Pulitzer Prize for international reporting and the Sigma Delta Chi award in 1967 and 1971.

KEYES BEECH, Far Eastern correspondent for the Chicago *Daily News* from 1947 to 1980, received both the Pulitzer Prize for international reporting and the Sigma Delta Chi award in 1951. He is the author of *U.S. Marines on Iwo Jima* (1945), *Tokyo and Points East* (1954), and *Not Without Americans* (1971).

PETER BRAESTRUP, author of *The Big Story: How the American Press and Television Reported and Interpreted the Crisis of Tet in 1968 in Vietnam and Washington* (1978), is currently editor of *The Wilson Quarterly.*

BUI DIEM was chief of staff under Interim Premier Phan Huy Quat and served as special assistant to Prime Minister Nguyen Cao Ky. He is executive director of the Indochinese Economic Development Center in Washington, D.C.

CECIL B. CURREY ("Cincinnatus"), a professor of history at the University of South Florida, Tampa, has served as chaplain in the National Guard since 1961. He is the author of *Self-Destruction: The Disintegration and Decay of the United States Army During the Vietnam Era* (1981).

PETER DAVIS has produced many television documentaries, including "The Heritage of Slavery" (1968) and "The Selling of the Pentagon," the movie documentary *Hearts and Minds,* and the PBS series *Middletown.* He is the author of *Hometown* (1982).

DAVID DELLINGER, a pacifist during World War II and a leader of the Vietnam War protest movement, was one of the "Chicago Seven" arrested and tried for conspiracy as a result of antiwar demonstrations staged at the Democratic National Convention in Chicago in 1968.

DOANG VAN TOAI, author of *Le Goulag Vietnamien* (Paris, 1979), is currently writing a book about Vietnamese Communism.

ROBERT ELEGANT has been the Asian correspondent for *Newsweek* and the Los Angeles *Times,* and has covered Vietnam since 1955.

DANIEL ELLSBERG, who was senior liaison with the American Embassy in South Vietnam from 1965 to 1966, provided the Pentagon Papers to the Senate Foreign Relations Committee in 1969, and later to the *New York Times.* He is the author of *Papers on the War* (1972).

GLORIA EMERSON wrote *Winners and Losers: Battles, Retreats, Gains, Losses and Wins from a Long War* (1976). She was a *New York Times* correspondent in Indochina during the early 1970s.

GEORGE EWALT, JR. served in Vietnam with the First Infantry Division. He has spoken and written articles on Agent Orange and worked actively with veterans' organizations.

JAMES FALLOWS, an editor of *The Atlantic,* was associate editor of *Texas Monthly* in the mid-1970s and chief speech writer for President Jimmy Carter from 1977 to 1979.

FRANCES FITZGERALD, a free-lance writer in Vietnam in 1966, is the author of *Fire in the Lake: The Vietnamese and the Americans in Vietnam* (1972), which won both the Pulitzer Prize and the National Book Award in 1973, and *America Revised* (1979).

EDWARD FOUHY, CBS bureau manager in Saigon and senior producer of the *CBS Evening News* during the Vietnam War, is now vice-president of ABC News, Washington, D.C.

MURRAY FROMSON was a correspondent for CBS News and the Associated Press in Asia and the Soviet Union. He is a visiting professor at the USC School of Journalism and host of *California Week in Review* on PBS.

TODD GITLIN, a professor of sociology and director of the Mass Communications Program at the University of California at Berkeley, is the author of *The Whole World Is Watching: Mass Media in the Making and Unmaking of the New Left* (1980) and, most recently, *Inside Prime Time* (1983).

DAVID HALBERSTAM was a reporter for the *New York Times* in Vietnam (1962–63) and received the Pulitzer Prize for international reporting in

1964. He is the author of *The Making of a Quagmire* (1965), *The Best and the Brightest* (1972), *The Powers That Be* (1979), and *The Breaks of the Game* (1982).

GEORGE C. HERRING, professor of history at the University of Kentucky, has written *Aid to Russia, 1941–1946: Diplomacy and the Origins of the Cold War* (1973) and *America's Longest War: The United States and Vietnam, 1950–1975* (1979).

SEYMOUR HERSH has worked as a correspondent for both United Press International (1962–63) and Associated Press (1963–67). In 1970, he received the Pulitzer Prize for international reporting. He has written *My Lai 4: A Report on the Massacre and Its Aftermath* (1970) and *The Price of Power: Kissinger in the Nixon White House* (1983).

ROGER HILSMAN, who teaches political science at Columbia University, served as assistant secretary of state for Far Eastern affairs under President John F. Kennedy, resigning in opposition to the Vietnam War. His books include *To Move a Nation* (1967) and *To Govern America* (1979).

MICHAEL HUYNH is executive director of the Southeast Asia Resettlement Program, San Francisco, California.

PHILLIP KNIGHTLEY has been a feature writer for the *Sunday Times* of London since 1963, and is the coauthor of *The Philby Conspiracy* (1968) and author of *The First Casualty* (1975), winner of the Overseas Press Club Award.

JOHN LAURENCE, a free-lance correspondent for ABC News, PBS, and the BBC, worked as a CBS correspondent in Vietnam between 1965 and 1970.

LAWRENCE LICHTY, professor of communication arts at the University of Maryland, is director of research for the WGBH series *Vietnam: A Television History*.

DON LUCE served with the International Voluntary Services as a director in Saigon from 1958 to 1967 and now works for the Southeast Asia Resource Center in New York. He is the author of four books based on his Vietnam experience.

JOHN MCAULIF was active in the antiwar movement from 1967 to 1975 and has served for the last ten years as director of the Indochina Program of the American Friends Service Committee in Philadelphia.

RALPH MCGEHEE retired after twenty-five years with the CIA, during which he served in Vietnam from 1968 to 1970. He is author of *Deadly Deceits: My Twenty-five Years with the CIA* (1983).

ROBERT MANNING, assistant secretary of state for public affairs (1962–64) and editor of *The Atlantic* for fourteen years, is editor-in-chief of Boston Publishing Company, publishers of a sixteen-volume history, *The Vietnam Experience*.

PETER MARIN is a culture critic who has contributed articles on the Vietnam War and Vietnam veterans to a number of journals, including *Harper's* and *The Nation.* He is currently completing a book on conscience in America.

SHAD MESHAD, a Vietnam veteran and counselor, wrote *Captain for Dark Mornings* (1982).

ARTHUR MILLER is author of *Death of a Salesman, The Crucible,* and *After the Fall,* among many plays. With Inge Morath, he wrote *Chinese Encounters* (1979).

JOHN MUELLER, professor of political science at the University of Rochester, is the author of *War, Presidents and Public Opinion* (1973).

ROBERT MULLER is national president of Vietnam Veterans of America.

NGO VINH LONG, author of *Before the Revolution: The Vietnamese Under the French* (1973), is a consultant to WGBH's series *Vietnam: A Television History* and the Boston Publishing Company's sixteen-volume history *The Vietnam Experience.*

MADAME NGUYEN NGOC DUNG took part in the resistance movement in Vietnam and attended the peace negotiations in Paris from 1969 to 1973 as assistant to Madame Nguyen Thi Binh. She is currently Ambassador, Deputy Permanent Representative of the Socialist Republic of Vietnam to the United Nations.

ARCHIMEDES L. A. PATTI, then a major in the OSS, acted as liaison between Ho Chi Minh and the American forces fighting the Japanese in Indochina in 1945. He has written about his experiences in *Why Vietnam? Prelude to America's Albatross* (1980).

LT. GEN. WILLIAM R. PEERS (USA-Ret.) was a combat commander during the Vietnam War, mainly with the Fourth Division in the Central Highlands. He directed the official army inquiry into the massacre at My Lai.

DOUGLAS PIKE, a retired U.S. Foreign Service information officer, teaches in the Institute of East Asian Studies at the University of California at Berkeley. He is the author of three books on Vietnamese Communism, including *Viet Cong: The Organization and Techniques of the National Liberation Front of South Vietnam* (1965).

GEORGE REEDY has been congressional correspondent for United Press International, press secretary to President Lyndon B. Johnson in 1964 and 1965, and dean of journalism at Marquette University. He has written *The Presidency in Flux* (1973) and *Lyndon B. Johnson: A Memoir* (1982).

MORLEY SAFER opened the Saigon bureau for CBS News in 1965. A winner of the Polk Award, the Peabody Award, and three Overseas Press Club awards, he is in his thirteenth season as coeditor of *Sixty Minutes* (CBS).

HARRISON E. SALISBURY, former correspondent and editor for the *New York Times,* has written twenty-two books, including *Behind the Lines: Hanoi* (1967), *Orbit of China* (1967), *The Unknown War* (1978), *Without Fear or Favor: The New York Times and Its Times* (1980), and *A Journey for Our Times: A Memoir* (1983).

ROBERT SCHEER, former editor of *Ramparts* magazine, is a national correspondent for the Los Angeles *Times.* His most recent book is *Without Enough Shovels: Reagan, Bush and Nuclear War* (1982).

PAUL SCHRADE, former regional director of the United Automobile Workers, was active in the antiwar movement.

ROBERT SHAPLEN is a staff writer for *The New Yorker.* His books include *The Lost Revolution* (1965), *Time Out of Hand* (1970), *The Road from War* (1971), *The Face of Asia* (1972), and *A Turning Wheel* (1979).

WILLIAM SHAWCROSS has been a writer for the *Sunday Times* of London and is the author of *Sideshow: Kissinger, Nixon and the Destruction of Cambodia* (1979).

MAJ. GEN. WINANT SIDLE (USA-Ret.) served as chief of information for Gen. William Westmoreland in Saigon (1967–69), then as the U.S. Army's chief of information (1969–73), and as deputy assistant secretary of defense—public affairs (1974–75).

CLANCY SIGAL teaches at the University of Southern California School of Journalism and is a free-lance journalist and critic in Britain. He is the author of three novels.

FRANK SNEPP, the CIA's chief strategy analyst in Saigon in the mid-1970s, resigned from the agency in 1976 to write *Decent Interval* (1977).

RONALD STEEL is the author of *Pax Americana* (1967) and *Walter Lippmann and the American Century* (1980).

JOHN STOCKWELL worked for the CIA as a field officer in Vietnam from 1973 to 1975. He is the author of *In Search of Enemies: The CIA Story* (1978).

GEORGE SWIERS served in Vietnam (1968–69) and was decorated for valor. He represents the Vietnam Veterans of America, Capital District.

JAMES THOMSON served as an aide to the assistant secretary of state for Far Eastern affairs and as a staff member of the National Security Council (1964–65). He is curator of the Nieman Foundation for Journalism and the coauthor of *Sentimental Imperialists: The American Experience in East Asia* (1981).

RUBEN TREVISO, an intelligence case officer in Vietnam (1971–72), is staff coordinator for the Forum of National Hispanic Organizations and an associate editor of *Hispanic Link.*

WILLIAM TUOHY, a Pulitzer Prize winner for international reporting in 1968, spent four years in Vietnam as Saigon bureau chief for *Newsweek* and the Los Angeles *Times*. He is currently London bureau chief for the Los Angeles *Times*.

GARRICK UTLEY, a correspondent for NBC News, has been assigned to Brussels, Vietnam (1964–66), Berlin, Paris, London, Chicago, and New York City.

FRANK WALKER, a Marine who fought in Vietnam, is a veterans' counselor in Los Angeles.

BRUCE WEIGL, a Vietnam veteran, teaches English at Old Dominion University, Norfolk, Virginia.

ROBERT E. WHITE, former ambassador to El Salvador and a twenty-five-year veteran of the Foreign Service, has served as senior associate with the Carnegie Endowment for International Peace.

WILLIAM APPLEMAN WILLIAMS, a professor of history at Oregon State University, was president of the Organization of American Historians (1980–81). He has written over a dozen books, including *Empire As a Way of Life* (1980).

BARRY ZORTHIAN served as program manager for the Voice of America (1956–61) and was in charge of the Joint United States Public Affairs Office in Vietnam from 1964 to 1968. From 1969 to 1979 he was a vice-president of Time, Inc., and is currently senior vice-president of Gray and Co.